Amerikastudien

American Studies

A Quarterly

Edited for
the German Association
for American Studies by

GENERAL EDITOR

Oliver Scheiding

EDITORS

Christa Buschendorf
Andreas Falke
Hans-Jürgen Grabbe
Alfred Hornung
Sabine Sielke

ASSISTANT EDITORS

Tanja Budde
Patricia Godsave

Volume 58 · 1 (2013)

Universitätsverlag
WINTER
Heidelberg

EDITORIAL OFFICE

Professor Dr. Oliver Scheiding,
Amerikanistik / American Studies,
Department of English and Linguistics,
Johannes Gutenberg-Universität Mainz,
Jakob Welder Weg 18,
D-55128 Mainz
Telefon ++49-6131-39-22357
Telefax ++49-6131-39-20356
E-Mail: redaktion@amerikastudien.de
Website: http://www.amerikastudien.de

Subscriptions
Amerikastudien ★ *American Studies (Amst)* is published quarterly. The subscription price is € 79,70 plus postage. The subscription is renewed automatically for the following year, if notice of cancellation is not received by December 1 of the current year.

Universitätsverlag WINTER GmbH, Heidelberg
Postfach 10 61 40, D-69051 Heidelberg

Typesetting:
OLD-Media, D-69126 Heidelberg
Printing and bookbinding:
Memminger MedienCentrum GmbH, D-87700 Memmingen

Contents

ARTICLES

DOMINIK NAGL	The Governmentality of Slavery in Colonial Boston, 1690-1760 5
JASON S. POLLEY	Race, Gender, Justice: Storytelling in *The Greenlanders* 27
MARTA PUXAN-OLIVA	A Mysterious Heart: 'Passing' and the Narrative Enigma in Faulkner's *Absalom, Absalom!* and *Light in August* 51
SARAH HEINZ	"Not White, Not Quite": Irish American Identities in the U.S. Census and in Ann Patchett's Novel *Run* 79
ANDREW MILLER	Taking Fire from the Bucolic: The Pastoral Tradition in Seven American War Poems 101
DIMITRIOS LATSIS	Nature's Nation on the Screen: Discursive Functions of the Natural Landscape in Early American Film 121

FORUM

FRANK MEHRING	The 1946 Holocaust Interviews: David Boder's Intermedia Project in the Digital Age 139

REVIEWS

JASPER M. TRAUTSCH	Charlotte A. Lerg, *Die Amerikanische Revolution* (2010); Charlotte A. Lerg, *Amerika als Argument: Die deutsche Amerika-Forschung im* Vormärz *und ihre politische Deutung in der Revolution von 1848/49* (2011) 151
WOLFGANG SPLITTER	UDO SCHEMMEL, *Laien in lutherischen Kirchenordnungen: Die unterschiedliche Entwicklung ihres Beeinflussungspotentials auf Gemeindebelange im 18. Jahrhundert in Pennsylvania im Vergleich zu Kirchenordnungen des Landesherrlichen Kirchenregiments—dargestellt an der Genese der Kirchenordnung der St.-Michaelis-Gemeinde in Philadelphia, Pennsylvania* (2012) 155
MARCUS GRÄSER	Alex Jansen, *Alexander Dallas Bache: Building the American Nation Through Science and Education in the Nineteenth Century* (2011) 158

WOLFGANG HOCHBRUCK	Andrea Mehrländer, *The Germans of Charleston, Richmond and New Orleans during the Civil War Period, 1850-1870* (2011) 159
MARTIN SEIDL	Eve Tavor Bannet, *Transatlantic Stories and the History of Reading, 1720-1810: Migrant Fictions* (2011) 161
MICHAEL DOPFFEL	Nicole Waller, *American Encounters with Islam in the Atlantic World* (2011) 162
DAMIEN SCHLARB	Bradley A. Johnson, *The Characteristic Theology of Herman Melville: Aesthetics, Politics, Duplicity* (2011) 165
STEFANIE SCHÄFER	Günter Leypoldt and Bernd Engler, eds., *American Cultural Icons: The Production of Representative Lives* (2010) 167
KLAUS H. SCHMIDT	Ulrich Eschborn, *Stories of Survival: John Edgar Wideman's Representations of History* (2011) 168
DANIEL STEIN	Jared Gardner, *Projections: Comics and the History of Twenty-First-Century Storytelling* (2012) 171

CONTRIBUTORS   175

The Governmentality of Slavery in Colonial Boston, 1690-1760

DOMINIK NAGL

ABSTRACT

This article explores slavery in colonial Boston as a contradictory legal, cultural, and religious institution by introducing the concepts of 'pastoral power' and 'governmentality' as analytical instruments to the study of slavery. New England slavery was a culturally specific form of bondage that still rested upon pre-modern and religious notions of contract. An all-pervasive Puritan religious culture, and the spatial and social proximity of the slaves and their masters, gave New England slavery its unique character and produced a distinct way of slave management that is best described as 'Puritan governmentality of slavery.' In addition, it is suggested that the concept of governmentality addresses some of the criticisms leveled against Eugene Genovese's model of slavery as 'paternalism,' as it allows for the recognition of resistance as a defining feature of slavery.

Introduction

In colonial British North America, slavery was an institution still in the making as the early modern period saw the evolution of a variety of different systems of slavery. Starkly contrasting geographic, demographic, socioeconomic, and cultural conditions produced manifold power relations that allowed a plurality of diverse forms of slavery to evolve. While there exists a large body of literature on slavery in the southern colonies, the scholarship on slavery in colonial New England is slight and lacks detail. This neglect of attention is unfortunate since the case of New England slavery is marked by some curious peculiarities that make it an interesting counterpart to the southern slave systems. Slavery in British North America was an inherently contradictory institution; it rested on the legal assumption that certain groups of racially, socially, and culturally stigmatized persons could lose their status as legal subjects, become servants for life, and thus be turned into chattel—moveable property not much different from tools or livestock. From this vantage point, a slave was simply a means of production that could be owned, sold, and inherited. In this regard, the governance of slavery was a matter of the law of property. The necessary precondition for reducing wayward living human beings into property, however, was their deprivation of rights and the development of control mechanisms that should guarantee obedience to their masters. Consequently, the law of property was never enough to regulate slavery.

Below the surface of property definitions, slavery was a complex social relationship created and reproduced by the interaction of the slaves, the masters and their household members, the state, and society as a whole. Thus, it clearly transcended the confines of individual households and families and could not be treated simply as a matter of private law. For this reason, colonial assemblies tried to regulate racial relations and slave behavior by passing public laws and ordinances. This contradiction is most apparent in the legal treatment of slaves in New England, as slaves occupied a remarkable dual legal status there: they were property *and* persons at the same time. I claim that this paradoxical legal situation can be attributed to New England's all pervasive Puritan religious culture and, rooted in the region's relations of production, a peculiar spatial and social proximity of the slaves and their masters. Puritan slavery was a culturally specific form of bondage that rested upon pre-modern and religious notions of contract. Religion and the slaves' position in the northern work force decisively shaped slavery in New England and produced what I would like to a call distinct Puritan 'governmentality' of slavery.

The concept of governmentality, borrowed from Michel Foucault, refers in its most general usage to the nexus between the self-governance of individuals, i.e., individual behavior/conduct, and the government of society by the state, or political rule (cf. Dean 9-39; see also Burchell, Gordon, and Miller). According to Foucault, this connection became increasingly problematic in the early modern era. In the absence of a single, unified center of government, the question of 'good governance' was raised in many different fields at the same time. The idea of governmentality implies that there existed not one, but a multiplicity of 'governments' that included the government of individual behavior, the government of the family/household, the government of church congregations, and the political government of the state (Foucault, "Subject" 221). Thus, the concept of governmentality promises to be a productive analytical tool for the exploration of early modern slavery in New England; it is highly sensitive to the complex relationship between Puritan religious beliefs, family life, and slave management and allows for a description of it as a form of pastoral power. This approach resembles American historian Eugene Genovese's famous analysis of antebellum slavery in that it attempts to grasp the interaction of micro- and macro-levels of governance and emphasizes the role of culture and religion. However, I am going to show that concept of governmentality avoids some of the criticisms leveled against Genovese's model of slavery as 'paternalism,' which he derived from a problematic adoption of Antonio Gramsci's Marxist theory of hegemony and class rule in modern capitalist societies to slave societies. In addition, I will illustrate how the subtle subjectivity transforming psychological and cultural micro-techniques of power proved to be insufficient to guarantee the slaves' obedience and had to be augmented by disciplinary instruments based on force. In Massachusetts, where slavery was largely an urban phenomenon, there was constantly a strong pressure from the local level to pass ever stricter laws for the regulation of the behavior of slaves and free blacks. I will point out, however, that these repressive regulations were largely ineffective; they never developed into a coherent and reliable system of slave control as they left ample room for uncontrolled and sometimes even rebellious activities.

The Emergence of Slavery in Massachusetts

Compared to the South, the relatively small slave population of New England only grew to substantial numbers in the eighteenth century. The first black slaves, however, came to New England in 1638 when Massachusetts sent Native Americans captured during the Pequot War to the Caribbean in exchange for black slaves.[1] According to Edmund Morgan, the enslavement of Indians and Africans, as well as the coercive servitude of Scottish and Irish prisoners of war in New England, was justified by claiming they had forfeited their liberty by being vanquished in 'just wars' as a punishment for sin (Morgan, *Puritan Family* 109-11), a belief that derived from the writings of church father St. Augustine. It is important to note, however, that in New England, voluntary and involuntary forms of servitude existed at the same time and that the so-called voluntary forms of servitude dominated by far in terms of numbers. The group of voluntary servants consisted of children who had been apprenticed to masters by their parents to learn a trade, servants who were hired as laborers for a couple of years, and the famous indentured servants—those who wanted to get to America but could not afford to pay for the voyage, and for this reason contracted with a master to serve for seven years in exchange for passage to the New World. Involuntary servitude, on the other hand, could be afflicted on criminals and prisoners made in (just) wars as punishment. In contrast to the enslaved Indians and Africans, however, white servants were never held in perpetual bondage (Morgan, *Puritan Family* 109-11). The perpetual enslavement of 'heathens' was justified by reference to the Old Testament, and the Puritans claimed that God had given them Indian and black servants as part of their biblical inheritance (L. Greene, *Negro* 151). The old Hebrews knew two types of servitude: the servitude of male Jewish servants was legally limited to six years unless they decided to stay voluntarily with their masters in order to remain with an enslaved wife (Exod. 21.2-6); non-Jewish slaves (gentiles), in contrast, could be kept in perpetual bondage and be inherited in the family (Lev. 25.44, 46).[2] Thus, biblical example, the just war theory, and a religious sense of mission towards the indigenous 'devil worshippers,' combined with an ethnocentric sentiment of cultural superiority, helped the Puritans to reconcile slavery and Christianity from early on.[3] It is hardly surprising, therefore, that Massachusetts had already legally recognized slavery in 1639. The "Body of Liberties" stated that "there shall never be any bond slaverie, villinage or Captivitie amongst us unles it be lawfull Captives taken in just warres, and such strangers as willingly selle themselves or are sold to us" (Whitmore 53; par. 91).

During the early decades of the colony, however, the number of slaves remained small and saw a sharp increase only in the first half of the eighteenth century. The years of the largest growth, between 1700 and 1750, coincided with a time of economic prosperity that also was characterized by an increase in New England's

---

[1] "We sent 15 of the boys and 2 of the women to the Bermudas by Mr. Pierce; but he missing it carried them to Providence Isle" (Winthrop 227-28). For a closer examination see Jennings 225-26; Mason 616-20; Fickes 58-81; L. Greene, *Negro* 15-18; Moore 4-7; Hyde 12-13.

[2] See Reiss 3. For the distinction of the two different types of servitude described in the Old Testament, see Cobb xxxviii-xlix.

[3] For an overview on the debate on Indian-White relations and the settlers' ethnocultural self-perception in Puritan Massachusetts, see Thomas 3-27. The title is somewhat misleading since the author admits that Puritan attitudes were (albeit despicable) not 'racial' in the modern sense of the word. See also Bailey 39-73.

agricultural and industrial productivity and a rise of market oriented activities (Melish 19-20). The eighteenth century also saw the rise of New England's commercial involvement in the slave trade, which affected New England's economic development far more directly than slave holding (L. Greene, "Slave-Holding" 502). In the first decades of the eighteenth century, before they were surpassed by Rhode Island towns such as Newport, Bristol, and Providence, Boston merchants played a leading role in the slave trade (McManus 10). The African slave trade racialized slavery by turning perpetual bondage into an almost exclusively black institution, even threatening the liberty of free blacks, because skin color became increasingly synonymous with social status.[4]

One example of this development is the story of Thomas Barter, a black man who was in danger of becoming enslaved in Boston in 1712.[5] Thomas Barter was the son of Edward Barter, a black African interpreter working for English slave traders on the coast of Guinea. Edward Barter had been educated in England and had a close relationship with his European business partners (Nagl 645); one of his daughters was even married to an English slave trader. Around 1708 Edward Barter decided to put his son Thomas into the custody of the ship captain John Sadler who should take him to England. Thomas was supposed

> to be Educated & Instructed to read & write, & to learn such other things as should be thought proper & Convenient, and at the End of the six years [...] [he] was to be returned to his said Father again". Edward Barter promised John Sadler to pay "what he [Sadler] should Expend & lay out in his Education & bringing [him] up [...].

When the young man left the coast of Africa, however, he was to embark upon an unforeseen odyssey around the 'Black Atlantic.' As promised, Captain Sadler took him to London, but as the captain was obliged to continue his trip to Weymouth, he decided to leave Thomas Barter "under the Care & Keeping of One John Ingleton of London Brandyman where he was to Continue till the sd. Sadlers return back from Weymouth." But John Ingleton, far from keeping his promise, soon disposed himself of Thomas Barter by handing him over to the ship captain Jeremiah Turner. They then "proceeded from London to New York in America." On the voyage back to Lisbon, the ship was captured by two French battle ships and "& Carryed into Cadiz in the Kingdom of Spain" where Thomas Barter was imprisoned with the rest of the crew. When they were finally released six month later, Barter was allowed to leave with them, as two crew members confirmed that he was not a slave. But Barter's unlucky destiny did not stop there. He decided to remain with Captain Turner and join him on a trip to Virginia. When they got back to London, Barter was left in the custody of a Mr. Benjamin Barnes. Barnes was a man of sinister intentions, for he embarked on a ship to Boston with Barter and as soon as they arrived there, he tried to sell the surprised young African man as a slave. In order to prevent himself from being enslaved, Barter desperately wrote a petition to "His Excellency the Governor and to the Hono[ra]ble. Her

---

[4] For a comprehensive analysis of the Massachusetts slave trade, see Desrochers, "Slave" 623-64 and Desrochers, "Every Picture" 146-216.

[5] The following story is reconstructed from court file papers found in *The Suffolk Files Collection*. All following quotations are taken from these pages.

Maj.[es]ties Council, or to any Court of Justice whom it may Concern" in which he begged that no injustice should be done to him. Paul Dudley, a Justice of the Peace in Boston, upon receiving this information, ordered that Benjamin Barnes and his brother James Barnes post a security of fifty pounds each to ensure that they would not sell "the sd. Negro out of this Province without the Knowledge & Consent of Her Majesties Government or some Court of Justice within ye Province." While the ultimate fate of Thomas Barter cannot be determined from the surviving documents, there exists a court testimony of a Boston slave trader who claimed to know Thomas Barter's father in Africa, a fact that lends some credibility to the whole story.

The Law and the Economy of Slavery in Massachusetts

The case of Thomas Barter is a fascinating example of the contradictory legal and social relations slavery produced in Massachusetts. The fact that Barter took recourse to court in a desperate attempt to escape his enslavement points to a rather unique feature of slavery in the colony, as Barter was not the first black person in Massachusetts to contest his legal status in court. In 1701, Adam, a slave to the Judge John Saffin, had entered a protracted legal battle against his master, who had broken his promise to set him at liberty if he faithfully served him for seven years.[6] The case was even brought before the highest court of the colony, and Adam finally was declared free in 1703. What had enabled Adam to sue his master in the first place was the curious legal form slavery had assumed in New England. Lorenzo Greene points out that New England slavery was a "blending of servitude and bondage" (*Negro* 168),[7] and for this reason New England slaves occupied a dual legal status: they were property *and* persons at the same time—property in the sense that they could be traded and treated as commodities, and persons because they still were entitled to certain rights under the law. In New England, slaves were legal subjects who could make contracts, were allowed to participate in church service, could testify in court as witnesses against both blacks and whites, and were even able to file law suits (L. Greene, *Negro* 179). This observation is an important deviation from the sociological concepts in which slavery is usually conceived, as theoretical notions of slavery often entail an idea of "social death" in the sense that slaves did not belong to the community and had no social existence independent from their masters (Patterson 38). This resonates with what Italian philosopher Giorgio Agamben has recently analyzed with recourse to the antique figure of the "homo sacer." Slaves resemble Agamben's "homines sacres" because they might be said to lose their political lives (zoé) by becoming excluded from society and by being reduced to their bare biological lives (bíos) (6-12). A closer look, however, reveals that these

---

[6] See Greene, *Negro* 184-85; Towner, "A Fondness" 201-19; Towner, "Sewall-Saffin" 40-52; Goodell, "John Saffin" 85-112. See also Peterson; Von Frank; Sands; Saffin, *His Book*.

[7] For a recent discussion of the old controversy as to whether the slaves in early seventeenth century had the same legal status as indentured servants, see Berg.

theoretical constructs can be misleading when they are applied to the history of the institution of slavery. Slavery evolved gradually over time, with the initial situation of relative openness giving way to the step-by-step codification of the system of chattel slavery around 1700. The 'social death' of the slaves, therefore, was neither instant nor sudden. In New England masters could not claim a boundless sovereignty over death and life. Slaves did not completely lose their political lives and legal bodies, and for this reason they could not be killed with impunity (L. Greene, *Negro* 177). New England slavery, after all, was not that much different from other forms of early modern bondage such as indentured servitude (Towner, *"A Good Master"* 149-50).

This special legal status was fostered and supported by the slaves' socioeconomic position in New England's social structure. Most of the slaves were male and could be found in the commercial and agricultural seaport towns along the coast and in a few agricultural areas. With the significant exception of Rhode Island, large-scale slave plantations, such as those that existed in the southern colonies, did not exist in New England, and in the colonial era blacks never constituted more than 2.5% of New England's population (McCusker 652; "Boston Census" 95-97). In Massachusetts the highest number of slaves could be found in Suffolk County; Boston in particular harbored a substantial number of the colony's black population. According to a census taken in 1754, there were 4,489 slaves in Massachusetts and 989 of them—22%—lived in Boston, thus making up 10% of the city's population. Lawrence Towner has even estimated that in the 1730s and '40s black servants and slaves became the largest single source of imported labor in Massachusetts (*"A Good Master"* 151). While the slaves of Boston—like elsewhere in New England—seem to have been employed in a great variety of functions, a majority were employed in domestic service. Some performed unskilled labor in shipbuilding, and a minority were even trained in skilled trades such as carpentry, blacksmithing, and tailoring. In 1795 Reverend Jeremy Belknap recalled that "in the maritime towns, the negroes served either in families or at mechanical employments" (200). An eighteenth-century author noted that "there is no house in Boston, however, small may be its means, that has not one or two [Negroes]" (Shurtleff 48-49.) However, from the surviving names of slave holders, it appears that a large number were members of the city's political and social elite, even though there were also some wealthy artisans among them (Horton and Horton 14). Eminent men of the Boston community—doctors, lawyers, ministers, deacons, merchants, sea captains, justices, and even governors—owned slaves. These slaves typically did not live physically separated from the white members of their masters' family, but were housed, slept, and often worked under the same roof. And just like the white population of New England, slaves were required to legitimize their sexual relationships by marrying, and their intentions to marry had to be made public before the wedding. Furthermore, even though there seems to have been little effort among early Puritans to Christianize their slaves, there is at least anecdotal evidence that in New England slaves were more often encouraged to attend church service than their fellow sufferers in the south. When in the eighteenth century—after the Bishop of London had made a definite statement on the issue in 1727—fears waned that the slaves' conversion to Christianity would set them free, and a considerable number were even baptized into membership of their masters' churches.[8] In sum, in New England the spatial proximity, together with the strong Puritan foundation of the colony's culture, contributed to the slave's social integration into their master's family and the larger society. William D. Pierson describes the familiar nature of this type of slavery with the term "family slavery," which drew heavily on the biblical example of the patriarchal family (25-26). Thus, in colonial Massachusetts slave management was part of a system of 'family government' that was characterized by an intimate cohabitation of masters and slaves.

'Pastoral Power' and 'Governmentality' in Puritan Massachusetts

A good example of this religiously grounded "family government" (Morgan, *Puritan Family*) can be found in the case of the famous Puritan theologian and Reverend of Boston's Old North Church, Cotton Mather. While Mather is chiefly remembered for his involvement in and his account of the Salem witch trials, it is less known that in 1717 Mather opened a short-lived night school for religious instruction for blacks and Indians (Horton and Horton 21), and that between 1706 and 1717 he himself owned a slave whom he called Onesimus.[9] In his diary entry for December 1706, Mather recounts their first encounter:

> Some gentlemen of our Church, understanding (without any Application of mine to them for such a Thing,) that I wanted a good servant, at the expence of between forty and fifty Pounds, purchased for me, a very likely Slave; a young man, who is a Negro of a promising Aspect and Temper, And this Day they presented him unto me. It seems to be a might Smile of Heaven upon my family; and it arrives at an observable Time Unto me. I putt upon him the name of Onesimus; and I resolved with The Help of the Lord, that I would use the Best Endeavors to make him a Servant of Christ. (*Diary* 1: 579)

Mather named his slave Onesimus after a biblical slave who had escaped from his Christian master Philemon. Apostle Paul eventually met the runaway slave, converted him to Christianity and sent him back to his old master with a letter that asked Philemon to take Onesimus in again, "not now as a servant, but above a servant, a brother beloved" (Philemon 1:10, 16) Around 1716 Mather, apparently having some quarrels with Onesimus, who now "proves wicked, and grows useless, Froward and Immorigerous," allowed Onesimus to buy his freedom by saving money to purchase for Mather the young black slave Obadiah, who was a "a better servant in his Room" (*Diary* 2: 363). After his release, however, Onesimus seems to have continued to work in Mather's household together with other servants. He became famous in 1721 when a devastating smallpox epidemic struck Boston, and Mather used information he had learned some years earlier from his former slave when he proposed "ye Method of Inoculation," a vaccination technique practiced in Africa and Asia Minor, as the best way to fight the disease. Mather's relationship with Onesimus seems to have been not without difficulties, but his diary clearly indicates his benevolent and educational intentions:

---

[8] See Hyde 86; Greene, *Negro* 268; Jernegan 32.
[9] See Niven 640-41; Winslow 539-59; Middlekauf 354-59; Silverman 264-65.

> There are several points, relating to the Instruction and management of my Servant Onesimus, which I would now more than ever prosecute. He shall be sure to read every Day. From thence, I will have him go on to writing. He shall be frequently Catechised. I would also invent some advantageous Way, wherein he may spend his Liesure-hours. (*Diary* 2: 271-72)

In January 1714 Mather recorded in his *Diary* the death of Onesimus' son and claimed to use the tragic event to "incalculate agreeable Admonitions of Piety upon him" (2: 282). When Onesimus became implied in "some actions of a thievish aspect," Mather gloomily noted "that I must keep strict Eye on my Servant Onesimus; especially with regard unto his company"; but at the same time Mather referred to him as a family member when he continued:

> But then, upon every observable Miscarriage of any Person in my Family, I must make my flight unto the Blood of my Savior, as a Family Sacrifice: so that Wrath of God may be turned away from my Family. (*Diary* 2: 139)

Mather's remarks on slavery reveal a distinct 'governmentalty' of slavery, a term I understand as a specific *Puritan* rationality of rule and practice of mastership that places the slave within the family.[10] This governmentality is not based primarily on force or coercive measures, but stresses forms of governance that make use of close social surveillance by the community and that apply discourses and symbols as means of domination. Mather summarized the essence of this Puritan governmentality of slavery in July 1713 when he wrote:

> My Negro-Servant, is [...] more easily govern'd and managed, by the Principles of reason, agreeably offered unto him, than by any other methods. I would oftener call him aside, and assay to reason him into good behavior. (*Diary* 2: 222)

Religious instruction, education, and the internalization of norms and rules stand out as key elements of a form of slave management directed at producing voluntary compliance and good self-conduct.

Puritan governmentality shows some similarities with the affirmative notion of slavery as a system of benevolent paternalism which was popular among southern slave holders in the nineteenth century. By applying Gramsci's concept of 'hegemony,' Genovese integrated the paternalistic view of slavery that had been prominently put forward by southern historian Ulrich B. Phillips into a Marxist analysis of southern slavery. It is important, however, to understand the differences and theoretical shortcomings of Genovese's approach.[11] Clarence E. Walker and others have convincingly argued that Genovese uses the notion of hegemony as an all-explaining grand narrative that simply dresses the slaveholders' view of slavery in Marxist clothing. Thus the concept obscures as much about antebellum slavery as it reveals. Hegemony allows Genovese to preserve his belief in class domination and yet explain the absence of visible class struggle. Viewed in this context, the idea of hegemony is part of the Marxist effort to explain why the great revolu-

---

[10] For a general analysis of the relationship between Puritanism and Slavery, which also addresses the problem of slave baptism, see Rosenthal 62-81.

[11] For a comprehensive treatment of the problem and a fundamental critique of the concepts of ideology, see Chartier; Kolchin 52-67; Walker 56-72.

tions (in this case slave revolts) did not occur as they should have and therefore glosses over the many existing social differences and non-revolutionary conflicts in southern society by presenting it as a static, almost unchanging social formation. Moreover, differences of opinion concerning disputes over political representation, taxes, and slavery have led some scholars to suggest that the planter's dominance was never so absolute as to constitute a 'hegemony.' The model of an all-pervasive planter hegemony exclude the idea that the slaves might have been able to develop an independent interpretation of religion. In Genovese's conception of American slave Christianity, religion is analyzed along functional lines and described as a vehicle of consent; it did not generate a sense of denial that would culminate in revolt. Slaves allegedly did not accept the idea of original sin and affirmed the 'joy in life in the face of every trial.' According to Genovese, this prevented the development of a revolutionary or politically militant millennialism and messianism. Thus, religion appears simply to have mystified the slaves' sense of political power and reconciled them to their position in society. Genovese's history, argues Walker, is all in all

> too logical to be an accurate picture of the past, for what Genovese has done is to take an ambiguous theoretical construct and make it precise. In brief, Genovese's hegemony coheres where Gramsci's may have not, for Gramsci's writings suggest that a ruling class's exercise of hegemony was never total nor static. Furthermore, hegemony's scope and impact, Gramsci argued, varied from one society to another. Genovese makes only perfunctory obeisance to these qualifications. Hegemony as he uses the concept is all-encompassing and pervasive (58).

In addition, Genovese tends to downplay the coercive nature of slavery by uncritically conflating the masters' proslavery rhetoric with the reality of power relationships under slavery in the antebellum South. He thus establishes paternalism as an umbrella term under which all master-slave relations can be subsumed. Walker claims, however, that slavery in the period discussed by Genovese necessarily involved mutuality or reciprocity. If this is the case, antebellum slavery was not paternalistic at all: "The planters may have defended slavery with a rhetoric whose imagery was domestic and familial, but this was only a smokescreen for exploitation or a technique of exploitation" (63). Another big problem is Genovese's emphasis on class at the expense of race when he argues that slavery is "by definition and in essence" (Walker 66) a system of class rule. Racism, however, argues Robert Blauner, "excludes a category of people from participation in society in a different way than does class hegemony and exploitation. The thrust of racism is to de-humanize, to violate dignity and degrade personalities in a much more pervasive and all-inclusive way than class exploitation" (qtd. in Walker 66).

One might, perhaps, argue that at least in some respects Genovese's model of a benevolent paternalist slave system (defined as a system of reciprocal obligations) is a more appropriate description of the family- and household-based slavery of Puritan New England than that of the antebellum South. However, given the relatively marginal role slave labor played in New England's economy, one can hardly portray Massachusetts slavery as a system of social class dominance of slaveholders and apply a Marxist notion of ideology in the sense of 'false consciousness' or 'hegemony' in the immediate interest of a ruling planter class. Besides, one must keep in mind that the proslavery argument of paternalism in nineteenth-century discourses on slavery evolved in a time when the institution of slavery seemed to be increasingly at odds with the principles of liberal democracy. Accordingly, paternalism served as an unveiled attempt to defend slavery against modern ideas of human rights. In contrast, the paternal elements in the discourse on slavery in colonial New England were not born of a need to justify the institution of slavery in face of liberal values (J. Greene 793) or dictated by the necessity to find a way "of mediating irreconcilable class and racial conflicts" (Genovese 6); they derived from a genuinely pre-modern and religiously based world view that produced a distinct form of human bondage. Moreover, the reality of slavery in colonial Massachusetts cannot be equated with Southern plantation slavery. Southern slaves—resembling Agamben's "homines sacres"—never possessed any legal rights comparable to those of the slaves in colonial Massachusetts. The examples of Thomas Barter and John Saffin's slave Adam show that slaves had recourse to courts which sometimes even enabled them to sue their masters. This peculiar legal status was an expression of a distinctly Puritan practice of slavery and a religious understanding of society which derived from medieval and ancient notions of servitude. In contrast to the simplifying, totalizing notion of slavery as a system of hegemonic class rule, a governmentality approach rejects the idea that individual social classes can exert total ideological control over society or permanently articulate coherent interests. It emphasizes that social and cultural domination cannot be reduced to the economic interests of one social class. Governmentality, rather, investigates historically, and beginning from the lowest level, determines how the multiplicity of dispersed local power relations shape subjectivities by weaving together micro-practices of self-conduct and macro-practices of government. Power is thus conceived as "action on actions" and government as the "the conduct of conduct" (Foucault, "Subject" 221). Within this framework resistance is not marginalized as in Genovese's model of hegemony, but is an ever-present possibility. It is a consequence of the subjects' freedom to act and a necessary outcome of Foucault's action-oriented notion of power.[12] Moreover, governmentality entails the idea that religion, and churches in particular, produce and maintain the knowledge, truths, and social order associated with self-regulated governance. It is this emphasis on religious and spiritual practices that make the governmentality approach a valuable contribution to the study of Puritan society (see Bendle).

The Puritan practice of slavery entailed a form of exercising power that noticeably resembles Foucault's description of "Christian pastoral power."[13] Foucault describes pastoral power as a predecessor of or a 'prelude' to the modern and secularized notions of political rule that—from the sixteenth century on-

---

[12] "Freedom is not only a necessary precondition of power, but also that which resists power. Precisely because freedom is an indispensable element of any power relation, there are no power relations without the possibility of resistance. [...] Foucault's novel conception of power as 'action on actions' redirects the theoretical orientation of his earlier works, which had stressed the anonymity of power and its strategies" (Lemke 305; translation mine).

[13] See Foucault, *Security*, especially lectures seven, eight, and nine (163-254); Foucault, "Subject" (213-14); Foucault, *History* (136).

ward—gradually evolved out of the earlier pastoral modes of governance. Pastoral power is based on the imitation of the example of pastoral leadership of religious congregations. While the origins of this notion of power are clearly religious, it also became a guiding principle for exercising social and political power in the early modern era. In this model the Christian pastor assumes the role of a 'good shepherd' who guards and leads his flock by providing spiritual leadership, teaching the religious truth, and seeing to it that the godly commands are obeyed. It is the ultimate aim of pastoral power to guide humans on the right way so that they are able to find the path to salvation. In order to reach this goal, pastoral power developed into an 'art how to govern humans.' This art of governance operates on the micro-level of the individual and makes use of confessional self-examination and internalization of practices of self-discipline (power techniques orientated towards individuals), that are the very same techniques described by Cotton Mather as the principles of good slave management (Foucault, *'Omnes'* 227). Moreover, the Christian pastorate is characterized by a collective responsibility between the group, the individual, and the pastor as their spiritual leader. Every soul is important to God, and the pastor (or his secular counterpart) will eventually be held accountable not only for the management of the group as a whole, but also for the failings of individual members. This aspect of pastoral power appears in Mather's diary in connection with Onesimus's involvement in criminal activities. Mather clearly expresses the fear that he and his family might be punished by God for Onesimus's wrongdoing when he writes: "I must make my Flight Unto to the Blood of my Saviour, as a Family-Sacrifice; that so the Wrath of God may be turned away from my Family" (*Diary* 2: 139). According to this view, both group and individual share a common destiny: on the one hand, the fate of the group affects every individual, but on the other hand, individual failings might lead to the punishment of the whole society. Edmund S. Morgan has convincingly explained how this principle was put into practice in Puritan New England. Since the whole community had promised obedience to God, the community as a whole could be punished for the sins of any delinquent individual if it did not prosecute that person. By publicly punishing him or her, the community expressed its disapproval of the sinful aberrations and so escaped collective responsibility for them. Constant vigilance should prevent sin from going unpunished: "It was as if a district occupied by a military force were given notice that for any disorder the whole community would be penalized, innocent and guilty alike" (*Puritan Family* 10). Additionally, pastoral power is characterized by a patriarchal and hierarchical notion of authority structures based on the all-pervasive family analogy and the concept of *patria potestas*—the legal authority of a father over his children. From this perspective, all forms of temporal rule are basically an earthly emulation of God's patriarchal rule of the universe, and the political order on earth can be described as a hierarchical continuum of authorities that goes from God down to the political ruler, then to the family father, and so on. Accordingly, Puritan pastors maintained that civil order and civil government were of divine origin. John Norton expressed this notion when he argued in 1659 that "order is a divine disposal, of superior and inferior relations, in humane or Christian societies" (qtd. in Morgan, *Puritan Family* 25).

Covenant, Government, and Family Slavery

As Perry Miller and others have shown, Puritan theology links the individual, God, and society by the Calvinistic concept of 'covenant' (*Errand* 48-98). It is this concept that inserted the mechanisms of pastoral power into the political and social institutions of New England, and it had a profound effect on slavery. A covenant was a form of contract derived from biblical examples in the Old Testament (Kline 27). It was not designed, however, as a treaty between equal parties, "but one between a king and his subjects, and it was a binding contract that stated each party's responsibilities and the punishment that would be meted if either side was delinquent" (Kuehne 36). In Puritan thought, almost all social and spiritual relationships were conceived as hierarchical contractual relationships which took the form of dualistic covenants that bound the participating parties in mutual obligation (Morgan, *Puritan Family* 25). A first covenant, the 'covenant of works,' was made between God and Adam, but it became invalid when Adam violated God's commands. Later God made a new covenant, the 'covenant of grace,' with Abraham (Knight 89). In it God promised to save Abraham (as an individual), his family, and his descendants (the people of Israel) by sending a redeemer (Morgan, *Puritan Political Ideas* xx-xxi). The prerequisite of God's deal with Abraham was a covenant which God had made with Jesus and which already existed "from the beginning of time, even before the transaction with Abraham" (Miller, *New England* 406). In this 'covenant of redemption,' "God covenanted with Christ that if he would pay the full price for the redemption of beleevers [sic], they should be discharged. Christ hath paid the price [...]" (Miller, *New England* 406). With the coming of Christ, every Christian who responds to God's grace by faith can receive salvation as God's gift. A holy way of life (sanctification) was interpreted as a sign of election (salvation), but—according to the theory of predestination—the former certainly could not cause the latter.

The Puritans' typological reading of the Bible led them to believe that Christians had inherited the covenant of grace from Abraham not only as individuals, but also as families and nations. On the group level, however, the covenant theory conflicted with the notion of predestination. The Puritans firmly believed that there were only a small number of persons elected for salvation, and so it could not be assumed that every member of their families, congregations, or political community would be spared from damnation. For this reason they were forced to develop the theological theory of the covenant of grace into a political theory of social contract that also knew family, church, and state covenants:

> The covenant, they said, when applied to a group, originated in, but was not the same as, the covenant of an individual. It had different terms and a different name. It was called a family covenant or a church covenant or a state covenant, instead of a covenant of grace, and the group engaging in it promised external obedience of faith and received external, temporal prosperity instead of eternal salvation. Since every group contained unbelievers, no group as such was capable of salvation. (Morgan, *Puritan Family* 9)

Echoing St. Augustine's distinction between an earthly and a heavenly city, Puritans distinguished between a temporal 'visible church,' which included true believers and outwardly righteous sinners, from the eternal 'invisible church,' which was reserved for true saints. The existence of 'black sheep'—not only in the visible church, but also in the families and in the state—and the reciprocal logic of pastoral power required that the 'governments' of these bodies should at least guarantee the knowledge of and formal obedience to God's commands. Otherwise, the whole collective would suffer under God's punishment. Thus it becomes understandable that the institution of the family did not exist as "a private retreat from the public world" but "was viewed as extension of, rather than escape from, all other institutions; it was the first filiation that led to all subsequent affiliations" (Kaufmann 20). The result of this covenantal construction of society was a web of mutual obligations and a social order in which individual identity "was defined by one's relation to, not independence from, institutions such as church, state and family" (Kaufmann 15).

Slavery as a coercive institution could not easily be integrated into this system of contractual relationships in which even forms of servitude such as indenture were based on the (theoretical) free will of its participants. When Richard Mather stated that "all relations which are neither naturall nor violent, but voluntary, are by vertue of some covenant" (22), there were two exceptions implied: children and prisoners of war. Since early Puritan law defined slaves as prisoners made in just wars, they belonged to the latter category. Although slaves and children were not active participants in the making of a covenant, because they were family members they were *indirectly* implied in the family covenant. This covenant required the head of the household to take responsibility for his family's religious instruction and good behavior; he could demand strict obedience from them because the Puritan world view "strongly emphasized the submission of children and other dependents within the family" (Anderson 159). Cotton Mather even claimed that masters "a little bear the image of God in that Government, which you have over your servants" (*Good Master* 7). In the words of the English seventeenth-century political theorist Robert Filmer, it was the duty of fathers and kings "to preserve, feed, clothe, instruct, and defend" the subjects under their care and keeping (10). Failure to comply with this command could be interpreted as a sinful abuse of power that would eventually be punished by God. For this reason, Cotton Mather reminded masters of their "pastoral" duties and warned them of the consequences—for both themselves and their slaves—of neglecting this responsibility. In 1706 he vehemently argued for the religious education of slaves in his essay *The Negro Christianized*:

> There are Servants pertaining to thy Household. It is a mighty Power which thou hast over them; A Despotick Power which gives thee numberless Advantages, to call them, and lead them into the Way of the Lord. Art thou Regardless of bringing them into Christianity? Then thou doest not Walk in the Steps of our Father Abraham; and art not like to call him thy Father [...] When such Christians appear before the Glorious LORD, it will be in vain for them to plead, that they call'd him LORD, and own'd Him for their LORD. If they did it why did they not bring their SERVANTS under Governement of the LORD? Verily, He will say to such Christians, I knew you not. (5-13)

Cotton Mather—and other ministers such as Ezra Stiles, Daniel Wadsworth, and Parson Ashley—not only threatened the slaveholders with eternal damnation (Mather's formulation clearly alludes to Matthew 7.21-23), but they were also eager to show that Christianizing the slaves would have immediate advantages for the masters themselves. "Yea, the pious Masters," Mather wrote, "that have instituted in their Servants in Christian Piety, will even in this Life have a sensible Recompence" (*Negro* 20). The "Recompence" the masters could expect was a "more Serviceable, and Obedient and Obliging Behaviour of their Servants" because the slaves—"tinged with Spirit of Christianity"—would be exceedingly dutiful, patient, faithful, and "afraid of speaking or doing any thing that may justly diplease you" (*Negro* 21). With the intention to disperse the slave holders' fears that baptism might entitle the slaves to freedom, Mather unambiguously declared that there existed no contradiction between Christianity and slavery:

> What Law is it, that Sets the Baptised Slave at Liberty? Not the Law of Christianity: that allows of Slavery; Only it wonderfully Dulcifies, and Mollifies, and Moderates the Circumstances of it. Christianity directs a Slave, upon his embracing the Law of the Redeemer, to satisfy himself, That he is the Lords Free-man, tho' he continues a Slave. [...] Will the Canon law do it? No; The Canons of Numberless Councils, mention, the Slaves of Christians, without any contradiction. Will the Civil Law do it? No: Tell, if you can, any part of Christendom, wherein Slaves are not frequently to be met withal. But is not Freedom to be claim'd for a Baptised Slave, by the English Constitution? The English Laws, about Villians, or, Slaves, will not say so. (*Negro* 26-27)

It is interesting to note that Mather's religious convictions led him to repudiate any racial justifications of slavery. For such an old-line Puritan, there was no spiritual gap between himself and a slave, and it could not be ruled out "that this Poor Creature may belong to the Election of God!" (*Negro* 3). The idea (originally derived from Aristotle) that certain groups of people were born to be slaves by their natural character was alien to Cotton Mather's thought. Acknowledging a need to 'civilize' the supposedly culturally backward black servants, Mather insisted that Africans were endowed with a "Reasonable Soul" and fiercely lashed out at the emerging racial thought:

> They are Men, and not Beasts that you have bought, and they must be used accordingly.'Tis true; They are Barbarous. But so were our own Ancestors. The Britons were in many things as Barbarous, but a little before our Saviours Nativity, as the Negroes are at this day if there be any Credit in Cæsars Commentaries. Christianity will be the best cure for this Barbarity. [...] The God who looks on the Heart, is not moved by the colour of the Skin. (*Negro* 23-25)

Mather, however, was living in a time when traditional values of Puritanism were in decline. In the eighteenth century, commercial activities and a materialistic mindset more and more replaced old religious attitudes. These changes might have affected the general attitude toward slavery, as well. It is likely that certain slaveholders perceived black servants merely as an instrument to generate profit. Racial arguments could emphasize the justification of their economic interest.[14] Such an attitude was displayed, for example, in 1701 by the merchant and slave-trader John Saffin, who wrote about "the Negroes Character" in response to Samuel Sewall's famous anti-slavery tract, "The Selling of Joseph":

---

[14] The emergence of early modern racial thought is sketched out in Jordan 3-98.

Cowardly and cruel are those Blacks Innate, Prone to Revenge, Imp of inveterate hate. He that exasperates them, soon espies Mischief and Murder in their very eyes. Libidinous, Deceitful, False and Rude, The Spume Issue of Ingratitude. ("Reply" 58)

Mather principally rejected such essentialist notions of race, and he challenged the popular belief that God had singled out black Africans to be enslaved. This religious explanation of black bondage was based on the interpretation of a passage in Genesis (9.20-27) that deals with Noah cursing one of his sons (Haynes 23-40). The Bible relates the story that one day Noah, after enjoying too much wine, was lying naked in his tent. When his son Ham (the name denotes 'dark' or 'black') stumbles upon Noah in this unflattering situation, he tells his brothers, who cover their father's naked body. When Noah awakes he curses Ham's son Canaan rather than Ham and his brothers, and declares that Canaan was henceforth condemned to be the lowest kind of servant. Mather did not oppose the institution of slavery as such, but the obscure theory that black Africans had to serve as slaves because they were the offspring of Ham seemed to him "not so very certain" (*Negro* 2). In 1693, having allegedly been approached by a "company of poor Negroes" in need of spiritual guidance, Cotton Mather propounded a set of nine rules for a "Society of Negroes" which was intended to promote their religious instruction and good behavior. The text, which is written from the slaves' perspective, is a good example of the kind of self-governance and subjectivity Mather expected from 'good' slaves. According to the rules, slaves commit themselves to help catch and punish runaway slaves, promise to "avoid all Wicked Company," and consent to admonish and isolate servants who "fall into the Sin of Drunkenneß, or Swearing, or Cursing, or Lying, or Stealing, or notorious Disobedience or Unfaithfulneß, unto their Masters" (Mather, *Rules*). In addition, slaves promise to "to Meet in the Evening after the Sabbath; and Pray together by turns," and assiduously learn the catechism. The rules emphasize the voluntary participation of slaves in their subjugation and demand good self-conduct and the constant surveillance of other slaves.

Sovereign Power or the Limits of "Soft Power": The Murder of Captain John Codman

The discursively constructed norms found in sermons and programmatic statements of Puritan slaveholders should not be identified naively with the reality of power-relationships under slavery in Puritan New England. The concept of governmentality forces the historian to carefully reconstruct and analyze concrete interactions between masters and slaves in everyday situations. The 'soft' mechanisms of power were neither reliable nor very effective and thus had to be supplemented by corporal disciplinary mechanisms. Gyan Prakash has convincingly argued that colonial forms of governmentality always violate metropolitan norms and conceptions of liberty because the colonized subjects are necessarily denied equal political and legal rights. In colonial societies we do not find a historical progression from sovereign to disciplinary and liberal forms of power that characterized European development according to Foucault.[15] Colonial constellations are usually built on some type of master-slave dialectic and thus can never solely rest on 'pastoral' and 'paternal' mechanisms of domination; they always require a certain degree of force and coercion as a necessary ingredient. Disobedient slaves in New England were usually punished by whipping. Reverend Jeremy Belknap of Boston remembered in the 1790s that his home town, which had a "house of correction, to which disorderly persons of all colours were sent, formed one object of terror to them; but to be sold to the West-Indies, to Carolina, was the highest punishment that could be threatened or inflicted" ("Queries" 200). Massachusetts was the first English colony to legally recognize slavery, and it repeatedly passed legislation concerning matters of race, slavery, and servitude. An "Act to Prevent Disorders in the Night," for example, imposed a 9:00 p.m. curfew on Indians, as well as black and mulatto servants and slaves, and another act forbade interracial marriages (*Acts* 535-36, 578-79). In addition to colony-wide regulations, in 1723 the selectmen of Boston drafted an additional bill for the "Regulation of Negroes, Mulattos and Indians in this town" (*Report* 173-75), which clearly shows the security concerns of white Bostonians. The bill imposed restrictions on the slaves' ability to meet, engage in business activities, drink alcohol, move freely around town, go out at night, and possess weapons.

In reality, however, the slaves were never subject to effective disciplinary control mechanisms. The diary of Reverend Stephen Williams from the town of Longmeadow, for instance, reveals his struggles to control his slave Nicolas. Williams complained on several occasions about the "ill carriage" of his "African boy," lamented that he stayed away at night, and reported that he had to be corrected for his "falsehood and wickedness" (91, 97). The most vivid and extreme example of slave autonomy in the Boston area is the murder of slaveholder Captain John Codman which, in the words of Lois and James Horton, shows that "urban slaves were likely to have a great more freedom of movement and therefore more opportunity for association" (25). Codman was a Charlestown merchant and artisan who owned several slaves. Three of them—house servants Phoebe and Phillis, and Mark, a blacksmith—found the treatment they received from their master unbearable. Mark, who seems to have been the ringleader, was a slave from Barbados who had been brought to Boston as a young child. Codman was his fifth owner, and Mark felt that his earlier owners had given him a much kinder treatment. One had even taught him to read, and had educated him as "tenderly as one of his own Children" (*Last*). According to Massachusetts Historical Society Proceedings as recorded by Abner C. Goodell in "The Murder of John Captain Codman," in a first, but unsuccessful, attempt to get away from their despotic master, the three slaves decided to burn down Codman's workshop by placing some chips of wood "between the Blacksmith's Shop & the Work House" and then throwing a "Coal of Fire" into them. Mark suggested setting fire to the building because "he wanted to get to Boston, and if all was burnt down, he did not know what Master could do without selling us" (131). When the burning of his workhouse did not force Cod-

---

[15] For a statement that emphasizes the ever present dialectics of despotism and self-governance, see Valverde.

man to sell his slaves, Mark conspired with Phillis and Phoebe to kill their master. Phillis later confessed that Mark had told them "that he had read the Bible through, and that it was no Sin to kill him if they did not lay violent Hands on him So as to shed Blood, by sticking or stabbing or cutting his Throat. [...] He said he was uneasy and wanted to have another Master" (127). It was Robbin, the slave of a doctor in Boston, who provided them with arsenic to carry out their plan. The events of the following weeks clearly show how the oppressive slave codes enacted to control the slaves were all in vain, and this story is a telling example of how slaves were able to avoid the laws.

Documental evidence indicates that Mark and Robbin met secretly at night on two occasions—once to receive the arsenic, and a second time to obtain more when the three conspirators lost the poison before their master had received a deadly dose (134). Mark traveled to Boston to obtain additional arsenic from Robbin, who pretended "to the Ferryman that he was a Country negro and wanted to see [...] [Mark] about [...] his Child" (129). Before Mark took the return ferry to Charleston, he and Robbin met another slave to have a "hot Toddy" at Mrs. Shearman's, who lived close "to the long Wharffe" and who was known to sell alcohol to slaves against the will of their masters (135). The following evening the slaves poisoned Codman by putting arsenic into his "barly Drink and into his Infusion, and into his Chocalate, and into his Watergrue" (127), and apparently supplemented the arsenic by mixing lead into their master's food. The day before Codman died, Phoebe went to her master's blacksmith shop to meet her fellow slave Tom, who was suffering from an injured eye. There she "got to dancing & mocking master & shaking herself & acting as master did in the Bed; And Tom said he did not care, he hop'd he wou'd never get up again for his Eye's sake" (136). But as fate would have it, the coroners of the county of Middlesex immediately realized what the slaves had done to Codman. The punishment they received was merciless and intended as a warning to all slaves. While Phoebe seems to have been transported to the West Indies, the fate of Mark and Phillis was reported by the *Boston Evening Post* on September 22, 1755:

> Thursday last, in the Afternoon, Mark, a Negro Man, and Phillis, a Negro Woman, both Servants to the late Capt. John Codman, of Charlestown, were executed at Cambridge, for poisoning their said Master [...]. The fellow was hanged, and the Woman burned at a Stake about Ten Yards distant from the Gallows. They both confessed themselves guilty of the Crime for which they suffered, acknowledged the Justice of their Sentence, and died very pentitent [sic]. After Execution, the Body of Mark was brought down to Charlestown Common, and hanged in Chains, on a Gibbet erected there for that Purpose.

Conclusion

Slavery in colonial Massachusetts distinguished itself by a distinct social character and a unique legal form that separated it from slavery in other English colonies. While it is true that racial stereotypes and discourses on racial difference were of increasing significance in the eighteenth century, slavery in Massachusetts—anachronistically combining elements of biblical bondage, indentured servitude, and early modern slavery—nevertheless retained its peculiar legal structure. For this reason slaves were able to legally challenge their status and sometimes even successfully sued their masters for freedom. The explanation for this peculiarity is to be found in the religious beliefs of the seventeenth-century Puritan settlers, which incorporated the slave into the master's family by means of extending the theological concept of covenant to the community and household levels. According to this concept, the family was not a private retreat from society, but formed its smallest social, religious, and political unit. Slaves, intimately integrated both spatially and socially into their masters' households, were conceived as dependant family members. The head of the family was not only the undisputed patriarchal ruler and responsible for the family's material well-being, but was also obliged to provide for spiritual guidance. If a father failed in performing his pastoral duties, God was likely to collectively punish him and his family or even the entire community. The Calvinistic theory of predestination demanded consideration of the slave as a human being, culturally backwards perhaps, but nonetheless endowed with a soul and principally eligible for salvation, just as any other person. Thus, the religious instruction of the slaves should not be perceived as merely a benevolent enterprise or a utilitarian act of paternalistically minded slaveholders. It must be understood as an earnestly felt religious duty that sprang from Puritan theology and fear of punishment. Nevertheless, Massachusetts slaveholders and Puritan ministers knew, of course, that religion also could be beneficially employed as an instrument of behavioral control. Those 'governmental' mechanisms of slave control aimed at the voluntary internalization of norms, rules, and patterns of deferential behavior. They were not reliable, however, in bringing about the desired outcomes, and they sometimes even had paradoxical consequences. Mark and other rebellious slaves in colonial Massachusetts embraced Christianity on terms that were at odds with dominant Puritan beliefs, for they creatively adapted the religious messages to their own needs, thus transforming them into a resource of obstinate and resistant behavior. This double-edged nature of the slaves' religious education appears to have been a problem of slaveholders in general, as it is a well-established fact that some of the prominent leaders of the nineteenth-century North American slave rebellions were religiously motivated. Soft power was never enough to maintain control of the slaves. Slavery is an inherently coercive and exploitative system that cannot dispense with physical violence and despotic forms of power, and colonial Massachusetts was no exception to this rule.

Works Cited

The Acts and Resolves, Public and Private, of the Province of the Massachusetts Bay from 1692-1780: to Which Are Prefixed the Charters of the Province. With Historical and Explanatory Notes and an Appendix. Vol. 1. Boston: Wright and Potter, 1692. Print. 21 vols.

Agamben, Giorgio. *Homo Sacer: Sovereign Power and Bare Life*. Stanford, CA: Stanford UP, 1998. Print.

Anderson, Virginia DeJohn. *New England's Generation: The Great Migration and the Formation of Society and Culture in the Seventeenth Century.* Cambridge: Cambridge UP, 1991. Print.

Bailey, Richard A. *Race and Redemption in Puritan New England.* Oxford: Oxford UP, 2011. Print.

Bendle, Mervyn F. "Foucault, Religion and Governmentality." *Australian Religion Studies Review* 15.1 (2002): 11-26. Print.

Berg, Manfred. "Die Ursprünge der Sklaverei in Nordamerika." *Zeitschrift für Geschichtswissenschaft* 54.9 (2006): 741-60. Print.

"Boston Census." *Collections of the Massachusetts Historical Society: Vol. III [of the Second Series].* Boston: John Eliot, 1815. 95-97. Print.

Burchell, Graham, Collin Gordon, and Peter Miller, eds. *The Foucault Effect: Studies in Governmentality with Two Lectures by and an Interview with Michel Foucault.* Chicago, IL: U of Chicago P, 1991. Print.

Chartier, Roger. *Cultural History: Between Practices and Representations.* Ithaca, NY: Cornell UP, 1988. Print.

Cobb, Thomas R. *An Inquiry into the Law of Negro Slavery in the United States of America.* Philadelphia: Johnson, 1858. Print.

Dean, Mitchell. *Governmentality: Power and Rule in Modern Society.* London: Sage, 1999. Print.

Desrochers, Robert E., Jr. "Every Picture Tells a Story: Slavery and Print in Eighteenth-Century New England." Diss. Johns Hopkins U, 2001. Print.

---. "Slave for Sale Advertisements and Slavery in Massachusetts, 1704-1781." *William and Mary Quarterly* 59.3 (2002): 623-64. Print.

Fickes, Michael L. "'They Could Not Endure That Yoke': The Captivity of Pequot Women and Children after the War of 1637." *New England Quarterly* 73.1 (2000): 58-81. Print.

Filmer, Robert. "Patriarcha, or the Natural Power of Kings." 1640. *Patriarcha and Other Writings.* Ed. Johann Sommerville. Cambridge: Cambridge UP, 1991. 1-63. Print.

Foucault, Michel. *The History of Sexuality.* Vol. 1. New York: Pantheon, 1978. Print. 3 vols.

---. *'Omnes et Singulatim: Toward a Criticism of Political Reason': Two Lectures Delivered at Stanford University, California, on October 10 and 16, 1979. The Tanner Lectures on Human Values.* Ed. Sterling M. McMurrin. Vol. 2. Salt Lake City: U of Utah P, 1981. Print.

---. *Security, Territory, Population: Lectures at the College de France, 1977-1978.* New York: Picador, 2007. Print.

---. "The Subject and Power." *Beyond Structuralism and Hermeneutics.* Ed. Hubert L. Dreyfus and Paul Rabinow. 2nd ed. Chicago, IL: U of Chicago P, 1983. 208-28. Print.

Genovese, Eugene. *Roll Jordan Roll: The World the Slaves Made.* New York: Pantheon, 1974. Print.

Goodell, Abner C., Jr. "John Saffin and His Slave Adam." *Colonial Society of Massachusetts Publications* I (1895): 85-112. Print.

---. "The Murder of John Captain Codman." *Massachusetts Historical Society Proceedings* XX (1883): 122-57. Print.

Greene, Jack P. "'A Plain and Natural Right to Life and Liberty': An Early Natural Rights Attack on the Excesses of the Slave System in Colonial British America." *William and Mary Quarterly* 57.4 (2000): 793-808. Print.

Greene, Lorenzo J. *The Negro in Colonial New England*. New York: Columbia UP, 1942. Print.

---. "Slave-Holding New England and Its Awakening." *Journal of Negro History* 13.4 (1928): 492-533. Print.

Haynes, Stephen R. *Noah's Curse: The Biblical Justification of American Slavery*. Oxford: Oxford UP, 2002. Print.

Higginbotham, A. Leon, Jr. *In the Matter of Color: Race and the American Legal Process*. Vol. 1. New York: Oxford UP, 1978. Print. 2 vols.

Horton, James Oliver, and Lois E. Horton. *In Hope of Liberty: Culture, Community, and Protest Among Northern Free Blacks, 1700-1860*. New York: Oxford UP, 1997. Print.

Hyde, Laura Hutchison. "Negro Slavery in Colonial New England." Diss. U of Chicago, 1914. Print.

Jennings, Francis. *The Invasion of America: Indians, Colonialism, and the Cant of Conquest*. Chapel Hill: U of North Carolina P, 2010. Print.

Jernegan, Marcus Wilson. *Laboring and Dependent Classes in Colonial America, 1607-1783: Studies of the Economic, Educational, and Social Significance of Slaves, Servants, Apprentices and Poor Folk*. Chicago, IL: U of Chicago P, 1931. Print.

Jordan, Winthrop D. *White Over Black: American Attitudes Toward the Negro 1550-1812*. Chapel Hill: U of North Carolina P, 1968. Print.

Kaufmann, Michael W. *Institutional Individualism: Conversion, Exile and Nostalgia in Puritan New England*. Hanover: Wesleyan UP, 1998. Print.

Kline, Meredith G. *The Structure of Biblical Authority*. Grand Rapids: Eerdmans, 1978. Print.

Knight, Janice. *Orthodoxies Massachusetts: Rereading American Puritanism*. Cambridge, MA: Harvard UP, 1994. Print.

Kolchin, Peter. "Eugene D. Genovese: Historian of Slavery." *Radical History Review* 88 (2004): 52-67. Print.

Kuehne, Dale S. *Massachusetts Congregationalist Political Thought, 1760–1790*. Columbia: U of Missouri P, 1996. Print.

The Last & Dying Words of Mark Aged about 30 Years. A Negro Man who belonged to the late Captain John Codman of Charleston; Who was executed at Cambridge, the 18th of September, 1755, for Poysoning his abovesaid Master. Boston, 1755 (Imprint housed at Massachusetts Historical Society).

Lemke, Thomas. *Eine Kritik der Politischen Vernunft: Foucaults Analyse der Modernen Gouvernementalität*. Hamburg: Argument, 1997. Print.

Mason, Van Wyck. "Bermuda's Pequots." *Harvard Alumni Bulletin* 39 (1937): 616-20. Print.

Mather, Cotton. *A Good Master Well Served*. Boston, 1696. Print.

---. *Rules for the Society of Negroes*. Boston, 1693. Print.

---. *The Diary of Cotton Mather.* 2 vols. New York: Ungar, 1957. Print.
---. *The Negro Christianized: An Essay to Excite and Assist that Good Work, the Instruction of Negro Servants in Christianity.* Boston, 1706. Print.
Mather, Richard. *An Apologie of the Churches in New-England for Church-Covenant.* London, 1643. Print.
McCusker, John J. "Colonial Statistics." *Historical Statistics of the United States.* Ed. Susan B. Carter. Cambridge: Cambridge UP, 2006. 627-772. Print.
McManus, Edgar J. *Black Bondage in the North.* Syracuse, NY: Syracuse UP, 1973. Print.
Melish, Joanne Pope. *Disowning Slavery: Gradual Emancipation and "Race" in New England, 1780-1860.* Ithaca, NY: Cornell UP, 1998. Print.
Middlekauf, Robert. *The Mathers: Three Generations of Puritan Intellectuals, 1596-1728.* Berkeley: U of California P, 1999. Print.
Miller, Perry. *Errand into the Wilderness.* New York: Belknap, 1956. Print.
---. *The New England Mind: The Seventeenth Century.* 1939. Boston: Beacon, 1961. Print.
Moore, George H. *Notes on the History of Slavery in Massachusetts.* New York: Appleton, 1866. Print.
Morgan, Edmund S., ed. *Puritan Political Ideas: 1558-1794.* Indianapolis, IN: Bobbs-Merrill, 1965. Print.
---. *The Puritan Family: Religion and Domestic Relations in Seventeenth-Century New England.* New York: Harper, 1966. Print.
Nagl, Dominik. *No Part of the Mother Country, but Distinct Dominions— Rechtstransfer, Staatsbildung und Governance in England, Massachusetts und South Carolina, 1630-1769.* Berlin: LIT, 2013. Print.
Niven, Steven J. "Onesimus." *African American Lives.* Ed. Henry Louis Gates, Jr. and Evelyn Brooks Higginbotham. Oxford: Oxford UP, 2004. 640-41. Print.
Patterson, Orlando. *Slavery and Social Death: A Comparative Study.* London: Harvard UP, 1982. Print.
Prakash, Gyan. *Another Reason: Science and the Imagination of Modern India.* Princeton, NJ: Princeton UP 1999. Print.
Pierson, William D. *Black Yankees: The Development of an Afro-American Subculture in Eighteenth-Century New England.* Amherst: U of Masschusetts P, 1988. Print.
Peterson, Mark A. "The Selling of Joseph: Bostonians, Antislavery, and the Protestant International, 1689-1733." *Massachusetts Historical Review* 4 (2002): 1-22. Print.
"Queries Respecting the Slavery and Emancipation of Negroes in Massachusetts, Proposed by the Hon. Judge Tucker of Virginia, and Answered by the Rev. Dr. Belknap." *Collections of the Massachusetts Historical Society: Vol. IV [of the First Series].* Boston: Phelps and Farnham, 1795. 191-211. Print.
Reiss, Oscar. *Blacks in Colonial America.* Jefferson, NC: McFarland, 1997. Print.
Report of the Record Commissioners of the City of Boston. Vol. 8: Boston Records from 1700 to 1728. Boston: Rockwell, 1884. Print. 39 vols.
Rosenthal, Bernhard. "Puritan Conscience and New England Slavery." *New England Quarterly* 46.1 (1973): 62-81. Print.

Saffin, John. *His Book (1665-1708): A Collection of Various Matters of Divinity, Law & State Affairs Epitomiz'd Both in Verse and Prose*. New York: Harbor, 1928. Print.

---. "Reply to Judge Sewall." 1701. *Racial Thought in America: From the Puritans to Abraham Lincoln*. Ed. Louis Ruchames. Amherst: U of Massachusetts P, 1969. 47-58. Print.

Sands, Alyce E. "John Saffin: Seventeenth-Century American Citizen and Poet." Diss. Pennsylvania State U, 1965. Print.

Silverman, Kenneth. *Cotton Mather: The Life and Times of Cotton Mather*. New York: Harper, 1984. Print.

Shurtleff, Nathaniel. *A Topographical and Historical Description of Boston*. 3rd ed. Boston: City Council, 1890. Print.

The Suffolk Files Collection, Vol. 86, papers - 87779 to 8782 (Microfilm Reel # 46), pages 7-9 (Massachuttes State Archives).

Thomas, G. E. "Puritans, Indians, and the Concept of Race." *New England Quarterly* 48.1 (1975): 3-27. Print.

Towner, Lawrence W. "'A Fondness for Freedom': Servant Protest in Puritan Society." *William and Mary Quarterly* 19.2 (1962): 201-19. Print.

---. *"A Good Master Well Served": A Social History of Servitude in Massachusetts, 1620-1750*. Diss. Northwestern University, 1954. Print.

---. "The Sewall-Saffin Dialogue on Slavery." *William and Mary Quarterly* 21.1 (1964): 40-52. Print.

Valverde, Mariana. "'Despotism' and Ethical Liberal Governance." *Economy & Society* 25.3 (1996): 357-72.

Von Frank, Albert J. "John Saffin: Slavery and Racism in Colonial Massachusetts." *Early American Literature* 29.3 (1994): 254-72. Print.

Walker, Clarence Earl. "Massa's New Clothes: A Critique of Eugene D. Genovese on Southern Society, Master-Slave Relations, and Slave Behavior." *Deromanticizing Black History: Critical Essays and Reappraisals*. Ed. Clarence E. Walker. Knoxville: U of Tennessee P, 1991. 56-72. Print.

Whitmore, W. H., ed. *The Colonial Laws of Massachusetts*. Boston, MA: Rockwell, 1890. Print.

Williams, Stephen. *Diary of Reverend Stephen Williams*. Vol. 1. WPA typescript. Richard B. Storrs Memorial Library, Longmeadow, MA. *The Storrs Library Historical Documents*. Web. 9 July 2013.

Winslow, Ola. *A Destroying Angel: The Conquest of Smallpox in Colonial Boston*. Boston, MA: Houghton, 1974. Print.

Winthrop, John. *History of New England, 1630-1649*. Vol. 1. Ed. James K. Hosmer. New York: Scribner's, 1908. Print. 2 vols.

Race, Gender, Justice: Storytelling in *The Greenlanders*

JASON S. POLLEY

ABSTRACT

In *The Greenlanders* (1988), a novel that I read as a meditation on the nature of justice, Jane Smiley crafts indispensable links between survival, legality, and shared narrative. In her critically ignored masterwork, the Pulitzer Prize-winning novelist posits how increased seclusion leads to the loss of collective stories in Greenland, the only established European civilization to fall apart and disappear. At the height of her fictional case study of justice, Smiley's ill-fated characters disband their annual tribunal (evocatively titled the 'Thing'). In doing so, they forfeit their chances of survival. To put it simply, the law equals life in Greenland. Without the Thing and its inherent—and essential—ironies, ironies that tie the practice of justice to memory, debate, and liability, the colony cannot endure. For Smiley, irony is the preserve of justice. Since irony is one way of creating correctives to the law, justice integrates incongruity in order to serve and protect. Without a system of law to question, however, there can be no corrective, no means by which to redirect the unjust courses of legality.

I.

Jane Smiley's masterwork posits a link between the law and survival in Greenland between 1345 and an indeterminate period sometime after 1415—the historical time at which the last Norse settlement in Greenland vanished due to factors such as the harsh environment, deficient trade, internecine conflict, and resistance to social change. Jared Diamond's *Collapse* devotes two chapters to the demise of Greenland, a place Diamond qualifies as "European civilization's most remote outpost" (212). First settled in 985, the far-flung colony survives for nearly five centuries—the last ship leaves Greenland in 1410, and none return until sometime between 1576-1587 (212, 271). This decade and a half cease in communication between the Greenland Norse and the outside world is likely due to the beginning of what Diamond calls "a Little Ice Age" around 1420 (219). Smiley herself concedes her fictionalized saga was inspired by the very singularity of the Greenlander's demise: "One of the first things that intrigued me about [the fate of the colony] was that it was the only attested case of an established European civilization or culture falling apart and vanishing" (qtd. in Nakadate 106).

In her fictional case study of a people she describes as having "fall[en] through a hole in history and disappeared" (*Greenlanders* 106) Smiley's narrative technique is as merciless as the harsh Greenlandic way of life. At a presentation in 1996, eight years after the publication of *The Greenlanders*, the author congratulates herself for the remorseless style of her saga, and at the same time reveals her textual influence: "After writing *The Greenlanders*, I rather prided myself on my cruelty to my characters. I was pleased at how readily I could sacrifice them to principle. Sudden, accidental death, for example, is a prominent feature of the Icelandic saga" ("Shakespeare" 171). Smiley's cruelty, or harsh reality, extends to her understated configurations of gender and race. Though she incorporates momentary female triumph in *The Greenlanders*, she ultimately sacrifices these characters and their intuitive qualities to the will of the leading white men on the colony. And while Diamond differentiates between Greenland's nomadic populations as "Inuit, Dorset, and Indian" peoples (261), Smiley leaves these groups undefined, referring to them all as 'Skraelings.' Smiley's recounting of the Greenland colony thus makes skillful interventions into critical race theory, critical race feminism, critical legal studies, and aboriginal studies.

Critical race theory accentuates how "institutional racism 'originates in the operation of established and respected forces in the society'" (Gillborn 253). As Laura E. Gomez articulates, "race *is* complicated, and the relationship between race and law is messy. Race does not exist outside of law; it is constituted by law" (453). Raymond Wacks turns to scholars influenced by Jacques Derrida and Julia Kristeva to point out how these critical projects converge in their critiques of essentialist paradigms, and cites Deborah Rhode, who claims that "these traditions share a common goal: to challenge existing distributions of power" (qtd. in Wacks 316). Wacks posits that critical race theory, feminism, and legal studies are "sceptical of many Enlightenment concepts such as 'justice', 'truth', and 'reason' since they 'reveal their complicity with power.' [They] also attemp[t] to expose the manner in which these ideas are 'racialized' in American law" (321). Not unlike native and aboriginal studies, these theories consider how "the law's formal constructs reflect, it is argued, the reality of a privileged, elite, male, white majority. It is this culture, way of life, attitude, and normative behaviour that combine to form the prevailing 'neutrality' of the law. [...] A racial minority," Wacks concludes, "is consigned to the margins of legal existence" (322). Speaking of aboriginal cultures, Leroy Little Bear stresses the irredeemable link between law and life: "Law is not something that is separate and unto itself. Law is the culture, and culture is the law" (83). Little Bear notes how "all colonial people, both the colonizer and the colonized, have shared or collective worldviews of the world embedded in their languages, stories, or narratives. It is collective because it is shared among a family or a group. However, this shared worldview is always contested, and this paradox is what it means to be colonized" (85). David Gillborn explains how critical race theory aims to untangle these paradoxes through the stories Little Bear discusses: "A particular striking aspect of some CRT is the use of storytelling and counterstorytelling. Here myths, assumptions, and received wisdom can be questioned by shifting the grounds of debate or presenting analyses in ways that turn dominant assumptions on their head" (256). This paper consequently develops according to several overlapping trajectories as I endeavor to deliver a measure of justice to Smiley herself. Despite her Pulitzer Prize-winning novel *A Thousand Acres*, which adapts *King Lear* to the Midwestern farm crisis in the 1980s, and a canon that includes twelve additional novels, four nonfiction books, and a book of short stories, Smiley receives scant attention from the academy.

While *The Greenlanders* deserves an extended close reading in and of itself, the novel is also important because it can contribute to our understandings and prompt deeper studies of several of Smiley's contemporaries. To talk about *The Greenlanders* is also to talk about other North American novels of the 1980s and 1990s that address gender, race, and law—and how the law itself institutionally encodes the subjugation of females and non-whites (cf. Gillborn 245; Wacks 315; Gomez 455). Patricia Ewick plainly states that "power and privilege are embedded in institutions and language," and she quotes Susan Silbey in order to reify the inherent social reproduction of dominant ideologies: "Unfortunately, the emphasis on the choosing subject's selecting from toolkits of available symbols, metaphors and strategies elides the actions of collectivities seeking to privilege their vision of the world as reality, and the efforts of others in turn to find the means to resist such attempts" (83). Diamond highlights how the Norse define themselves as "Christians, Europeans—not Inuit," and how their non-adoption of "useful Inuit technology" leaves them to starve "in the face of abundant unutilized food resources" (246, 274). "Why," Diamond wonders, "did the Vikings eventually fail while the Inuit succeeded?" (255). *The Greenlanders* does not simply concern the telltale fate of what Diamond describes as the "communal, violent, hierarchical, conservative, and Eurocentric" Greenlanders, nor does it merely recreate how, as "church-oriented Christians, the Norse shared the scorn of pagans widespread among medieval Europeans" (235, 265). In Smiley's fourth novel, the Norse of Greenland inherit a particular worldview, one that leads to their decline and disappearance. Denise Kimber Buell remarks on the potential insidiousness and exclusion of particular cultural inheritances, claiming that "the idea that one 'inherits' characteristics from one's 'blood' or environment has been an insidiously powerful and flexible one, used to naturalize binary, heterosexist notions of gender as well as race, ethnicity, national identity, class, and religious identity" (171). Buell turns to Derrida to stress the critique liberationism entails: "[A]n inheritance is the *'injunction* to *reaffirm by choosing* [...] *one must* filter, sift, criticize; one must sort out the several different possibilities that inhabit the same injunction'" (170).

The Greenlanders is markedly contemporary because it considers how dated archetypes and officialized narratives silence the stories of minority voices. "No matter how dominant a worldview is, there are always other ways of interpreting the world," and of speaking of that world, and of defending it (Little Bear 77). What Smiley does in *The Greenlanders* is to reconstruct Greenlandic demise in order to enter into dialogue with modern "terrains of struggle" to which, Smiley and her contemporaries demonstrate, we are very much culturally connected (Ewick 85). Neil Nakadate quotes Smiley, who remarks: "The whole time I was writing [the saga], I felt very socially responsible" (106). To illustrate Smiley's alignment with other contemporary indictments of the master narratives that subjugate contrasting worldviews with allusions to some of her fellow North American novelists, I examine works by Louise Erdrich, Margaret Atwood, Audrey Thomas, Guy Vanderhaeghe, and Thomas King—all of whom equally illustrate the virtues of storytelling through different voices in different forms.

Smiley sets great store by the manipulation of narrative conventions, as attested by her preoccupation with historical narratives and continued experiments with genre. *Duplicate Keys*, for instance, is crime fiction; *A Thousand Acres* is contemporary tragedy; *Moo* is social comedy; *Lidie Newton* is a bellum romance; *Good Faith* is a cautionary suspense-fiction; and *Ten Days in the Hills* a celebrity-culture satire. And Smiley is unpityingly true to the stylistic conventions of the Scandinavian sagas in *The Greenlanders*. Nakadate points out how "the dominant mode of the sagas and chronicles was a direct and dispassionate 'plain style'" (104–05). Smiley utilizes parataxis to create a biblical feeling; her repeated 'ands' evoke chapter one of The Book of Genesis. The 'plain style' she employs for almost 600 pages—incredibly her *Greenlanders* "manuscript exceeded 1,100 pages" (Nakadate 110)—reflects the Nordic lifestyle she represents: measured, repetitive, bleak. She also integrates iterated indexes of time by using the word 'now' to link paragraphs. Her steadfast form speaks to the Greenlanders' importunate decline; their days are numbered from the beginning.

II.

The Greenland colony is originally comprised of two settlements. At the onset of the novel, the Western Settlement—consisting of about one thousand residents—is inexplicably found "abandoned [with] all of the livestock dead or scattered to the wastelands" (6). According to Diamond, a clue to the settlement's failure lies in a simple clarification: The Western settlement is in fact "300 miles north of the other," so Western settlers must thereby contend with arctic summers—when high temperatures never exceed 10°C (50°F)—that are two months shorter than those of their 4000 cousins in the 'East' (215). Smiley's saga unfolds in the Eastern Settlement, where the Greenlanders live on steadings in districts separated by fjords. Society in Greenland is made up of concentric circles: the clerics in the priestly district of Gardar, the wealthy with one or more steadings, the poor with small steadings, and the servants who insinuate themselves onto steadings by contributing livestock and handicrafts. Women complicate the relations of this social structuring, since like servants and Skraelings, they belong both everywhere and nowhere. Women do not merely have domestic skills in *The Greenlanders*, as their attributes include second sight and prescience. The men, however, often misinterpret these qualities, and ignore or suppress the forewarnings—the stories—of the women. Not unlike the privileged ranking of the sexes in Audrey Thomas's historical novel *Isobel Gunn*, "the women ha[ve] no say in the matter" (Thomas 2).

Norse Greenland's male population also has strained relations with the Skraelings, the Icelanders, the Norwegians, and the papacies in Rome and France. Each of these tense ties is determined by water. Similar determinations define *Isobel Gunn*, set in the equally inhospitable Orkney Isles (which have a history of Viking raids) and Canada's Hudson Bay (home to Indian natives). For these early nineteenth-century Scottish settlers and traders, the "sea is, and always has been, the central fact of [their] lives" (Thomas 26). Fjords separate the Greenlanders' several districts, so Skraelings show up in canoes for trade activities. Other visitors arrive on ships. Water symbolically demonstrates the fluidity of Greenland's social system, and although people routinely go both up and down in the social ranks due to a variety of factors, the mobile tendency for Smiley's main characters—as it is for the entire population of the remaining settlement—is downward.

Nakadate provides the only extended examination of *The Greenlanders*. He accentuates dissolution: "*The Greenlanders* conveys the bewilderment of a slowly weakening, steadily fraying civilization in which meaningful conviction, civil obligation, and the skills of everyday life endure from year to year but decline over the decades" (112). While his emphasis on dwindling surety, duty, and adroitness is apt, his summary ignores Smiley's main strategy. She does not single out inevitable decline. The Greenlanders, after all, are aware they live through cycles of hunger, sickness, respite, and bounty (473). Smiley focuses her treatment on the relation between general decline and the law because as Greenland loses its laws, lives are lost as well. Smiley also links legality to orality—to memory and storytelling—and the sharing their legal forum entails. Nakadate, however, finds fault with the oral nature of Greenland and condemns Greenlandic reliance on the conventions of orality, claiming that the "Greenlanders' orality-dependent, highly subjective, and fallible memory does more to sustain the debilitating enmities of clans than to nurture a sense of shared experience and a productive understanding of the world" (132). Nevertheless, orality is not summarily counterproductive for the Greenlanders or any culture, 'orality-dependent' or not. J. Edward Chamberlain takes issue with the still-enervating choice that "colonialism" and "the academy" impose: "the choice between oral and written traditions" (138). Chamberlain underlines how "we should be deeply uncertain about where to draw the line between oral and written traditions," since every culture

> has eyes and ears, as it were, and the woven and beaded belts and blankets, the carved and painted trays, the poles, doors, and veranda posts, canes and sticks, masks, hats, and chests that are variously part of many oral performances among Aboriginal peoples [...] *these* forms of writing are often just as important as the stories and songs. (138)

Smiley, in tune with what Chamberlain describes as the non-transparency of any kind of text as a vehicle of abstract meaning (140), or what we might simplify as mimetic and interpretive fallibility, investigates the justness of communally recounting *and* debating the laws. *The Greenlanders* illustrates how parity requires communal engagement. Their justice system, called the 'Thing,' relies on contrasting memories, on different renderings of the past. The Greenlanders are what comparative and procedural law scholar H. Patrick Glenn calls a chthonic society. Glenn marks the importance of the dialogic over less public forms of transcribed verbal culture and describes the egalitarian agenda of chthonic legal systems: "The law is vested in a repository in which all, or most, share and in which all, or most, participate. Transmission of the tradition is through the dynamic procession of oral education, in daily life, and the dialogical character of the tradition is a matter of daily practice, for all ages of people" (59).

The Greenlanders chthonic-modeled 'Thing' solicits communal deliberation. Though leading men monopolize Thing cases, the law calls on a vocal public. Women and men look forward to and depend upon the Thing. Originally a seven-day annual affair, nearly every Greenlander attends the event in order to launch, resolve, defend, or audit legal cases, as well as to organize communal hunts, brandish marriageable offspring, engage in team games, acquire news of other districts, and retell traditional stories. The undefined, elusive, and deliberately frustrating title of this legal system speaks to its adaptation. Because it is oral, memorial, and public, the Thing evolves; its transformative nature makes it ineffable. The Thing transcends legal cases and criminal sentencing; it influences every facet of ordinary life in a harsh environment whereupon no one component alone is "sufficient for survival" (Diamond 234). The Thing also sponsors the obligatory acquisition of "social capital" that refers to, as Robert D. Putnam explains, productive "connections among individuals." Social capital extends "the norms of reciprocity and trustworthiness" within communities (19).

The Thing is not solely what Nakadate defines as the "fundamental tool for articulating and distributing justice" (120). The Thing involves recreation as well—diversions that allow for a shared break from the hardship of daily life in the colony. Songs are sung. Tales are told. Storytelling encourages interpretation and the exchange of opinions, and games allow for relatively safe risk; each activity reflects and mediates the strictures of a colony defined by constant threat. Smiley's saga links the law to the social system, as the discussions and diversions of the Thing are essential for the survival of the colony. Even though the Greenland colony survives through six centuries, notwithstanding cycles of hardship, the men of Greenland choose to abolish this legal forum. Most importantly, they discontinue the time-honored Thing without consulting the women, consequently crumbling the social fabric that holds their civilization together. The law betokens a just social system—a system that promises survival. The law, and its gesture toward the impossible ideal of justice, equals life. And in the absence of a legal (and communal) system, revenge replaces legislation and discussion.

The conclusion of *The Greenlanders* does not mirror its opening. The author does not depict the abandonment of the Eastern Settlement, thus signaling the end of this remote outpost. Instead, Smiley leaves her Greenlanders in a state of lawlessness; in fact, in Smiley's reconstruction of the colony the whole of Greenland turns into a lawless wilderness. Since Outlawry—as both a place and a state—best represents the end of legality, Thing law creates a zone for outlaws—the wilderness—to which laws do not extend. General outlawry ultimately replaces Greenland's legal and social systems, and Outlawry itself becomes the story.

Cases are publicly presented at the annual Thing, right after the lawspeaker recites the laws, which are not recorded but are passed down through the generations only as oral history. Glenn explains how the "most evident feature of chthonic legal tradition has been its orality. The teaching of the past is preserved through the informal, though sometimes highly disciplined, means of human speech and human memory" (58). Glenn underscores the indispensability of memory: "The tradition only survives by constant decisions, based on previous decisions, and hence previous information." The reliance on precedence, however, does not limit change; instead, it allows for change in small measures. Glenn clarifies how chthonic legal procedure is always "open to endless debate as to its interpretation and application; it can be rejected in its fundamental teaching and disappear" (73). A chthonic-based forum, the Thing makes essential demands on the civilization it governs, as laws evolve via collective deliberation. The demands of public debate foster community while legislating change.

Andrew Ross speaks to the evolution necessary to legal systems. The law is "constantly in a state of redefinition" even as it is "already fully formed" (48). No system of law can remain stagnant, either in definition or in practice. There is always already a gap between the formation and the institution of laws; their strictures are always in a process of renegotiation. Laws come from the past, so precedents remain pertinent to present circumstances because of adaptation. Michael Walzer remarks on the pluralism, cultural diversity, and historical circumstance influencing justice systems and implies that every implementation of justice is a unique appropriation: "Justice is a human construction, and it is doubtful that it can be made in only one way" (5). Oral legal systems make this process of human construction very clear. The Greenlanders revise legal understandings when they recite the laws they commit to memory, a process that necessarily puts old laws into practice in new ways. S. L. Hurley correspondingly stresses how justice is not about regnant views, but about impartial ones: "The mere fact that some normative views are prevalent does not immunize them if they compromise the demands of justice" (238). Greenland, of course, is removed from the parity—if not the pluralism and diversity—that Walzer and Hurley describe. The colony is comprised, nonetheless, of distinct social classes and peoples from a variety of districts, all of whom are invited to the Thing. And chthonic law, by virtue of communal debate, must accommodate competing claims to justice.

The Greenland colony integrates people of Scandinavian extraction with Christian émigrés from other areas of Europe. The arrival of Christianity distorts the transparency of legality. In "The Greenlanders' Saga," reported by Thorfinn Karlsefni around 1010 and orally transmitted until preserved in manuscript form sometime in the thirteenth century, Eirik the Red tells his son Leif the Lucky that the first priest in Greenland is a "shyster." Eirik eventually converts to Christianity in this version of the saga, but Gwyn Jones, author of *The Norse Atlantic Saga*, prefers the alternate account where Eirik remains a "heathen" to the end (145). Whether or not Eirik adopted the teachings of the Catholic Church promoted by King Olaf of Norway at the millennial turn, the effects of Christianity on Nordic law remain deleterious; Glenn convincingly explains how "the massive character of European settlement has generally been debilitating for chthonic law" (78). He revisits eras predating substantial colonization as he clarifies the simplicity of chthonic traditions: "A tradition which is oral in character does not lend itself to complex institutions. So the tradition faces less danger of pecuniary and institutional corruption, offering fewer positions of prestige and authority" (60).

Glenn associates increased settlement with growing complexity, in this case what Denise Kimber Buell might call "the double-edgedness of Christian universalizing aspirations, aspirations that similarly produce 'others' as those left behind—Jews, idolators, heretics, heathens—and by implication, inferior humans or less than fully human" (185). Chthonic law values an open understanding of a judicial process that relies on orality, not on written-down laws. A component of increased religious institutionalization, the technology of writing alters the historical nature of legality. The first fallacy here is that orality somehow refines itself into written culture—"which is to say toward sophisticated thought and civilized behaviour" (Chamberlain 139). Chamberlain laments how, because of the huge impact of largely discredited theories by Walter Ong and Marshall McLuhan, "people are inclined to think of oral traditions as less evolved than written traditions and of communities in which oral traditions flourish as correspondingly less developed—socially, culturally, and perhaps emotionally and intellectually" (139). The second fallacy is that the strength of the Church improves the fate of the Greenlanders. Diamond writes:

> Greenland was a hierarchical society, with great differences of wealth justified by the Church, and with disproportionate investment in churches. Again, we moderns have to wonder if the Greenlanders wouldn't have been better off had they imported fewer bronze bells, and more iron with which to make tools, weapons to defend themselves against the Inuit, or goods to trade with the Inuit for meat in times of stress. (245)

Because the Church dismisses so-called "pagan ways" as anathema, the Norse in Greenland refuse to "adopt useful features of Inuit technology" and consequently starve to death (247).

The Greenlanders begins three centuries after the arrival of the Church. The narrator relates the tortuousness of the colony's institutionally corrupted legal system:

> At this time the Greenlanders had three types of law, the Thing law, the bishop's law, and the king's law, of which the last two were sometimes combined, depending on whether the bishop or the representative of the king was living in Greenland. Thing law and the law of the bishop were intended to concern the different matters of secular and Church law, but sometimes the Thing was less powerful, and sometimes the bishop was not in residence, so the men of most of the fjords settled disputes among themselves, and this was a habit the Greenlanders had gotten into since the death of the last bishop and the aging of the lawspeaker Gizur. (47)

The law loses accountability and clarity as the convergence of multiple legal systems complicates the meting out of justice. Self-governance or the settling of disputes amongst themselves becomes a more just method to determine legality, particularly when commonplace oral exchanges remain unimpeded by the institutionalized privilege and obscurity of three combined legal approaches (Thing law plus bishop law plus king law). Self-governance likewise bespeaks the values of community; it offers the transparency of public scrutiny.

The Greenland Norse population paradoxically attests the positive influence of lawspeakers when they bypass the incapable Gizur. Since the control held by a lawspeaker indicates the sway of the law, the lawspeaker symbolizes Thing values as he presides over a thirteen-judge panel. When he is replaced, the law is revived. A seasoned lawspeaker exemplifies an essential tie to tradition, while a fresh lawspeaker embodies the need for modern revision. In order to be lawful, belated laws require renewal. In Greenland, where heritage and legacy reign, justice too evolves as colony members rally behind competent lawspeakers in the same way they question less competent ones. Early in Smiley's saga the narrator discusses the proactive Osmund who "was known as a lucky man, who stepped forward and spoke up in all things. His mother's brother, Gizur Gizursson, was the lawspeaker, but it was well known that Osmund knew the laws better than any man in Brattahlid district" (9). The Greenlanders thus elect Osmund Thordarson as their new lawspeaker at the Thing following the death of Gizursson, who has no heir (69).

III.

Glenn's moderated explanation of gerontocracy is helpful in explaining why living lawspeakers, regardless of perceived competency, tend not to be replaced in Greenland. He observes the diversity of chthonic peoples and the applications of chthonic law:

> The most common feature appears to be a council of elders, individual people who, by their assimilation of tradition over a longer period of time, often speak with greater authority. There is no guarantee of this, no process of screening out those faltering with age, but it appears to have been generally held to be true. This has been referred to as gerontocracy, but it may be preferable to see it as an expression of a link with past generations. (60)

In other words, elders are living links to the past, and each ruling lawspeaker occupies an integral place in the culture he governs. Nassim Taleb also provides useful ways of reading the term gerontocracy: "Respect for elders in many societies might be a kind of compensation for our short-term memory. The word *senate* comes from *senatus*, 'aged' in Latin; *sheikh* in Arabic means both a member of the ruling elite and 'elder.' Elders are repositories of complicated inductive learning that includes information about rare events. Elders can scare us with stories" (78). If we extend Taleb's informed speculation to native and aboriginal worldviews in the face of colonial and neo-national discourses, it is likely, as Louise Erdrich remarks in *Love Medicine*, that elders speak "in the old language, using words that few remember, forgotten, lost to people who live in town or dress in clothes" (81). Elder lawspeakers discourage unreflective tears from the past. If a lawspeaker's memory of the laws noticeably wanes, his judicial authority is transferred to the council of judges or to the community at large. Whether or not members of the colony annually attend The Thing, they subscribe to its conventions. As the major plot event in *The Greenlanders*, the dismantling of the Thing jeopardizes survival on the remaining Greenland settlement.

The community that supports and questions a lawspeaker also mitigates the influence of the Church in Greenland. The narrator equivocally suggests how the bishop and community complement one another early in the first of *The Greenlanders'* three books: "Bit by bit, the bishop had learned the ways of the Greenlanders, and often judged cases as the Greenlanders themselves would have judged them" (69). Local concerns, as Walzer implies, alter the terms under which we invoke justice, and although rendered more complex via Church intervention, the law still entails consensus. Glenn explains how community relations restore the balance of justice, as "crime becomes the responsibility of civil society, in the form of the groups, clans or families which make it up. Injury to a member was the responsibility of the group" (64). The chthonic logic of communal responsibility is shared by native peoples, to whom we might liken the pre-Christianized Greenlanders; early Norse custom and culture in far-flung Greenland is colonized by the institution of the Church as well.

"Aboriginal traditions, laws, and customs," Little Bear points out, "are the practical application of the philosophy and values of the group" to explain how these values, how this communal law, is disseminated mainly through "praise, reward, recognition, and renewal ceremonies and by example, actual experience, and storytelling. [...] Storytelling is a very important part of the educational process. It is through stories that customs and values are taught and shared" (79, 81). "Because the shared heritage is recorded in the minds of the members of a society," Little Bear stresses, "honesty is an important Aboriginal value. Honesty is closely related to strength and sharing and may be seen as a commitment to these values." Lies are thus equally debilitating to the values of social harmony, as they "result in chaos and establish false understanding" (80). Therefore the memories and narratives of elders are necessary correctives to what Guy Vanderhaeghe sadly historicizes as the Christianizing, so-called civilizing mission of the Methodists in the Canadian West in the 1920s (145-47). *Love Medicine*'s Lynette knows that her generation needs the instructive counter-stories of its their elders: "Tell'em Uncle Eli," she drunkenly cautions; "They've got to learn their own heritage! When you go it will all be gone!" (32).

What Glenn, Little Bear, and Erdrich refer to as group responsibility incorporates both sides—criminal and compensatory—of chthonic law. If we remove the immeasurable hegemonic violence and cultural erasure attending the so-called civilizing mission of institutionalized Christian imperialism, physical violence is the principle social wound in chthonic societies: "There was to all intents and purposes no law of theft or burglary, no law of drugs, no organized crime; no money laundering; no white collar crime; no fraud. The list could go on. Crime was a serious social wound, usually involving physical violence" (Glenn 64). In Greenland, while murder is the gravest offence, the Thing also presides over other acts of justice, such as cases dealing with rape, foul play, servant abuse, driftage rights, land disputes, and squatters' claims to abandoned steadings. The kind of justice Smiley offers for these crimes typically pertains to property in one form or another. Settlers can lay claim to abandoned steadings or be legally divested of properties. Depending on the magnitude of a conviction, guilty parties customarily lose parts or the whole of their land and livestock as payment to their victims. With the exception of a greater outlawry conviction (capital punishment), to judge a case is to consider the rightful allocation of property. Even an arraignment of lesser outlawry (banishment to the wilderness at the dystopian fringes of the settlement and the law) involves property, as these lesser outlaws lose rights to civilized territory when they are charged with heinous acts, but are not considered threats to the colony's survival.

Smiley elaborates on the manner in which the law must question its application: every crime instigates a causal sequence, a series that precedents cannot predict, and the job of the law is to redirect these sequences toward the ideal of justice. Thing law stresses this process by demanding the immediate announcement of killings (125). Distinct from murder, a killing can be a lawful compensatory act that must undergo communal evaluation in order to be understood as just. Because crimes and judgments have serious repercussions, and because law is never fully comprehensive, justice demands ongoing renegotiation. In *The Greenlanders*, lawspeakers are liable for their memories of the laws, judges are responsible for their applications of the laws, and criminals are accountable for their infractions of laws. And since the law does not stop with remunerative acts, remunerators are answerable for their compensatory legal acts. Court and civilization evolve as legal precedent is remembered, law is debated, and parity is privileged; life in the colony persists because of these checks and balances.

The Greenlanders' new lawspeaker, Bjorn Bollason, who replaces the dead Osmund, dispenses with the transparency requisite to Thing law and makes unprecedented changes to the Thing. He institutes these changes in hope of preserving fairness in the face of falling Thing attendance:

> Bjorn Bollason established a new type of judge, to be known as an at-large judge, and to be appointed by the lawspeaker to sit in on cases when judges failed to come to the Thing, and these new judges were to be appointed from among the most prosperous farmers at the Thing who did not have cases pending, and they were to remain judges-at-large until they should have cases before the Thing, which would disqualify them for that year and two years after that. (328)

The amendment speaks to the everydayness of Thing cases. Bollason's proviso aims to secure continued equality for the Greenlanders with the caveat that the prosperous are institutionally 'more equal.' Just as most colonists (which includes judges) are called to the Thing, most (including judges) are ranked the same at the Thing. Bollason's changes may seem just if, again, we disregard the fact that "institutional racism [or in this case classism] 'originates in the operation of established and respected forces in the community'" (Gillborn 253). Bollason's amendments recall what Ross describes as the shifting qualities of the justice system (48), and speak to what Walzer sees as the necessarily different implementations of justice (5). Bollason, however, breaks with tradition. While it is true that "[u]nlike almost anything else, only the law can change itself" (Ross 55), the Greenlanders depend on change moderated by communal debate. Bollason ignores legal convention by changing the law rather than letting the law change naturally by slow degrees. The new lawspeaker devalues the effectiveness of the legal system and obscures its legislative function while ironically undercutting his own privileged position. The knowledge of the lawspeaker ensures that traditional customs are preserved as they are reiterated and reformulated. Bollason second-guesses his own authority when his actions undermine the law that his own position epitomizes—actions that consequently catalyze other changes to the law.

Instead of cross-examining Bollason's competency by means of avoiding him and the Thing—the customary way of redistributing a lawspeaker's authority to the community-at-large—Jon Andres Erlendsson, a respected member of the colony, prepares a Thing case against lawspeaker Bollason. Jon Andres elucidates the demands law makes upon itself by accusing Bollason for an injustice he commits as lawspeaker at a Thing several summers earlier; Jon Andres charges lawspeaker Bollason with murder. He specifies how murder is always murder, whether performed by a man or "a man in the guise of a lawspeaker," before "demand[ing] a judgment of full outlawry and deprivation of property against Bjorn Bollason, [a verdict that entails] exile into the wastelands, loss of position as lawspeaker, and any other punishments as self-judgment might allow" (556).

The lawspeaker's response works against the principles of law, and Bollason's reaction to the charge reveals how his changes to the legal system are executed under "the shield of pragmatism [so as] to pack a truncated court with his own judges" (Nakadate 114–15). More valuable than obvious vested interests, however, is the fact that Bollason's response outlines what justice is not. He says:

> Bjorn Bollason established a new type of judge, to be known as an at-large judge, and to be appointed by the lawspeaker to sit in on cases when judges failed to come to the Thing, and these new judges were to be appointed from among the most prosperous farmers at the Thing who did not have cases pending, and they were to remain judges-at-large until they should have cases before the Thing, which would disqualify them for that year and two years after that. (328)

Bollason refuses to disqualify himself from the position of lawspeaker "for that year and two years after that" as his amended laws prescribe (328). He removes himself from legal accountability, thus reminding readers of Juvenal's famous dictum: *Quis custodiet ipsos custodes*, and strategically places himself beyond the law, as a watcher who should remain unwatched, as a judge above judgment. Smiley thus exposes how the "central aim of critical legal theory is to doubt the prospect of uncovering a universal foundation of law based on reason. It repudiates the very project of jurisprudence which it generally perceives as clothing the law and legal system with a bogus legitimacy" (Wacks 332). As Bollason rallies behind a priority he revamped—precedence—in order to reject the challenges law needs, Smiley gestures toward the uneasy and tenuous position of the law. The Thing sustains itself by questioning its inconsistencies: justice marches forward because of its incongruities, is constrained by the cultural milieu it regulates, and governs a self-regulating discourse. When Bollason disallows the deliberation Jon Andres lawfully proposes, he cancels the justness of Thing law. This denial of the contradictions demarcating the praxes of legality is a turning point for the colony, as the disappearance of the Greenlanders arises from their failure to maintain the contradictions of the law.

Jon Andres and his backers anticipate the unlawfulness of "Bollason and his hand-picked judges" and physically attack the lawspeaker (557). Because the assailants do not set aside their weapons when they arrive at the Thing, as the law prescribes, a one-sided battle ensues (557–59). But Jon Andres and his group do more than disband Thing partisanship: devised over several years, the assault suspends longstanding legal procedure, thus exposing the wide compass of law in Greenland. The narrator reveals the Greenlanders' dependency on due process after Jon Andres's coup d'état: "The Thing was broken up without deciding any more cases, and the judges went home to their steadings, as if in flight. Indeed, everyone there went home as if in flight, for they knew not how to regain the normal ways that had been lost through this event" (559). The catalogue of victims of the planned attack includes Bollason and his three sons, and the absence of a lawspeaker, along with the erasure of legal legacy as symbolized by the death of the lawspeaker's sons, is foreign to the Greenlanders. While over the past six centuries Thing attendance often waned, "and [as] such times come and go" (562), the Thing always prescribed 'normal ways.'

The communal loss following the razing of the court recalls the predictions of Ulfhild the Widow, who loses a son in what comes to be known as "the great battle of the Brattahlid [district] Thing" (562–63). Playing up the would-be naïveté of her social positioning as an aging woman in the colony, she confronts Jon Andres to call him to account for his battle plans: "The powerful men of this district have been quiet enough for the last few years. Something is hatching, it seems to me." She also formulates an adage that functions as a version of legal counsel: "The great ones will bring us down in the end, and that is a fact" (540). Jon Andres does not observe Ulfhild's admonition, nor does he acknowledge her two insights: "It is a fact that men love to fight" and "women can do little enough about it." Jon Andres avoids a *tête-à-tête* with the widow and declares: "No one cares to fight" (540-41). In contrast to the men, Ulfhild sees the eventual ramifications of the situation. For the men of Greenland, the law cannot predict real outcomes; it can only be concerned with and work towards the unprecedented and unpredictable.

Most colony members endorse the attack against the Thing, saying that it "was generally agreed that [Andres and his followers] had been strongly provoked in the case, and were not to be blamed too harshly for what had come about, for men must avenge the injuries done to them, if they are strong enough to do it" (559). The Greenlanders stress the cultural timbre of law, they still discuss the law, and they retrospectively assess Bollason as an inadequate lawspeaker: "Bjorn Bollason could be said not to have learned the laws especially well himself, since the telling of them had shrunk in his time from a three-day cycle to less than a one-day cycle." Not-so-distant Things, Greenlanders remember, lasted seven days (562). Despite their remembrances of the Thing, they do not restore it, blaming the dead Bollason, who "had not sought to teach the body of the law to anyone, except perhaps [his son] Sigurd," who was also a victim of the battle (561).

The aggressors plan the murders of Bollason's sons for the purpose of suppressing lawful compensatory killings. Because they are killed, the lawspeaker's sons are incapable of "avenging the injuries done to them" (559). Jon Andres and his men terminate the oral transmission of the laws through the generations when they eliminate the possibility of legal redress, and they guarantee their immunity from the law by eliminating just recourse. Justice disappears with the laws, and what comes to pass as a result insinuates the truth of Ulfhild's prognostication. The Greenlanders resign themselves to a laissez-faire variety of reciprocity within a year of destroying the court: "Though no one knew all the laws, did not everyone know, in a general way, what was to be expected of one another?" (562). But without a formal legal system, clashing overtakes conversing, unannounced killings supplant legal accountability, and individual agenda supersedes social consensus. This state of lawlessness reflects the approach Jon Andres and his men adopt to overthrow the Thing. They present a case that questions the head of the legal system because they judge a former ruling unjust. The accusers destroy the cross-examined court when it fails to consider the case's legitimacy. This retaliation creates nuances of irony and complexity, especially if law is understood as nonpartisan, even though laws, like ideologies, "legitimate systematic asymmetries by depicting situations as worthy of support" (Ewick 86). Yes, Jon Andres questions the fairness of the court. Yes, Jon Andres eliminates an unjust court. Yes, he eliminates injustice in the name of justice. However, he performs these acts unjustly. To appropriate a germane case of twentieth-century legal and martial logic from Smiley's novel *Ten Days in the Hills*: "The war itself was just, but the means by which it was conducted were unjust and unimaginable" (246). Jon Andres and his men illegally overthrow Bollason's illegality and replace a partiality with a competing one. Neither legislative body privileges disinterestedness, neither assembly argues its case, and each cluster of men dismisses dialogue. Still, Jon Andres's injustice highlights and eliminates a perceived injustice. Unjust actions can redirect unjust legal courses just as unjust actions emphasize just renegotiation. Smiley shows that irony is the preserve of justice.

Illegal acts draw attention to legal necessities. Law provides for exchanges within a dynamic lawful-unlawful dialectic. The only way to right a lack of legality is to formulate a legal system. The Thing needs to be restored. After "some talk," however, the men decide against "reinstituting" the Thing they leveled a few years earlier, because "the Greenlanders would have to make up a whole new set of laws for a new lawspeaker to learn, and this seemed both an impossible task and an unnecessary one, since almost everyone agreed on what actions were the proper ones and what were the improper ones" (570). The Greenlanders oust legal process in favor of propriety, and replace fluid law with vague morality.

Walzer emphasizes how any goodness that masquerades as inevitability or propriety is by definition contentious: "No account of the meaning of the social good, or of the boundaries of the sphere within which it legitimately operates, will be uncontroversial" (21). Social goods are not social givens; they are arguable and changeable—an understanding that extends to the field of ethics as it pertains to social justice. J. Hillis Miller remarks on the groundlessness of ethical judgment: "An ethical judgment is always a baseless positing, always unjust and unjustified, therefore always liable to be displaced by another momentarily stronger or more persuasive but equally baseless positing of a different code of ethics" (55). The only stability for ethics is certain instability, as ethics compels ongoing appraisals of principle propositions. Not unlike justice, ethics relies upon incertitude and transformation, neither of which is ever a *fait accompli*. Ethics is unethical when it discludes point and counterpoint. David Gillborn observes how critical race theory makes poignant use of "storytelling and counterstorytelling. Here myths, assumptions and received wisdom can be questioned by shifting the grounds of debate or presenting analyses in ways that turn dominant assumptions on their head" (256). Thomas King makes a virtue of storytelling in his novel *Green Grass, Running Water* (1993), wherein he acknowledges the generosity of his former colleague Little Bear. King frames his Native American novel, set mainly in Southern Alberta, with two playful, yet sardonic references to stories. When the Lone Ranger utters the platitude: "Everybody makes mistakes," an unnamed character replies: "Best not to make them with stories" (11). Near the novel's end, readers encounter the following equally allegorical exchange:

> 'I got back as soon as I could,' says Coyote. 'I was busy being a hero.'
> 'That's unlikely,' I says.
> 'No, no,' says Coyote. 'It's the truth.'
> 'There are no truths, Coyote,' I says. 'Only stories.' (432)

King playfully deconstructs the essentialism of Western master-narratives.

The Thing is democratic because of its agonistic or polemical structure. Chantal Mouffe underlines the conditional nature of ethical and political accord when she says that "every consensus exists as a temporary result of a provisional hegemony, as a stabilization of power." Democracy "always entails some form of exclusion." Democracy endorses controversy by legitimating diversity. Democracy makes "room for the expression of conflicted interests and values" (92). Ethical principles define functioning democratic processes. Developing change ought— "Ethics is the *ought* in thought" (Harpham 404)—to be a corollary of dissent. Laws governing social collectives evolve as individuals question the law, so democratic orderliness is pliable and temporary. This is the point of Margaret Atwood's first dystopian novel, *The Handmaid's Tale* (1985). The author outlines how the work speaks to religious oppression and its affinity to nationalism's reproductions of imperial hegemony:

> The early Puritans came to America not for religious freedom, as we were taught in grade school, but to set up a society that would be a theocracy (like Iran) ruled by religious leaders, and monolithic, that is, a society that would not tolerate dissent within itself. They were being persecuted in England for being Puritans, but then they went to the United States and promptly began persecuting anyone who wasn't a Puritan. My book reflects the form and style of early Puritan society and addresses the dynamics that bring about such a situation. ("Notes" 393)

"I wish this story were different," the handmaid says near the end of her tale, "more civilized" (*Handmaid's* 333). She then appropriates Samuel Beckett: "So I will go on. So I will myself to go on," and finds a refuge in writing, in storytelling (334).

The consequence of the Greenlanders failure to revive lawful dissent is a complete feeling of exclusion on the colony. Because there is no Thing, because "no one kn[ows] the laws," there is no way for lawbreakers to be "punished or outlawed" (*Greenlanders* 575). Without a place for discussion, compensatory killings go unannounced, legislated answerability disappears, and colony members look upon relationships with trepidation since they lack legal mediation. The narrator waxes nostalgic: "many folk in many districts were afraid, and no longer spoke to one another as Greenlanders once had, in open jest about many things" (575). The result is a telltale absence of commemorative (and democratically imperative) "talk, and jesting, and tale-telling" on the remaining settlement (158).

IV.

The Greenlanders come to fear disagreement, which includes the camaraderie of banter, play, and dispute. The avoidance of others ironically becomes crucial to survival when undecipherable codes of propriety replace law; we hide from lawlessness when the law no longer serves us, since "a man might do anything and be in the wrong. There was no way to tell. It was better to stay on the steading and mind the cows and be content with such days as are left to one" (577). Like survival in Greenland, justice requires social capital, and the sequestration to steadings calls attention to the former movements between farms and districts. Diamond explains the necessities of economic and spatial integration in the colony: "[N]ot even the richest Greenland farm was self-sufficient in everything required to survive through the year. That integration involved transfers between inner and outer fjords, between upland and lowland farms, between Western and Eastern Settlement, and between rich and poor farms" (231). Diamond stresses how a "complexly integrated economy" enables the "Greenland Norse to survive in an environment where no one [component] alone was sufficient for survival" (234). The place is necessarily communal because "one person could not go off alone, make a living by himself or herself, and hope to survive" (235).

Chthonic law encourages movement and interconnection. Since Thing verdicts are influenced by the number of followers of individual claimants, case presenters circulate between farms (Ulfhild becomes aware of Jon Andres doing so) to petition support by offering help in the form of livestock or allegiance. Friendships, like foodstuffs, are practical and essential investments. The Thing draws attention to the dialogic nature of public deliberation, where to offer support is to receive support. At the midpoint of the saga certain residents recall the conviviality of their annual tribunal during a downswing in Thing attendance:

> [N]ow it seemed to some powerful men in the largest districts that certain benefits of the Thing assemblies that had once gone unremarked upon, such as the opportunity to view prospective brides, or to trade goods, or to make plans for the seal hunts and the reindeer hunt, had come to be distinctly missed. (292)

The Greenlanders survive because of what Putnam, clarifying the sociological conception of resource, describes as the efficiencies and conciliations of trust. Like Little Bear, Putnam emphasizes how "[h]onesty and trust lubricate the inevitable frictions of daily life" (135). Hunting is diminished and trading is underprivileged in the absence of annual chthonic assembly; in the absence of law, the odds of survival in the colony drop.

The Greenlanders live as outlaws when there are no laws. Leading male figure Gunnar Asgeirsson's account of outlaw justice sets forth the gravity of the Greenlanders' final predicament. Near the beginning of the third book, Gunnar considers forming a Thing case against Ofeig Thorkelsson. He explains: "If [Ofeig] is made an outlaw, then he must live as an outlaw, for if he comes into the districts of men, they may kill him with impunity" (400). Ofeig is the devil figure of the saga, and as "The Devil" (which is the title of the second book of the novel), Ofeig symbolizes the Greenlanders' ultimate fate. Nakadate recognizes this synecdoche, saying that the "Devil enters Greenland through the door of disorder" (115). Disorder is the lawlessness (or devilishness) that compels the Greenlanders to isolation on their farmsteads, and it is this self-seclusion, alas, that compounds devilry.

That the Greenlanders sentence themselves to self-detention on their steadings is a cruel twist of fate, as most in Greenland believe that "devils sought out those who were alone and entered into them and possessed their souls" (185). Devilishness, which develops allegorically, translates into the annulment of social interaction—the end of civilization. Isolation relocates "the waste districts, where the Devil holds sway" (489) to the residual farms on the colony. Gunnar's bear story clarifies this conclusion by redefining the incursion of the wilderness into civilization as a form of self-consumption. In the parable, Kari, a Greenlander, captures a bear cub while hunting. He and his wife Hjordis name the cub Bjorn and resolve to raise him alongside their son, Ulf. Kari releases his bear son to the wild a year later (498) only to have his human son die shortly thereafter. Lonely, Kari beckons the now wild-eyed bear to return to his steading. The bear consents and, inevitably, he consumes Kari's food and livestock. Finally, in order to sate Bjorn's hunger, Kari offers the bear his arm knowing that "the bear would never be satisfied with only one arm, but must, in the end, eat him up" (501). Wildness devours the steading.

The bear story also reflects the devil Ofeig's relations to wilderness and confinement. While preparing for the Thing at which Ofeig receives a greater outlawry conviction, Jon Andres and Kollgrim discuss how they might "hunt" and "kill" this "devil among [men]" in the same way they would a "bear" (432). Jon Andres iterates Ofeig's resemblance to a bear when he and his men are summoned to the widow Ulfhild's sheep byre, where she has latched the door behind Ofeig, locking the brigand inside with her livestock. Jon Andres shouts, "Folk say that bears have returned to Greenland." He threatens Ofeig's life: "Folk say that in former days, it took ten men to capture a bear, but only six to kill it, we have ten men here, and would hate to use only six of them, for all are ready to fight" (446). Notwithstanding their readiness, the 'bear' breaks down the barn door and flees. The bear-like, devil-inspired Ofeig also overpowers the men who later sequester him in Undir Hofdi church (448–50). Ofeig routinely breaks into structures only to get locked inside them. With the exception of the events at Undir Hofdi church, a symbol of institutionally entrenched power and privilege, these entrapments occur on properties owned by women.

The site of Ofeig's last reported crime is particularly female coded. Jon Andres, the proprietor, is away soliciting support for his Thing case against Bollason, and his male servants are visiting a neighboring farm. Ofeig forcibly enters the steading by crashing through the roof, and lands in a uniquely female space. Taking advantage of cunning and luck, the seven women, including Jon Andres's young girl Gunnhild and his baby girl Unn, outmaneuver Ofeig using food as their main defense. They feed him and feed him. He eats and eats. Smiley then evokes a connection between female savoir faire and good luck. Just after baby Unn randomly "whimpers," the startled Ofeig abruptly writhes, doubles over, and falls to the ground (547–48). The interloper has overeaten, and the haphazard cry combined with the calculated surfeit of food upsets Ofeig's ordinarily strong stomach and he collapses in pain. Jon Andres's wife, her sister, and her servingmaids proceed to hector him for his "gluttony" and other criminal acts (548). They beat him, but before they can lawfully kill him, he "scrabbles" to his feet and decamps into the "moonlight," a tableau reiterating the figurative connection between aloneness and devilry (548).

Ofeig's overindulgence brings about his death. There are no more reports of his lawlessness, and the offender is soon found dead, by "all appearances [...] from starvation" sometime between the razing of the Thing and the decision not to reinstate it. The uncertain time of his death—"the devil had been dead for some time"—speaks to the unique moment in the history of Greenland (565). The Norse people sentence themselves to legal deregulation when they disband the Thing. Ofeig is the last legally condemned outlaw in the colony, as he dies in the transitional period between legal justice and outlaw justice. The Devil no longer needs Ofeig for a vehicle. Isolation lures the devilry he personifies into the zeitgeist of the colony.

Ofeig's story, however, does not directly foreshadow the end of a struggling yet enduring civilization. His entrances and exits stress the peripheries of the colony, his flights showing how borders determine Greenland's marginal characters. Ofeig's crimes lead to encounters with privileged members (leading men) and the underprivileged (everyone else), but his lasting confrontations are with the latter as he swiftly penetrates bands of vigilant men. He also spends considerable time within the female spaces he invades, so it is no surprise that Ofeig's burial is conducted by a woman rather than by a customary male priest. The elderly maidservant is a marginal figure par excellence—crack-voiced, "incontinent [...] blind and bent"—and only she can "lay [this] evil spirit" (566). In outlawry as in death, Ofeig's story focuses on the qualities of fringe figures: women, servants, and children.

Ofeig's relation to women recasts the moral of Gunnar's bear parable. Gunnar's story concludes with the bear's consumption of his foster father. Still, the tale does not necessarily end where he stops relating it. Bjorn the bear's foster mother Hjordis was not consumed like everything else on the steading, and is still present, and her conspicuously untold story can develop beyond the limits of Gunnar's narrative. Ofeig's actions elucidate how criminality, like community, involves every member of the colony. Women, servants, and children bring about Ofeig's death, and an old, blind, incontinent, serving-woman lays his spirit to rest. Marginal characters ameliorate the lawlessness Ofeig represents. These underprivileged figures make invaluable contributions to the colony and increase the odds of survival.

Women are marginalized in *The Greenlanders* as most male characters see them as mere "trinket[s]...lying in the grass" (493). They are, however, crucial to survival, and their indispensability is apparent when outlawry reigns. Women in Greenland figuratively always live and cope with outlaw parameters. They tend to be isolated on steadings, as Ofeig's recidivist incursions show. They tend to have little or no say in the exacting of justice, as Ulfhild's confrontation with Jon Andres demonstrates (540), and they tend readily to accept the condition Sigrid Bjornsdottir calls "incomprehension" (532). Not unlike the "*wives and sweethearts*" of the Rupert's Land colonizers in *Isobel Gunn*, they "[*d*]*id not understand but accepted: the women had no say in the matter*" (Thomas 2). The women of Greenland, akin to those of the Orkney Islands, are inured to unknowns and are well-adapted to unforeseen change. The condition of acquiescence and acceptance is the reason women manifest gifts of second sight and prognostication in Greenland, while the men rely upon rules of reason they themselves determine. Angela P. Harris describes the hegemonic apparatus of this normalizing of masculinity: "The masculine point of view is point-of-viewlessness. [...] The force of male dominance," Harris continues, quoting Catharine MacKinnon, "is exercised as consent, its authority as participation, its supremacy as the paradigm of order, its control as the definition of legitimacy" (35). Some women in Greenland, nevertheless, do not reduce the unexplainable to the monitory. They *prima facie* see because they do not *de facto* limit what they see. They envision freely, and conventional boundaries do not delimit what or how they see.

Birgitta Lavransdottir's first experience of second sight is telling. Her vision incorporates a scene recasting the brief montage of a young woman and stumbling child in Ingmar Bergman's 1957 film *The Seventh Seal*, set in fourteenth-century Sweden. Bergman's germane-to-*The Greenlanders* Nordic film is also discussed at length by all ten main characters in Smiley's *Ten Days in the Hills* (502–06). In book one of *The Greenlanders*, titled "Riches," young bride Birgitta has just moved to Gunnars Stead. She witnesses a woman in white, who carries "in her arms a child of about one winter's age, also clothed in white." The newlywed watches the "woman lift the child to her face and kiss it, then set it among the flowers on the grass." Birgitta sees the child laugh, carefully stand up, and stagger "forward with its arms in the air." Called by a servant, Birgitta momentarily looks away, and returns her gaze to a blank tableau: woman and child are gone. Birgitta, "later well known for having second sight" (64), relates this episode to Sira Pall and Sira Jon. The priests directly conclude Birgitta has seen the Virgin and Child, as the story is already written according to their institutionally sanctioned interpretations. Like three women before her, Sira Jon explains (65), Birgitta observes the ideal woman and her perfect son. The meanings of this vision, the ministers of archetypal Christian essentialism clearly state, are self-evident. The men dispense with prescience and look only to the past.

In "Love," the final book of *The Greenlanders*, Margret Asgeirsdottir beholds an apparition that recalls to us Birgitta's vision. Margret is likewise on Gunnars Stead, the childhood dwelling to which she returns as an old woman. She sees a child in white "running and stumbling forward, her arms raised happily in the air." Engaged in the scene before her, she watches the "mother, also in white, sway in attentive pursuit, now smiling, now laughing, at the child's antics." When the swaying child then "stumble[s] into a circle of flowers and f[alls] down," she sees the "mother step forward and sweep it into her arms and cover its neck with kisses, just below the ear, so that the child laugh[s] out in glee" (527). Margret sees Birgitta's first vision, a vision Margret recollects because she lives with Birgitta at the time of the newlywed's strange experience. In fact, Margret is the first person Birgitta encounters after the incident. Margret's first-hand experience of this remembered second-sight, however, is not a moment of virginal visioning as she does not see the Virgin and Son. The spectacle Margret witnesses is not a vision at all, but only Birgitta's daughter Helga playing with her own daughter Unn. Birgitta's original vision does not affirm a religious—and exclusionary—paradigm, but forecasts her own descendants. Her second sight, in turn, accentuates the individuals who can play an integral part in the preservation of the Greenland Norse. Yet it is less than possible to predict the ways in which Helga and Unn help to kill the outlaw Ofeig. Still, the vision focuses on a woman and her child. These characters stand, step, stumble, and stand again without speaking, without recourse to a privileged form of social power. The revelation consequently reads as a behest to men to pay attention to peripheral figures on the colony. Women see valuable things. Women say valuable things. Women, servants, and children disseminate invaluable stories. To use the language of Angela D. Gilmore, "The transformation of silence into language and action is an act of self-revelation, and is therefore dangerous; however, the alternative, remaining silent, is more dangerous, and eventually, on some level, deadly" (117).

Smiley populates *The Greenlanders* with resilient, autonomous women—characters who complicate Smiley's original focus on leading men. Gunnar's older sister Margret, who is born on the novel's first page, is the deferred hero of the text, and her role ironically lays emphasis upon the consensus that women are "eternal strangers" in the colony (116). Margret is tricked into marrying Olaf, whom she later names Odd and likens to a repugnant polar bear, when she finally relates her long-suppressed story (428–30). She falls in love with Skuli Gudmundsson, a Norwegian. When they "lay together as man and wife" (100), they are discovered. Gunnar and Olaf peremptorily kill Skuli for his part in the tryst, and they banish Margret from her steading and district (125–27). Foreshadowing the difficulties of her long exile (or what we might call an unofficial counter-narrative silenced by an official narrative), Margret's illicit child dies at a young age. She spends the fifty winters between Birgitta's vision and its actualization away from Gunnar's Stead. Initially she appropriates an abandoned farm, but dwindling resources soon force her to live as a servant. She eventually insinuates her way onto steadings by contributing her conserved livestock and her equally valuable needlework skills.

Margret's movements accentuate the enigmatic or asymmetrical qualities of several young women in Greenland, the most compelling of whom is Asta Thorbergsdottir. When Margret occupies her own property, she lives with Asta, "a girl so strong that she liked to compete with boys and men in swimming contests" (132). Asta also vies with the men by engaging in a relationship with and having a son by "a skraeling boy" (225). She is the only woman on the colony to couple with a Skraeling, although Greenlandic men regularly pair with Skraeling women. As unlikely as it may seem, the archeological record contains no proof of Skraeling-Norse interrelations. Diamond explains:

> As far as archeological evidence for contact is concerned, the Inuit might as well have been living on a different planet from the Norse, rather than sharing the same island and hunting grounds. Nor do we have any skeletal or genetic evidence of Inuit/Norse intermarriage. Careful study of the skulls of skeletons buried in Greenland Norse churchyards showed them to resemble continental Scandinavian skulls and failed to detect any Inuit/Norse hybrid. (263)

Perhaps Smiley's hybrid pairings likewise speak to the exclusionary practices of the Church. In death as in life, the Inuit and those who defect to them remain an anathema on consecrated land. Or maybe the Inuit themselves observe particular death rites, ones not delimited by Christian practice. The larger issue here is how Smiley envisions different forms of national integration. She particularly focuses on Asta's unprecedented coupling with a male Skraeling, which counteracts the dominations of colonial white male privileging. Thomas also comments on institutionalized racial and gender privilege in *Isobel Gunn*. Through eavesdropping, the title character learns that country wives are exclusively Native women. Another character contemptuously clarifies the term country wife: "Country marriages, we call them. Lots of children running around. No white women, is what I meant. Plenty of the other kind" (40). Like Smiley, Thomas, and their characters, women offer narratives that amplify or offset prevailing (normativized) assumptions. In the case of Norse Greenland, Smiley claims that the men need the counter-stories of the women.

V.

English pirates from Bristol attack the colony a decade after the Thing is dismantled, epitomizing the outlawry that finally besets Greenland. If not harbingers of forthcoming imperial expansion, pirates are prototypical outlaws. The freebooters restock their ship with what is left of the colony's goods, thereby exposing Nordic Greenland's eroded social network. The saga's two-page epilogue stresses the devastation of the Western colony, and the opening paragraph illustrates the general outlawry that lies in the pirates' wake. As he recounts the concentric circles of the colony, narrator Gunnar mourns the fact that "news between the districts was slow, [...] every district turned in upon itself, [and] all the families were in a turmoil of accusations and retaliations" (583). Survival is improbable in the absence of a legal system and its attendant social web. Outlawry waxes in inverse proportion to the waning of the communal accountably that is the preserve of justice. This is why Gunnar, famous for his bad luck (cf. 55, 224, 329, 413, 417, 436, 509, 577), turns out to be the narrator of the saga. The last line of the epilogue reveals *The Greenlanders* as "his tale" (584). Though Gunnar kills "eight men" in the narrative, a tabulation inducing him "to weep and weep and weep" (581–82), Smiley—who revels in sacrificing her characters to principle—does not abbreviate his life. Gunnar suggests his survival is a result of his identification with the traits and stories of Greenland's women, children, and servants. Like no other male in the narrative, Gunnar listens to and learns from women. As a boy, he shares stories with serving-women (19), has "little bent for hunting" (34), and "resort[s] to spinning wool, like a woman, in order to earn his place at the table" (44). He challenges Sira Pall by admiring what he sees as the "bold resolve" of the woman the priest chides in a didactic sermon (72). Gunnar, in fact, begins writing on parchments in an effort to correct what he sees as Einar Bjornsson's unjust rendition of the Greenlanders' story (236–37).

Gunnar stresses the value of women in light of general outlawry on the colony. The dwindling population isolates itself on private farmsteads, which is the normal condition of womanhood in the colony. The Greenland Norse are finally deprived of what Asgeir Gunnarson, father of Margret and Gunnar, once christened "real wealth": the infrequent "news of other places" (8). The Greenlanders "get the greatest pleasure out of a curious event"—whether these are tidings from the faraway continent, accounts from the North Atlantic, or reports from a neighboring district (281). Gunnar praises novelty by way of his enthusiasm for play and storytelling in the saga's final paragraph. He consolidates consciousness, existence, and play as indispensable for children. (Joyce Carol Oates makes the same observation in her short essay "Transformations of Play" [254]). As Gunnar looks over his chessboard, he says, "folk may not contemplate their fates all the time, and must play as well as work" (584). Surrounded by children, and in "the shadow" of "the great loom" spun by his sister, mother, and "many generations of wives before them" (584), Gunnar recalls his introduction to play in the form of storytelling. He spins his story belatedly, positioning the reevaluations of orality as antithetical to non-transparent memory. Gunnar concludes by correlating storytelling and justice, making *The Greenlanders* Margret's epitaph. As testament to his sister, a victim of the pirates (582), Gunnar shows how law, in order to be just, must circulate every story—especially the rich, curious stories of eternal strangers.

The fact that Jane Smiley's male narrator ultimately circulates the story of a silenced female speaks to the institutionalizing of privilege and power. Smiley speaks as Gunnar in order to give Margret a voice, and while not the first to do so, Smiley speaks as a man in order to give herself a voice. Thomas utilizes the same narrative technique in *Isobel Gunn*. Her narrator, a chronicler not unlike Gunnar, is tellingly named Inkster. He documents the unusual story of Isobel Gunn, a young woman who escapes a preordained life of sexism and drudgery in the Orkney Islands by disguising herself as John Fubbister, a laborer-for-hire, and sets forth to the colonies in Rupert's Land. Each female writer ironically adopts a male voice in order to deliver the counter-story of a disenfranchised or declassed female. Both writers accentuate how counter-narratives succumb to the institutional filtering—the archetypal dominations—of master narratives.

Works Cited

Atwood. Margaret. "Notes for Further Thought." *The Handmaid's Tale*. 1985. Toronto: Doubleday, 1998. 391-402. Print.

---. *The Handmaid's Tale*. 1985. Toronto: Doubleday, 1998. Print.

Buell, Denise Kimber. "God's Own People: Specters of Race, Ethnicity, and Gender in Early Christian Studies." *Prejudice and Christian Beginnings: Investigating Race, Gender, and Ethnicity in Early Christian Studies*. Ed. Laura Nasrallah and Elisabeth Schlusser Fiorenza. Minneapolis, MN: Fortress, 2009. 159-90. Print.

Chamberlain, J. Edward. "From Hand to Mouth: The Postcolonial Politics of Oral Written Traditions." *Reclaiming Indigenous Voice and Vision*. Ed. Marie Battiste. Vancouver: UBC, 2000. 124-41. Print.

Diamond, Jared. *Collapse: How Societies Choose to Fail or Succeed*. New York: Penguin, 2005. Print.

Erdrich, Louise. *Love Medicine*. 1984. New York: Harper, 1993. Print.

Ewick, Patricia. "Consciousness and Ideology." *The Blackwell Companion to Law and Society*. Ed. Austin Sarat. Oxford: Blackwell, 2004. 80-94. Print.

Gillborn, David. "Critical Race Theory beyond North America: Toward a Trans-Atlantic Dialogue on Racism and Antiracism in Educational Theory and Praxis." *Critical Race Theory in Education: All God's Children Got a Song*.

Ed. Adrienne D. Dixson and Celia K. Rousseau. New York: Routledge, 2006. 241-63. Print.
Gilmore, Angela D. "It is Better to Speak. *Critical Race Feminism: A Reader*. Ed. Adrien Katherine Wing. 2nd ed. New York: New York UP, 2003. 114-17. Print.
Glenn, H. Patrick. "A Chthonic Legal Tradition: To Recycle the World." *Legal Traditions of the World: Sustainable Diversity in Law*. New York: Oxford UP, 2000. 56-85. Print.
Gomez, Laura E. "A Tale of Two Genres: On the Real and Ideal Links Between Law and Society and Critical Race Theory." *The Blackwell Companion to Law and Society*. Ed. Austin Sarat. Oxford: Blackwell, 2004. 453-70. Print.
Harpham, Geoffrey Galt. "Ethics." *Critical Terms for Literary Study*. Ed. Frank Lentricchia and Thomas McClaughlin. 2nd ed. Chicago, IL: Chicago UP, 1995. Print.
Harris, Angela P. "Race and Essentialism in Feminist Legal Theory." *Critical Race Feminism: A Reader*. Ed. Adrien Katherine Wing. 2nd ed. New York: New York UP, 2003. 34-39. Print.
Hurley, S.L. *Justice, Luck, and Knowledge*. Cambridge, MA: Harvard UP, 2003. Print.
King, Thomas. *Green Grass, Running Water*. Toronto: Bantam, 1993. Print.
Jones, Gwyn. "The Greenlanders' Saga." *The Norse Atlantic Saga: Being the Norse Voyages of Discovery and Settlement to Iceland, Greenland, America*. London: Oxford UP, 1964. 143-62. Print.
Little Bear, Leroy. "Jagged Worldviews Colliding." *Reclaiming Indigenous Voice and Vision*. Ed. Marie Battiste. Vancouver: UBC, 2000. 77-85. Print.
Miller, J. Hillis. *The Ethics of Reading: Kant, de Man, Eliot, Trollope, James and Benjamin*. New York: Columbia UP, 1987. Print.
Mouffe, Chantal. "Which Ethics for Democracy?" *The Turn to Ethics*. Ed. Marjorie Garber et al. New York: Routledge, 2000. 85-94. Print.
Nakadate, Neil. *Understanding Jane Smiley*. Columbia: South Carolina UP, 1999. Print.
Oates, Joyce Carol. "The Life of the Writer and the Life of the Career: First Principles and 'Transformations of Play.'" *New Literary History* 27.2 (1996): 251-57. Print.
Putnam, Robert D. *Bowling Alone: The Collapse and Revival of American Community*. Toronto: Simon, 2000. Print.
Ross, Andrew. "The Private Parts of Justice." *Race-ing Justice, En-gendering Power: Essays on Anita Hill, Clarence Thomas, and the Construction of Social Reality*. Ed. Toni Morrison. New York: Pantheon, 1992. 40-60. Print.
The Seventh Seal. [*Det Sjunde Inseglet*]. Dir. Ingmar Bergman. 1957. Criterion, 2002. DVD.
Smiley, Jane. *The All-True Adventures of Lidie Newton*. New York: Alfred A. Knopf, 1998. Print.
---. *Duplicate Keys*. 1984. New York: Ballantine, 1993. Print.
---. *Good Faith*. New York: Knopf, 2003. Print.
---. *The Greenlanders*. 1988. New York: Ballantine, 1996. Print.
---. *Moo*. New York: Knopf, 1995. Print.

---. "Shakespeare in Iceland." *Transforming Shakespeare: Contemporary Women's Re-Visions in Literature and Performance.* Ed. Marianne Novy. New York: St. Martin's, 1999. 159-79. Print.

---. *Ten Days in the Hills.* New York: Anchor, 2007. Print.

---. *A Thousand Acres.* 1991. New York: Ballantine, 2001. Print.

Taleb, Nassim Nicholas. *The Black Swan: The Impact of the Highly Improbable.* New York: Random, 2007. Print.

Thomas, Audrey. *Isobel Gunn.* Toronto: Penguin, 1999. Print.

Vanderhaeghe, Guy. *The Englishman's Boy.* Toronto: McClelland, 1996. Print.

Wacks, Raymond. *Understanding Jurisprudence: An Introduction to Legal Theory.* New York: Oxford UP, 2005. Print.

Walzer, Michael. *Spheres of Justice: A Defense of Pluralism and Equality.* New York: Basic, 1983. Print.

A Mysterious Heart: 'Passing' and the Narrative Enigma in Faulkner's *Light in August* and *Absalom, Absalom!*

MARTA PUXAN-OLIVA

ABSTRACT

This essay argues that William Faulkner's *Light in August* and *Absalom, Absalom!* use the device of the narrative enigma to effectively tell stories in which the cultural practice of 'passing for white' in the United States under the Jim Crow system is strongly suggested. The secret is the essential feature of the social practice of passing, which makes the construction of the plot around a narrative enigma especially suitable. By not resolving the narrative enigma, the novels not only preserve the secret of the supposed 'passers,' but construct a narrative that departs from the most important conventions of the so-called genre of the passing novel. The truly modernist narrative strategy of placing an unresolved mystery to drive the plot even allows Faulkner to go a step further: the narrative can portray the Southern white fear of passing with even more significance than the actual act of passing itself. It is precisely the fact that the main characters, Joe Christmas and Charles Bon, have uncertain blood origins that allows and even urges the white community of Jefferson to build a story set only upon conjecture along established racial patterns. Therefore, the effect of the narrative enigma is twofold: it retains the racialization of the story and preserves the secret of the passers, while ambiguously uncovering the false grounds upon which the fear of miscegenation constructs and maintains racial boundaries.

> He passes away under a cloud, inscrutable at heart, forgotten, unforgiven, and excessively romantic.
>
> Joseph Conrad, *Lord Jim*

Sometimes literature illuminates in a striking way the emotional and historical effects that contemporary social practices—no longer operative today—had in the past, providing an understanding that an analysis from the viewpoint of our transformed, contemporary societies cannot offer. This is the case with the practice of 'passing' in the United States, and with the series of novels that constitute what has been labeled the passing novel genre. Joel Williamson defines 'passing' as "crossing the race line and winning acceptance as white in the white world" (100). Movement in the opposite direction is less common. Even though the practice survives—broadened to include gender passing, but still primarily denoting racial or ethnic mobility—the force and historical function that passing for white had during the Jim Crow period, which peaks in the late nineteenth century and the interwar period, perished with the end of segregation.[1] Viewed as a genre, the

---

* I am grateful to professors Enric Ucelay Da Cal at the Universitat Pompeu Fabra in Barcelona, Kenneth W. Warren at the University of Chicago, and John T. Matthews at Boston University for their insightful comments on a shorter version of this essay.

[1] Juda Bennett refers to 'gender passing,' and reflects on the practice historically. See Sollors and Fabi for the evolution, transformation, and recuperation of several motifs and values

passing novel shares features that exhibit both historical opinions about the practice itself, and a motif that is explored in literature. Although most passing novels focus on concerns with the nature of African American identity and its social circumstances, passing narratives also delve into some specifically white concerns. In this latter vein, William Faulkner's novels saliently deploy the characteristic features of the genre. According to M. Giulia Fabi, although passing novels share many common elements when they represent white or African American concerns, "they have been put to distinctively different uses" (3).[2] I do not intend to establish any narrative of author-based 'racial' divisions in the shaping of passing novels, but rather to show that, in some instances, the focus on what were common arguments and their related anxieties at the core of what were classified as white communities during periods of enforced social, economic, and political inequality in the United States, produced different patterns in the narratives from those that focused on the perception and experience of the passing of individuals classified as black. This is overwhelmingly the case in Faulkner's work.

Several scholars have developed the concept of passing in literature and a few have done so with a focus on Faulkner's novels.[3] Less attention has been devoted to the relationship between correlations linking the historical dimension and the narrative patterns of passing novels, except for the relevant works of Fabi, Werner Sollors, and Gayle Wald, in which the issue of 'passing' in Faulkner's work is not explored. In particular, it seems that insufficient attention has been paid to the 'secret' or the 'narrative enigma' in relation to the literary trope that concerns us in this essay. Scholarship has not yet unfolded the richness of this narrative device in its exploration of social practice. In attempting to fill this gap, I will focus on Faulkner's novels to highlight some of the most powerful uses of secrecy in passing literature. This essay intends to illustrate how Faulkner's use of passing in the novels *Light in August* (1932) and *Absalom, Absalom!* (1936) benefits from the idea that mystery is constitutive of the practice; he forges a narrative strategy that, in preserving the effectiveness of the characters' passing, emphasizes the very fear of miscegenation that gripped many Southern white minds during the Jim Crow era. The novels place an enigma at the center of the narrative that, by remaining unresolved, safeguards the mystery of racial identity, allowing the ambiguity of the characters' blood to haunt the racist minds that sanctified not only racial puri-

---

attached to the trope, which are not within the scope of this essay. Still, and despite the improvement in the last decade, the specifics of historical and literary treatment of passing seems to be insufficiently explored. On the decline of its popularity in literature, see Huggins's chapter "Passing Is Passé." I concur with Sollors's reluctance to consider the practice of passing during segregation and in a post-segregation U.S. society together and with the same parameters. However, some scholars insist on the survival of current practices. For a suggestion of ways in which passing might still be present today, see Wald; see also Kennedy's chapter "Racial Passing." In this latter vein, in being associated with performance, passing has recently been used—as a rather ahistorical point of entrance—to the question of identity, thus reconsidering passing as "those practices by which we try to refuse identities that have been historically offered to us, and that continue to structure our responses even as we seek to disavow them (often through that peculiar form of xenophobia I identified earlier)" (Caughie 404).

[2] On passing in literature, see Ginsberg.

[3] On Faulkner and passing, see Sugimori; Entzminger; Bennett; Ickstadt; and McKinley.

ty but also the segregated system that anchored inequality. It is the social practice of passing that specifically enables Faulkner to further the aesthetical possibilities of his narrative strategies while intervening in the contemporary racial debate of his time. In doing so, Faulkner's novels depart from the patterns adhered to by most novels of passing, utilizing the practice to explore the nuances of the external white perspective of the practice itself.[4]

From Murder to Race: Developing Narrative Mysteries

William Faulkner's *Absalom, Absalom!* and *Light in August* are structured by a narrative enigma pursued in the manner of a detective novel. The mystery of the novels lies at the heart of their central characters, but this is not always apparent. In both works, murder is an enigma that needs to be solved by storytelling. The question of why Henry Sutpen killed Charles Bon gives a centrifugal energy to the narrative of *Absalom, Absalom!*, just as the identity of Joanna Burden's murderer gives the earlier novel its structure, though to a somewhat lesser extent. Meanwhile, the narrative enigma of why Henry Sutpen killed Bon leaves the reader in doubt about Charles Bon's racial identity which is touched upon only in the novel's final act of conjecture. *Light in August* immediately transfers the heavy load of the novel's mystery to the doubt over Joe Christmas's miscegenation as being a likely key to solving Joanna's murder. Nonetheless, *Absalom, Absalom!*'s final revelation that Charles Bon is part black invites a refocused rereading that examines the evidence through the mulatto prism, necessarily relocating miscegenation to the heart of the narrative enigma. Similarly to *Light in August*, miscegenation functions as a proxy for the resolution of the assassinations. In fact, murder is the enigma that fits best here, since its association with miscegenation is well known, through both the stereotype of the razor murderer and lynching, the epitome of racial crime. Nevertheless, because the attribution of miscegenation to both Charles Bon and Joe Christmas are suspicions that the novels never definitively affirm or deny—for the racial composition of the characters' blood remains unknown througout—their racial identity becomes the mystery. It is through this narrative device that the characters' 'hearts' become mysterious. Faulkner writes modernist detective novels that sometimes feature murder as just the tip of the iceberg; beneath the water lurks a far more complex and obscure racial mystery.

Faulkner's use of mystery partakes of the modernist transformation of narrative form. In the lucid, insightful analysis by Argentinean writer and critic Ricardo Piglia, we find a rare illumination of the novel's evolution in its so-called transition to modernity. Piglia focuses on what he labels the narrative 'enigma' or the 'secret': the key narrative device structuring what he perceives as the generic seed of the modern novel, the *nouvelle*. The secret or enigma is a peculiarity, the essential void of which "allows us to link various narrative plots and diverse char-

---

[4] The perspective I adopt here thus considers the construction of whiteness as exposed by Toni Morrison in *Playing in the Dark*. For a study of Faulkner's exploration of whiteness, see Towner; Watson; Duvall, *Race*.

acters who live together in a space tied by that knot which is not explained. [...] Thereby we have this feeling of ambiguity, of uncertainty, of multiple meanings the story has" (200; translation mine). In Piglia's view, the detective novel is a subgenre of the novel that greatly contributes to the renovation of narration. Faulkner frequently develops this major narrative device in the genre of the novel.

Considering mystery in the same light, Spanish writer Juan Benet—an admirer and critic of Faulkner—highlights the particularly modern use of the device in the literature of the sea:

> In the legend of the ghost ship, certain things happen that invite thought. The invention of mystery (in the mystery novel or in any classic or modern genre of analogous configuration) fulfills a double objective when it shows the interest that the enigma arouses and when it benefits from all the intrigue that the process of investigation awakens, the progress that we today call 'suspense.' The enigma is invented to be solved, a scheme that has been repeated ever since *Oedipus, King*, right up to the modern detective novel. The novel of the sea, by contrast, very frequently bears an aura—I do not know exactly why— of a kind of permanent mystery, of vague and subtle confines. (181; translation mine)

Certainly, preceded by other narratives such as Henry James's "The Figure in the Carpet" or Joseph Conrad's *Heart of Darkness* and *Lord Jim*, the modern particularity of Faulkner's enigmas in these novels is that they are not solved. As Piglia notes, this modern turn of the screw allows uncertainty and ambivalence to lie at the heart of the narrative, opening the gates to multiple accounts, to rumors, and to an explosion of subjective perspectives, all of which are, in most cases, highly prejudiced. Faulkner uses a clandestine cultural practice to embody the narrative enigma of the novels in question here. Indeed, the well-known practice of passing was made possible by unsolved mystery. It was precisely in this requirement of secrecy that Faulkner found the most powerful incarnation of disorientation, in both modernist and Southern racial varieties.

To return to our previous point, the narrative enigmas remain unsolved in both *Absalom, Absalom!* and *Light in August*.[5] In a complex narration, Quentin and— much more clearly—Shreve both speculate, and later assume, that Sutpen's supposed son Charles Bon is "part negro." This assumption would have been a reason for Sutpen's legitimate white child Henry to kill Charles in order to prevent him from marrying his white sister Judith Sutpen. The narrative voice of the battle camp passage—in which Thomas Sutpen tells Henry that "*it was not until after he* [Charles Bon] *was born that I found out that his mother was part negro*" (292)—is so ambiguous that there is no way of verifying who is speaking or who is reporting this conversation. It is also difficult to determine whether the novel is presenting this information as something that actually happened, or if it is a constituent part of the imaginative play of Shreve and Quentin's narrative added in order to tell the story of Thomas Sutpen's downfall. This is precisely the crux of the mystery. Because the unreliable Shreve attempts to solve the mystery of Henry Sutpen's murder of Charles Bon by attributing the truth to what is uncertain, the mystery

---

[5] Many critics refer to the unresolved mystery of the novels. See Batty in particular for a radical interpretation that even questions the enigma itself, and see Novak for the relation between the mystery and the idea of loss.

of the murder remains unresolved.[6] However, since it is the emergence of racial mystery that impedes the resolution of the initial murder mystery, the novel realigns the narrative enigma that is thereafter centered on Bon's racial identity.

Likewise, Joe Christmas believes that he has "got some nigger blood" in him (543). Since childhood he has been called a "nigger," and the construction of his character suggests that he might be. There is ultimately, however, no reliable information either to confirm or deny this, and the affirmation of his race remains a mere rumor. Christmas's supposed grandfather Doc Hines—the only source of information about his origins—feels that he is black, something that would have motivated his family to abandon Christmas to an orphanage. Yet Doc Hines's wife states that "it was just that circus man that said he was a nigger and maybe he never knew for certain," leaving the certainty of Christmas's racial origins unresolved (678).

Seeing and Telling the Mulatto

The relationship between mystery and either narrative voice or narrative perspective is the basis of Faulkner's construction of an unresolved enigma, and thus it anchors the representation of racial passing in the novels. It is the conflicting perspectives or voices that produce the novels' effect of ambiguity with regard to race that lie at the core of both stories. Technically, *Light in August* develops multiple narrative perspectives told by one narrative voice, while *Absalom, Absalom!* gathers multiple narrative voices that encompass several narrative perspectives.[7]

This combination of narrative voice and narrative perspective generates a contrast between the individual narrative perspective of the supposed, or known, passing character on the one hand, and the external perspective of the same character on the other. This contrast constitutes a crucial feature of a reformulation of the passing novel, one that justifies the preeminent white perspective of both the mulatto character and of passing that is incapable of solving the novels' mysteries. When examined closely, the representation of mulattoes in both novels fully depends on other narrative voices: that of the authorial third-person narrator in *Light in August* and that of the character-narrators Rosa Coldfield, Quentin Compson, and, far more importantly, Mr. Compson and Shreve McCannon in *Absalom, Absalom!* However, this does not prevent the voices from granting the mulatto characters some degree of internal perspective, although it is never liberated from their dependency on the white characters.[8] This internal perception results in a crisis of self-recognition that is characteristic of the literary treatment of the mulatto figure. Likewise, in both novels there is an enforcement of the external perspective of mulattoes through the perspective of the town, and through

---

[6] I analyzed Shreve's unreliable narrative voice and these passages in particular in "Narrative Strategies." For an analysis of Shreve's language, see also Pitavy, "The Narrative Voice."

[7] I borrow Genette's and Bal's distinctions between narrative voice and focalization, otherwise called narrative perspective. Narrative perspective is the point from which the told object is seen or perceived, while narrative voice is the instance that utters the narration, or speaks.

[8] See Price for the construction of Bon and his subjective voice.

voices and perspectives other than their own, which is particularly true in the descriptions of Joe Christmas and Charles Etienne Saint-Valery Bon.

In *Light in August*, the narrator's focalization of Joe Christmas's inner self centers his overwhelming preoccupation with his racial identity. As Joanna and Christmas comment:

> 'You don't have any idea who your parents were?'
> If she could have seen his face she would found it sullen, brooding. 'Except that one of them was part nigger. Like I told you before.'
> She was still looking at him; her voice told him that. It was quiet, impersonal, interested without being curious. 'How do you know that?'
> He didn't answer for some time. Then he said: 'I dont know it.' (586)

This is the protagonist's personal explanation of the novel's mystery: he believes that he is black but cannot be sure. From the point of view of racial representation in literature, Christmas's internal perspective displays the already codified experience of the mulatto crisis. Evett V. Stonequist, a contemporary critic of Faulkner, reveals in his study *The Marginal Man* a widely acknowledged racial awareness of mulattos and 'marginal men' in general when these two novels were published. He explains both the experience of the crisis and its outcomes:

> Experiencing the conflict of cultures constitutes the turning point in the career of the individual. This is the period when the characteristic personality traits first appear. The experience itself is a shock. The individual finds his social world disorganized. Personal relations and cultural forms which he had previously taken for granted suddenly become problematic. He does not know quite how to act. There is a feeling of confusion, of loss of direction, of being overwhelmed. (140)[9]

The crisis experience places the 'marginal man'—in this case the mulatto—in an alienated position between two cultures, since "having participated in each he is now able to look at himself from the two viewpoints" (Stonequist 145). Left with the uncertainty of his parentage, Joe Christmas lives in a permanent state of identity crisis, in contrast to most other mulatto characters in fiction. The latter generally become acquainted with their racial identity in childhood and therefore experience a coming of age moment in which their own crises of identity take place, resulting in a decision about their future behavior and a choice about their affiliation with their chosen communities. In contrast, Joe's racial disorientation pervades the entire novel and peaks during his years in the South, for example, and during his time in the North before he goes to Jefferson. In rejecting both white and black cultures—or in assuming them both, as Thadious Davis and Bethany Lam argue—he clearly embodies the 'marginal man.' This status is highlighted, for example, in the follwing passage where we learn that:

---

[9] For the crisis experience and the novel of passing, see the chapter titled "Minds in Collusion: Miscegenation and Mulatto Crises." The bibliography on miscegenation in literature is extensive. In addition to the titles quoted and referred to in this essay, see the following in particular: the influential study by Kinney; Lemire for a study of miscegenation in the North between 1776 and 1865 with a sexual focus; Jones for a study since the end of segregation in the 1960s; Kaup and Rosenthal for a selection of essays comparing miscegenation in the Americas to the present moment. See also Mencke's still very informative study.

> [s]ometimes he would remember how he had once tricked or teased white men into calling him a negro in order to fight them, to beat them or be beaten; now he fought the negro who called him white. He was in the north now, in Chicago and then in Detroit. He lived with negroes, shunning white people. He ate with them, slept with them, belligerent, unpredictable, uncommunicative. He now lived as man and wife with a woman who resembled an ebony carving. At night he would lie in bed beside her, sleepless, beginning to breathe deep and hard. He would do it deliberately, feeling, even watching, his white chest arch deeper and deeper within his ribcage, trying to breathe into himself the dark odour, the dark and inscrutable thinking and being of negroes, with each suspiration trying to expel from himself the white blood and the white thinking and being. And all the while his nostrils at the odour which he was trying to make his own would whiten and tauten, his whole being writhe and strain with physical outrage and spiritual denial. (564)[10]

His recasting as an eternally misplaced character would impede his development along the lines of the literary passers who increasingly return to their black communities or receive some kind of reprimand for their betrayal of their race and the established order, as is the case with Rena Walden in Charles Chesnutt's *The House Behind the Cedars* (1900) and with Clare Kendry in Nella Larsen's *Passing* (1929). If these characters are trapped by their moral understanding of their passing and its social consequences, Christmas is trapped in the feeling that there is no escape for him, as if, as he affirms, "I have never got outside that circle" (650).

On the other hand, Christmas's perspective is framed by the town's own, which is feverishly engaged in trying to find out whether this central character is black or not. The town as teller is a composite of the subject 'town' or 'they,' as well as of the many scattered and fragmented individual voices. As Heinz Ickstadt notes:

> Even if we escape the temptation of wanting to (re)center the novel in one of its many different (and differing) voices (individual and communal ones telling or re-telling stories or rumors), these voices nevertheless occasionally overlap and echo one another. They seem to form or add up to a dispersed yet composite, collective voice celebrating the consolatory power of Southern light and soil suggestive of a peace that Christmas and Hightower long for, yet can attain only in death. (534)

The town is the main source not only of witnessed knowledge but also of judgment cast upon its inhabitants and newcomers, above all Lena Grove, Hightower, Byron Bunch, Joe Brown, and Joe Christmas. It acts as the collective narrative perspective to which Ickstadt alludes; it does this through repetition, and by the use of "they," the "workmen," and "the town"—terms that unify what is in actuality a cluster of character voices and perspectives. One example among a great number that can be used to illustrate this is when, in telling about Byron Bunch, the narrator borrows the town's insistant perspective by saying that the "other workmen, the town itself or that part of it which remembers or thinks about him, believe that he does it for the overtime which he receives" (433) and the repetitive use of "they told Byron" (443, 444). However, it is not only the town that provides an external perspective of Christmas: Byron Bunch, Joe Brown, Hightower, and Gavin Stevens, although watched themselves, create a portrait of Christmas that

---

[10] This passage is representative of the repulsion of miscegenation that Bluestein links to the illicit birth in particular, and to Faulkner's fiction in general.

is voiced individually but feels integrated.[11] Furthermore, as Scott Romine argues, this interaction of narrative perspective and narrative voice constructs a solid sense of community because the "narrator [...] (pseudo-diegetically) assumes the community's perspective not only at the level of focalization, but at the level of narration itself" (165). Romine fully illuminates how crucial the role of narrative is in the construction and preservation of the community, which he defines as "a social group that, lacking a commonly held view of reality, coheres by means of norms, codes, and manners that produce a simulated, or at least, symbolically constituted social reality" (3).

Certainly, the town as a compounded perspective relies on the detective-like hunt for predetermined features and attitudes that would help to elucidate Christmas's racial identity: he is treated as a "stranger" (421) and called "a foreigner for three years" (470); he lives in a "tumble down negro cabin" (424); he has a relationship with a "Yankee" who is "mixed up with niggers" and turns up murdered (437); neither the town nor Christmas himself know about his family origins; he escapes from the town and puts on the shoes of a 'Negro'; and his supposed sexual intercourse with Joanna is suggestive of rape when she is murdered.[12] If, as Wald argues, "it is precisely because it operates through representation that race acquires its authority to define" (11), these stereotypes shape a narrative that enables the town itself to determine Christmas's racial identity.[13] The language of racial discourse is even assumed by Joe to such an extent that, as Gena McKinley has pointed out, "because he accepts the racist ideology that there is a biological, 'blood' difference between blacks and whites he must classify himself as irreversibly black." Thus, "Faulkner can reveal more fully the horrifying power of society to shape an individual's identity according to its own perverse distortions" (154).

The prejudiced typology that assists both Christmas and the town in uncovering his identity is made effective with a narrative technique through which the characters create suppositions that will afterwards be confirmed. This insufficiently underlined core strategy encourages the reader, the town, and even Joe himself to rely on their own personal assumptions. The characters, generally either anonymous or secondary, make speculations based on what they witness, and their guesses are afterwards frequently confirmed as facts. For instance, in the scene where the country man who found Joanna's murdered body explains that "[s]he was lying on the floor. Her head had been cut pretty near off; [...] And how he was afraid to try to pick her up and carry her out because her head might come

---

[11] For an interpretation of the modulation of tone and vocabulary that creates this effect, see Pitavy's "Voice and Voices in *Light in August*" (171-75) and a broader approach to the language of the novel in his subsequent "A Stylistic Approach to *Light in August*" (177-201); both essays can be found in *William Faulkner's* Light in August: *A Critical Casebook*.

[12] McKee notes in regard to the stereotypical representations of white women and black characters: "Such masses belong, according to the rules of the public sphere, in holes and secret spaces. Prohibited from public expression and recognition in any form whatever, they are acknowledged only as hidden and formless phenomena" (131).

[13] For a general overview of the novel that emphasizes the reliance on stereotypes and fixed codes of conduct, see Berland. On the abstraction of the 'negro' and the necessity of this abstraction for maintaining the community, see T. Davis's insightful chapter on *Light in August*.

clean off," the conversation not only takes place, but the narrator also conveys the accuracy of the man's anticipation: "And he said that what he was scared of happened. Because the cover fell open and she was laying on the other side, facing one way, and her head was turned clean around like she was looking behind her" (466).[14] This repeated confirmation of the characters' various anticipations in a novel in which rumor plays such an important role prepares the way for the introduction of racial prejudice when judging Christmas's racial identity. Accordingly, Brown's assertion that Christmas is black is only reinforced by such—presumably clairvoyant—intuitions put forward by the marshall (471), the dietitian (489), and by the shopkeeper in Jefferson who says:

> 'Well, they found that nigger's trail at last,' the proprietor said.
> 'Negro?' Hightower said. He became utterly still, in the act of putting into his pocket the change from his purchases.
> 'That bah–fellow; the murderer. I said all the time that he wasn't right. Wasn't a white man. That there was something funny about him. But you cannot tell folks nothing until—.' (626)

In this sense, the communities in which Christmas lives make assumptions based on the aforementioned stereotypes that appear to suggest Christmas is a "Negro." Rumors are given narrative authority by the fact that, on many occasions, witnesses are able to anticipate facts. In *Light in August* then, the significant bestowing of narrative authority upon external observers has a powerful effect on the definition of Christmas's racial identity, including that which he, himself, perceives. Thus, the prejudices that function literally as intuitions assumed as true are endorsed by their confirmation in the narrative.

Concerning narrative perspective and the narrative voice in relation to the passing characters, *Absalom, Absalom!* establishes a similarly polarized pattern between the mulattoes' individual perspectives and the external perspectives others have of them. Yet there is a significant difference: Charles Bon's voice is entirely the construction of a character-narrator—mainly that of Mr. Compson and Shreve—and the perspective of Charles Bon is much less developed than Christmas's own. Whereas *Light in August* is narrated by an omniscient third-person narrator who, in spite of his or her all-knowing nature, does not reveal Christmas's racial identity and thus leaves the enigma unsolved, in *Absalom, Absalom!* the story is narrated by four character-narrators and is only framed by a third-person, non-characterized narrator. This means that the story is entirely dependent upon how the narrators present it, something that is further complicated at those junctures at which the characters are not in possession of the desired information.[15] Given that the main enigma is the figure of Charles Bon himself, of whom even Rosa says "*I had never seen him (I never saw him. I never even saw him dead. I heard a name, I saw a photograph, I helped to*

---

[14] The anticipation concerns also what Armstid speculates about Lena Grove's past (405, 408), which is also noted by Lalonde (111).

[15] The bibliography on narrative voice in *Absalom, Absalom!* is immense, and any attempt to adequately refer to it here would be impossible. As a guide, strong accounts and interpretations of the theme are offered by Kartiganer, *The Fragile*; Guerard; Ross; Ruppersburg; Matthews, *The Play*; Bassett; Parker; and Moreland.

make a grave: and that was all)" (121; italics in orig.), the construction of this character is completely external.[16] As narrators, however, Mr. Compson and Shreve also decide to provide an internal perspective of the characters through their own thoughts and words. Within their narrative voice we find various constructed perspectives that are generated by conjecture, as Albert Guerard has explained (332). It is within this level of the internal narrative that we find the mulatto characters' focalization: ultimately, they all depend on the narrative voice responsible for the story's delivery. From this viewpoint, in being subjected to characterized narrative voices, the internal perspective of the mulatto has thus less authority than in the free indirect discourse frequently adopted by the narrator of *Light in August*.

Even though the construction of Charles Bon is a collaborative effort by several narrators, it is Shreve's racial reading that imposes itself by the end of the novel, for it is he who places Bon at the center of both the narrative and its enigma, and who thus transforms the story—which had, until that point, been that of Thomas Sutpen's downfall—into the story of Charles Bon's assassination. Prone to conjecture, Shreve reads Bon through the lens of racial prejudice and uses this perspective to depict Bon's past, his behavior, and his personality. However, when the narrator invests his character with thoughts and words, he does not use Charles Bon's concern with his racial identity to enhance his skillful portrait; instead, he makes Bon focus on Sutpen's paternal acknowledgment of him. Indeed, in Bon's fabricated thoughts and utterances there is no mention of his 'negro blood' except in the ambiguous passage about the war quoted above. This is relevant because even Shreve deprives the character of any self-reflection about his racial identity at this point, even though he will eventually consider the racial factor to be the crucial justification for Henry's murder of him. Shreve takes up Mr. Compson's insinuations so as to prepare Charles Bon to be logically revealed as black by attributing to him several negro stereotypes: his need for pleasure and money (247), his wasting money "on his whores and his champagne" (248), his indifferent and almost sardonic smile (253), his insistence upon his New Orleans origins, his unofficial cohabitation with an octoroon and his lack of love for either her or for Judith (254, 266), and other references made by Shreve to Bon's flawed moral behavior. Indeed, as Thadious Davis argues, "their construct is quite believable. All rational investigations lead to a basic reality: Charles Bon as 'nigger'" (218).

Nonetheless, what is more relevant from the perspective of the present argument is that Charles Bon's racial indeterminacy does not constitute the heart of the mystery for him as it will for other characters. Indeed, this fact is so important to Shreve that he repeatedly converts conjectures about Bon's blackness into fact, as when he draws his conclusion about the end of the Sutpen family:

> 'So it took Charles Bon and his mother to get rid of old Tom, and Charles Bon and the octoroon to get rid of Judith, and Charles Bon and Clytie to get rid of Henry; and Charles Bon's mother and Charles Bon's grandmother got rid of Charles Bon. So it takes two niggers to get rid of one Sutpen, dont it?' (310)

---

[16] For an emphasis on character construction, see Brodsky. For the construction of the non-narrating characters' subjectivity, see Crist. For a combination of both, see Doody's chapter titled "Quentin and Shreve, Sutpen and Bon."

But racial identity primarily remains a mystery for Quentin, eventually for Mr. Compson, and finally for the reader.[17] Although the novel plays with the idea that Charles Bon could be such a light-skinned mulatto that he might attempt to pass for white, it takes the focus away from the passer's concern with his racial identity and from the resulting crisis experience—a significant deviance from other novels of passing. As much as the novel suggests that it might be a 'novel of passing,' the very absence of this central feature of the passing novel invites further interrogation of the relevance of racial lines for the story, as well as reinforcing the external judging of the conjectured 'passers.' To compensate for this lack of a central feature, Charles Etienne Saint-Valery Bon, the son of Charles Bon by his New Orleans octoroon, contributes to the main passing figure's concern with racial identity by means of introducing the mulatto's racial awareness.[18] Charles Etienne experiences the sharp racial divisions of the South when he is brought from New Orleans to Mississippi and told "that he was, must be, a negro" despite the fact that he "could neither have heard yet nor recognised the term 'nigger'" (165).

Mr. Compson long imagines Charles Etienne's crisis experience. In a passage that recalls the narrator's crisis in James Weldon Johnson's *The Autobiography of an Ex-Colored Man* (1912), Mr. Compson sympathetically describes how when Clytie and Judith brought Charles Etienne to Sutpen's mansion, they found a broken mirror in the garret in which he was to stay. Who knows, Mr. Compson speculates, "what hours of amazed and tearless grief he might have spent before it, examining himself in the delicate and outgrown tatters in which he perhaps could not even remember himself, with quiet and incredulous incomprehension" (165). When, in a difficult social relationship with Jefferson society, he is judged because he attacked some blacks at a party, Charles Etienne is prompted with the real question: "*What are you? Who and where did you come from?*" (168). If this question already alludes to the common trait of the passer as an immigrant *parvenue*, as suggested by Sollors, and thus to the fact that unknown origins may indicate blackness—as Jefferson also fears might be the case with Christmas—the suspicion is only strengthened by his New Orleans origins, which for the town virtually confirms that Charles Etienne is very likely a mulatto. Sollors's recognition that 'New Orleans,' 'creole,' and 'orphan' are three categories that invite thought about the discovery of blackness in interracial literature clearly shows that Faulkner subscribes to the motif of passing literature, delineating a parallelism between Charles Bon, Charles Etienne Saint-Valery Bon, and Joe Christmas (500).[19]

---

[17] The position of the listeners, especially Quentin, as reproducing the reader's own position, has generated many studies on metafiction in the novel. See, in particular, Brooks; Krause; Porter; Doneskey; and Robinson's remarkable study.

[18] Sugimori explores the figure of Charles Etienne to argue that language as a binary tool for classification ignores the physical denial of this opposition reflected in the white passing body of this character, thus evidencing the opposition between racial discourse and a reality of chaos.

[19] Ladd offers a full historical background for the significance of Charles Bon's New Orleanian origins in the conflicting relationship between the mulatto social status inherited from the old French Louisiana and the territories of the U.S. Deep South. Ladd also discusses this in relation to the construction of U.S. nationalism. See also Berzon's chapter on the subject.

Charles Etienne is forced to choose between passing for white or passing for black. Quentin's grandfather had told him that he must go away, must disappear, and he gives him money to do so. "Whatever you are" he continues, "once you are among strangers, people who don't know you, you can be whatever you will" (169). In an episode that echoes what happens to Joe Christmas, Charles Etienne is forced to learn that no one can stand on the color line, but that everyone must choose a side. His internal struggle results in the motif of the 'return' to the African American community, yet he does not feel fully comfortable there, either, again inscribing an overstated marginality. He experiences his mixed race with both violence and fury, forcing his black wife to agree to marriage even before she knows his name (170), "dragging her behind him, toward or from what, driven by what fury which would not let him rest" (171). If the novel does not present a guiding mulatto crisis for Charles Bon, it nonetheless dramatizes Charles Etienne's life as running parallel to that of Joe Christmas. As in *Light in August*, given Charles Etienne's extremely white skin, the town also struggles to classify him as either white or black based on his attitude and behavior. In contrast to the case of Christmas, however, both readers and some of the people in the town know about his ancestry. In *Absalom, Absalom!*, the external perspective thus not only depends on the town's views of Charles Etienne, but also on the narrators' voices that, in the process of constructing the characters based on stereotypes, also provide them with an internal perspective. Their self-perception ultimately emerges from the more authoritative, external white perception of them, relegating the characters to what Philip Weinstein terms "marginalia" (*Faulkner's Subject* 43).

Paradoxically, *Absalom, Absalom!* seems to deploy the reverse plot strategy to the one that structures *Light in August*. In *Absalom, Absalom!* external observation relies predominantly on known and witnessed information, rather than just the witnesses' intuitions. Facts do not necessarily fit what the narrators dream up when they do not have access to information, and speculation enters when facts pass by, unwitnessed by time. Thus, the novel cannot authenticate intuitions later through the presentation of facts, but rather does the contrary: it questions them by highlighting the difference between speculation and forgotten events. Shreve's account of Charles Bon's childhood, for example, appears almost grotesque in its detail because the novel makes it clear that there is no available information about it. The frame narrator frequently disavows these speculations by warning the reader that:

> the two of them creating between them, out of the rag-tag and bob-ends of old tales and talking, people who perhaps had never existed at all anywhere, who, shadows, were shadows not of flesh and blood which had lived and died but shadows in turn of what were (to one of them at least, to Shreve) shades too quiet as the visible murmur of their vaporizing breath. (250)

However, the key strategy of the narrators who draw the mulatto passer characters is to assume their speculations to be true facts in order to enable the development of the telling. Thus, as Peter Brooks observes, "it is a narrative in which we are always passing from the postulation of how it must have been to the conviction that it really was that way" (255). For the last two narrators, Mr. Compson and, in particular, Shreve, Sutpen's story apparently requires racial prejudice in order to exist.

Consequently, a relevant difference between the novels is that in *Light in August* the narrative strategy that shapes the external perspective produces the effect of investing conjecture with authority in the making of what Donald Kartiganer has named "the imagined mulatto" ("The Meaning" 10). Insofar as racial stereotypes become authorized beliefs, Christmas is almost taken for black. In *Absalom, Absalom!* relative authority is shaped by the lack of a counterpoint; only the narrators can shed light on the characters' racial identity.[20]

Passing for What? Faulkner's Borrowings from and Challenges to the Novels of Passing

The narrative strategies analyzed above powerfully underpin Faulkner's particular reading of both the social practice and the novels of passing. Though in different proportions, the external efforts to classify the mulatto characters in both novels only allow a difficult passing. It is difficult because it is uncertain what the characters are passing for. Both the African Americans and the whites of Jefferson suspect Charles Etienne's and Christmas's attempts to pass into their own communities. Charles Etienne has to face

> the negro stevedores and deckhands on steamboats or in city honky-tonks who thought he was a white man and believe it only the more strongly when he denied it; the white men who, when he said he was a negro, believed that he lied in order to save his skin or worse. (171)

Christmas faces a similar encounter when he meets a group of blacks on the road who say:

> 'It's a white man,' he said, without turning his head quietly. 'What you want, whitefolks? You looking for somebody?' The voice was not threatful. Neither was it servile.
> 'Come on away from there, Jupe,' the one who had followed the women said.
> 'Who you looking for, cap'm?' the negro said. [...]
> Christmas, turning slowly, watching them dissolve and fade again into the pale road, found that he had the razor in his hand. It was not open. It was not from fear. 'Bitches!' he said, quite loud. 'Sons of bitches!' (485)

However, the case of Joe Christmas passing is still more complicated, because although in Jefferson's judgment it seems clear that he is passing for white, Christmas finds it impossible to know exactly what he is passing for.[21]

---

[20] Kartiganer suggests that "this opposition of town and text to their own center is an irony underlying the whole novel, for Christmas as a character is as inaccessible to the community of Jefferson as he is to *Light in August*" ("The Meaning" 11). I read the reliance on the external perspective along the same lines as Wittenberg: "It might even be said that while the novel clearly exposes—in order to indict—the pernicious (though virtually inevitable) effects of the prevailing codes, its structure and other aspects of the narrative method to some degree subtly participate in the process of 'framing'" (153).

[21] It is interesting to note here briefly that Christmas's racial uncertainty challenges the distinction Wald makes between the narratives of white people passing for black and those of black people passing for white, both of which are also examined from a gendered perspective. As Wald argues: "Hence whereas the closure of narratives of 'passing for white' is typically predicated

Indeed, passing is a central issue in these novels. A peculiarly U.S. phenomenon because of its foundation on the 'one-drop rule,' according to which an individual is defined as black if he or she has any trace of black ancestry, passing initially became a way of escaping bondage—the origin of the expression probably comes from "passing for free" (Sollors 255)—and later of bypassing the anti-miscegenation laws that sought to define the line of segregation. The difficulties of defining *Who is Black?* (to borrow the title of F. James Davis's book) in state laws from the late-nineteenth and early-twentieth centuries were so blatant that, in most states, the 'one-drop' rule was just a customary law that differed from the more practical legal tracking of negro blood fractions in one individual (generally one eighth or one sixteenth), in part because it was virtually impossible, in most cases, to detect the one requisite drop.[22] The census of 1920 demonstrates the overwhelming arbitrariness of the classification because it was the last to count mulattoes, not only because that was a way of reinforcing the biracial society, but also because mulattoes were differentiated based on nothing but their "visibility," something that was becoming increasingly difficult (Williamson 114; J. Davis 57). When analyzing passing for white within this context, it is thus necessary to comprehend the practice as a way of obtaining a new social and economic status in reaction to anti-miscegenation laws, which aimed at stabilizing the color line that sustained segregation. As offspring of several generations of miscegenation, passers were a menace to the system because they embodied the violation of the anti-miscegenation laws, and also because they enacted the greatest defiance of the one-drop rule, exposing not only its absurdity but the limits of its effectiveness. In this sense, passing became the most provocative threat in the eyes of the defenders of the Jim Crow laws.[23]

Naturally, the African American perspective of passing at this historical juncture is almost diametrically opposite. Not generally threatened by miscegenation because their offspring had historically been counted first as slaves and later as blacks, African Americans tended to view passing either as an opportunity, as a betrayal of commitment to one's race, or as a way of making race "an object of affect." This was because, as Walter Benn Michaels points out, "the possibility of concealing one's racial identity—of looking and behaving in ways that do not reflect one's race—makes available the desire to reveal it," something that is commonly portrayed through the return to the black community (115, 118).[24] It is

---

on the subject's self-recognition within binary narratives of race, a process of recognition that is conflated with a symbolic 'homecoming' to black identity, white passing narratives—especially those of white middle-class male subjects—are contrastingly centered on the subject's ability to access passing as a means of leaving actual and metaphorical 'homes' and symbolically disciplining the 'other' as object of knowledge" (16).

[22] See Murray's compilation of State Laws. For state-specific studies focusing on law, see in particular Domínguez; see also Novkov.

[23] See Novkov for a solidly based legal study on the relation between segregation laws and anti-miscegenation in the case of the state of Alabama as illustrative of the crucial importance of the latter in the shaping of the former. A great number of the cases the author provides as historical evidence deal with individuals being accused of passing.

[24] See Fabi in particular for the tracing of these values and thematic representations, and for their specific use and transformation at specific moments.

precisely in the variety of responses it elicits that passing can offer disparate and enriching literary treatments.

To perform a passing, the individual must keep secret his or her racial identity; once it is discovered, that individual is no longer able to pass. As both Joel Williamson and Juda Bennett remark, because secrecy is essential "to the success of these passings, it has always been difficult for historians to document the phenomenon" (Bennett 2); this has resulted an absurd situation where even 'statistics' are derived from speculation. Because the essential ingredient of passing is mystery, secrecy is a main theme or device at the core of passing novels. The characters who pass must struggle to keep their secret and can share it only with trusted relatives or friends, such as Judge Straight in *The House Behind the Cedars* or Irene in *Passing*.[25] However, in most of the novels the plot progression does not depend on racial mystery; at most, in novels like Mark Twain's *Pudd'nhead Wilson* (1894), the plot is constructed towards the disclosure of the racial secret kept by one character. In almost all passing novels the reader shares the secret; it is only the white circles frequented by the passer that remain unaware. Other, more sophisticated, examples embrace secrecy at a metafictional level in the very act of publishing their novels. As Sollors explains:

> Literary hoaxes such as the anonymous publication of *The Autobiography of an Ex-Colored Man* and the invention of the author 'Vernon Sullivan' suggest the possibilities of connecting the theme of passing to formal plays with truth-telling and authenticity, as James Weldon Johnson and Boris Vian play hide and seek with their readers' expectation of an authentic identity of the author—even in fictions that thematize the fluidity of lines of identification. (271)

William Faulkner's use of secrets departs from the conventions of the genre because it is framed as the narrative enigma—unknown to narrators, readers, and even characters—upon which the narrative plot is built. By means of this narrative strategy, Faulkner's *Light in August* and *Absalom, Absalom!* benefit enormously from the element of secrecy in passing, displaying an innovative perspective that manages to turn the focus toward the portrayal and the inquiry into racial

---

[25] Although most discussions on passing deal with the complex dual reaction of African Americans in relation to the practice—that is to say, seeing it as a betrayal of the race as arged by Michaels, or as a mode of resistance and subversion—Kennedy offers a historically documented reflection on the issue. In documenting the "joke on racism" that both the trope and the practice offer—such as that represented in Langston Hughes's "Passing" or in George Schuyler's *Black No More*—Kennedy refers to historical cases that provide a basis for the idea that the secret was revealed by others in several dramatic instances not only because of "the desire to punish Negroes who aided Jim Crow exclusion, [... but maybe for] some vicarious pleasure in the knowledge that at least a few Negroes were enjoying facilities that racists had hoped to reserve exclusively for whites" (314). In this sense, the secret was sometimes disclosed not only by the passers themselves, but by those who shared their secret as a mode of resistance, a revelation that meant, paradoxically, the end of the practice and, most likely, dreadful consequences for the passer. Even though the secret was usually preserved by African Americans who may not have agreed with the option of passing, or did not have the privilege of making such a decision themselves, they remained silent because they shared the oppression of segregation; Kennedy points at the multilayered aspect of betrayal in relation to the secret of passing.

fear.[26] As we have seen, the novels unfold the mystery of racial identity through the threat of passing as experienced by the Southern white community. As long as the town does not know whether these very light-skinned subjects are classifiable as mulatto or white, they are likely to be performing a passing. It might be that Christmas himself is attempting to appear as white (since he only confides in the similarly suspicious Brown and to Joanna Burden) to avoid the law and to earn certain privileges; or it might be that Charles Bon is trying to pass for white to infiltrate a planter's family by marrying Judith Sutpen. But the town needs to know in order to decide how to behave toward, react to, and even to punish the intruders. It is precisely the fact that Christmas "never acted like either a nigger or a white man" that "made the folks so mad" (658).

Readers are warned that the town has the function of preserving social order, something that becomes clear when Hightower resigns his pulpit. The town, we learn, "was sorry with being glad, as people sometimes are sorry for those whom they have at last forced to do as they wanted them to" (449). Similarly, the town hopes that Joanna Burden will receive the punishment she deserves for being a "nigger lover" (611). By the same token, the town needs to know Christmas's racial identity in order to be able to punish him. It is the town that is inclined to make a decision about Christmas's ambivalent and changing appearance, just as Shreve decides where to place Charles Bon, based on his own imagination. This decision is made unilaterally in both novels, since the town does not know Christmas's racial identity, nor can Shreve be certain about Charles Bon's. In the case of Charles Etienne, it is only Charles Bon's relatives—the Sutpens—and a few other people in town who know he is a mulatto. Thus, his case does not provoke the same degree of social and narrative tension. As John Duvall demonstrates, it is precisely the urgent desire to know that leads readers frequently to assume that Joe Christmas is Joanna Burden's murderer, following the town of Jefferson's decision (see "Murder"). In fact, it is Brown's interests and some inconsistencies in his behavior that, along with the report of the murder, call Christmas's responsibility into question. As James Snead notes, the narrator's frequent support of the town's view creates the effect of "actively creating error. Society here turns arbitrary codes of dominance into 'fact.' To make matters worse, the reader helps accomplish the entire process" (160). Thus, as uncertain as racial identities are, the external perspectives that tell and judge the characters undertake the resolution of this all too uncomfortable mystery, therefore disclosing the secrets of the characters' passing. As an important variation on the passing novel, in these cases the secret is not uncovered by a character who already knows, as with *Puddn'head Wilson*'s Roxana, but by people who need to know. Insofar as knowledge is unattainable, it is replaced by belief.

In the light of these decisions, the characters pass. This is certainly the reason why *Light in August*—and, I would add, *Absalom, Absalom!*, which has not received sufficient attention from this perspective—should be considered "a culminating moment rather than an exemplary and popular expression of racial

---

[26] For a collection of historical writings on biological racism and the fear of miscegenation, see Smith.

passing" (Bennet 104). This is because Faulkner takes some basic conventions of this genre to the extreme. Even though readers are strongly persuaded to believe that Christmas and Bon are mulattoes, doubt about this remains. In contrast to most passing novels, the secret is undisclosed by the end of the novel, and racial identity thus preserves the mystery that enables passing to take place. Herein lies Faulkner's most remarkable device for his further elaboration of the genre: by leaving unsolved what is not only a secret but also a narrative enigma, the novels allow the figures of Charles Bon and Joe Christmas to preserve the effectiveness of their passing—if indeed they really are performing at all. If the secrets of racial identity were revealed, these characters would join the ranks of those recurrent protagonists in the passing novels who, because they are discovered or because they choose to return, are never able to pass.

Faulkner goes even further. Evidently, the very notion of passing involves some kind of belief in racial identity (whether personally held or maintained by society) on which it is dependent in order for it to operate. Because it is intrinsically based on the idea that racial identity is detectable—although this is, of course, not empirically true—passing "highlights an illusory sense of certainty in what is actually an area of social ambiguity and insecurity" (Sollors 250). This sense of certainty is mainly portrayed through the almost inevitable motif of the return to the black community, which also appears in Faulkner's novels with the added consequence of profound discomfort. Accordingly, Sollors concludes that

> the term "passing" is a misnomer because it is used to describe those people who are not presumed to be able to pass legitimately from one class to another, but who are believed to remain identified by a part of their ancestry throughout their own lives and that—no matter whom they marry—they bequeath this identification to their descendants. Ironically, the language speaks only of those persons as "passing" who, it is believed, cannot really "pass," because they are assumed to have a firm and immutable identity. (250)

Faulkner defies this idea by suspending belief in the characters' racial identity. Since their black blood is untraceable, they can really be whatever they want to be without ever having to pass. In an abstract sense, their mobility or their capacity for changing their present status is absolute because there is no traceable, reliable evidence upon which they could define a racial identity that would make any eventual passing happen.[27]

Fear to Uncertainties: White Narratives of Passing and Miscegenation

In Faulkner's novels the irresolution of the racial enigma has an ultimately striking effect that puts forward an intrinsically white portrait of miscegenation and passing; the doubt over racial identities remains because its texture alone shapes the latent fear of miscegenation—the fear of passing. Indeed, Faulkner's particular contribution to novels of passing is precisely his focus on fear. Accordingly, as John T. Matthews states, referring to Christmas, "we don't know if he is a passer or not, we only have the 'fear of passing'" (*William Faulkner* 165). The

---

[27] Accordingly, Kennedy refuses to call it "passing" (285).

fear of passing does not stem exclusively from its defiance of the established racial lines that legitimate segregation, thus constituting an insult to whites; the transgressive practice of passing also allows individuals classified as 'Negro' to actively contribute to engendering the silent 'bleaching' agents of a biracial society. In his final prophecy, Shreve foresees the consequences that the Sutpen family's downfall will have in the future, as inferred from his personal reading of the story. He activates racial fear by recalling Jim Bond, the miscegenated offspring of Charles Etienne:

> I think that in time the Jim Bonds are going to conquer the western hemisphere. Of course it wont quite be in our time and of course as they spread toward the poles they will bleach out again like the rabbits and the birds do, so they wont show up so sharp against the snow. But it will still be Jim Bond; and so in a few thousand years, I who regard you will also have sprung from the loins of African kings. (311)

This conclusion specifically voices the fear of miscegenation that produces the most acute anxiety when the black part of the interracial relationship is so light as to render it imperceptible. As Noel Polk reminds us,

> no matter how white we are, no matter how white the ancestors, whites fear that some residual drop of black blood, perpetuated through some inextinguishable half-life of blackness that will never be obliterated, no matter how many times halved or quartered or eighthed or sixteenthed, will lie there always, recessive but waiting like a bomb to explode at some inconvenient reproductive moment. (74)

The whites' fear is, therefore, twofold: that of already bearing the decisive 'residual drop of black blood,' and the fear of the invisible men who could stealthily introduce that single drop into the white community.

Faulkner's novels emphasize the fear of miscegenation and passing by emphasizing the problematic relationships between race and sex within the Jim Crow system. This emphasis is mainly portrayed through a focus on progeny: in order to prevent the blurring of racial lines and eventual passing, the anti-miscegenation policies concentrated on the mixed-race offspring and sought to prevent their birth. Furthermore, the fear of mixed-race children affected even the adoption system that, as a product of the Progressive reform, was concerned with how to manage orphans of unknown racial origin and is reflected in the novel and analyzed by both Jerng and Kennedy. It was feared that these orphans would eventually contribute to the 'bleaching' that would in turn permit defying practices such as passing to exist. Shreve's reference to Jim Bond, Charles Etienne's mulatto son, signals the fundamental importance of offspring in interracial conflict. It is relevant to Sutpen's story not only in the character of Charles Bon's actual son, Charles Etienne, but also—and primarily—in the future children of an interracial marriage with Judith Sutpen. The blurring of the races has its origins, therefore, in the relationship between race and sex, which the anti-miscegenation laws sought to forbid. This sexual interracial concern is evident when Bon is told to counter Henry's "*You are my brother*" with "*No I'm not. I'm the nigger that's going to sleep with your sister*" (294; italics in orig.).

Likewise, *Light in August* powerfully underscores the condemned relationship between race and sex. Both a pressing need for racial self-identification and a profound disgust overwhelm Christmas when he associates sex with women: when, for instance, the dietitian has sex in his presence, when he attempts to follow his white friends' example of raping a black woman, when Bobbie menstruates, or when he has sexual intercourse with Joanna. The sin of female sexual misbehavior—which Percy Grimm attempts to bring under control by finally castrating Christmas when he says, "[n]ow you will let white women alone, even in hell" (742)—sits in stark contrast with the image of the sacred white woman who protects her womb from intruders whose racial identity might be uncertain. Moreover, *Light in August* emphasizes the racially dubious offspring not only through the orphan's unknown racial origins but also through the repeated appearance of real or pretend pregnancy in Lena Grove, Joanna Burden, and Christmas's mother, Milly. The specter of miscegenation hovers over all of them.

As briefly as I have referred here to the relevance of the associations between sexuality and race, it is clear that it is the potential offspring who embody the fear of miscegenation, just as the bleaching effect sparks the consequent fear of passing.[28] Once again, this is in sharp contrast to the African American perspective of mixed-race offspring. In this particular game of chance, the passer fears having not light, but dark offspring, who might betray the parents' secret of having passed for white. As Clare Kendry admits in *Passing*: "I nearly died of terror the whole nine months before Margery was born for fear that she might be dark. [...] 'It's awful the way it skips generations and then pops out'" (26). It is to this "hallucinating 'possibility' of miscegenation" that Eric Sundquist refers when he states that

> such menace inevitably contained more fantasy than actuality is neither surprising nor mitigating; far from it, for it is precisely the hallucinating "possibility" of miscegenation, which in the white mind has often maniacally exceeded its grasp of the facts, that forms and propels the strange career of Joe Christmas. [... W]hat matters is the other point of view, the climate of fantasy in which the evidence, whichever way it may point, counts for little besides the suspicion that overwhelms and submerges it, repressing and distorting it at the same time. (68)

The focus of the novels is therefore not only the mulattoes who pass, but perhaps more importantly on the fear of whether they might actually attempt to do so. This fear becomes the crux of the racial mystery. At the point at which whites in Yoknapatawpha can no longer classify subjects on a racial basis, they feel the threat of miscegenation. In literature, however, these personified threats are, as

---

[28] For an extended analysis treating interracial sexual relations and their relationship to law, see in particular Kennedy's chapter titled "Race, Racism, and Sexual Coercion," and his illuminating focus on the conflictive location of the miscegenated offspring in the social order both during and after segregation in "Racial Conflict and the Parenting of Children: A Survey of Competing Approaches." *Absalom, Absalom!* displays interesting relationships between sexuality and miscegenation in the context of both homosexuality and incest. Sollors's chapter titled "Incest and Miscegenation" is also very illuminating. Peterson develops his perspective that the divided house is like a divided body, and sees in Henry, Bon, and Judith's triangular relationship "a tripartite transgression of the prohibitions on miscegenation, incest, and same-sex desire that in turn deconstructs the integrity of their bodies" (244). Entzminger discusses two of these issues similarly. Another author who treats miscegenation and the "life of the strangers in the self," and thus in the body, and links it to the episodes of Haiti in the novel, is Kutzinski.

Bennett observes, usually doomed to be self-defeating (52): the biological argument of degeneration in the fourth generation justifies Jim Bond's idiocy; a highly symbolical yellow fever kills Charles Etienne; Christmas's unbearable personal confusion makes his death resemble a suicide; and both Christmas and Charles Bon are lynched or murdered by butcher knives and pistols wielded by white supremacists. These characters' endings are canonical, yet the effects of their mysterious passing are not. The tense atmosphere of the novel is thus passed on to the reader, whose own sleeping reason—as Goya's distressing engraving would have it—produces monsters.

This threat of passing, a product of the population of whites who "became paranoid about invisible blackness" (Williamson 103), is reinforced by the limited presence of the mulattoes' direct and undistorted voice in the novels, and with the crucial role played by the town's rumor and external focalization in the shaping of the storytelling. This perspective certainly works for *Light in August* since the development of the story depends on the direction in which the town drives the events when deciding to place Joe Christmas on the black side of the color line, thereby justifying not only his ambiguous behavior but also a murder. Such an imposition receives the almost customary punishment: lynching.[29] The fear is brutally heightened because the uncertainty about Christmas's identity is real, as further demonstrated by his permanent experience of crisis. Thus, the terror of passing encounters its worst case scenario: an individual whose ancestry is untraceable.

Absalom, Absalom! emphasizes white fear as well, since the insistent mirror images and activation of negro stereotypes compel readers to believe in the mulatto character presented by Shreve. As in *Light in August*, negro stereotypes in the novel strongly encourage fearful external readings and are responsible for raising suspicions over the character's eventual passing. In contrast to *Light in August*, *Absalom, Absalom!* intensifies the external white perspective that "owns the horror" (303) by means of relegating the mulatto crisis to the foreshadowing story of Charles Etienne. It is only through him that we get a mulatto crisis in the novel. The fear involved in that crisis is diluted by the fact that, although he could have passed, he refused to do so. Instead, he publicly acknowledges his mixed blood and his place in society, thus erasing the threat of his exceptionally light skin. By displacing the crisis of racial identity by which the passer's internal perspective of

---

[29] The question the novel poses is, of course, 'who is the murderer and who has been assassinated?' For an interesting reference to the 'sacrificial' nature of lynching in the Southern white community, see Romine. See Hale's chapter titled "Deadly Amusements: Spectacle Lynchings and the Contradictions of Segregation as Culture" for an important account on how lynching developed the character of 'spectacle,' something that Christmas's own case certainly displays. Christmas's use of the razor, Grimm's initial use of the pistol and subsequent use of a butcher knife, and Henry's shooting of a pistol to kill Bon are all symptoms of the adherence to "race etiquette" that Banta dissects splendidly. Banta suggests that the progressive fear of miscegenation and the increase of mob violence in the decade between 1896-1907 gradually established the use of the pistol for white racial crimes as represented in *Life*. Banta also links this with the doubts of Lucas Beauchamp in *Go Down, Moses* and Christmas's clear choice to use a razor in *Light in August* as a symbol of his belief in his own blackness.

his own practice is located, *Absalom, Absalom!* leaves the judgment of Charles Bon's racial identity up to the intransigent, white, external perspective of him. Thereby, the white fear of miscegenation and passing is laid bare. As the enigma remains inextricable, the fear itself—which anxiously awaits disclosure—can be passed on to the reader, as Shreve quickly grasps in his prophecy.

Nevertheless, racial fear, reminiscent of the atmosphere created in Faulkner's short story, "That Evening Sun," ironically unveils its nightmarish origins in both novels. If the practice of passing itself simultaneously affirms and negates racial lines, the portrayal of racial fear also exposes its lack of foundation. It is precisely Faulkner's presentation of an undisguised white terror without counterpoint— justifiable neither on the basis of the characters' ancestry nor by of their internal African American perspective—that discloses its lack of rationale. The external portrayers cannot counteract the discourse of the passer precisely because it is almost nonexistent and clearly does not play a part of Charles Bon's concerns about racial identity, which he ignores regardless of whether he is passing or not. His indifferent attitude in respect to his racial identity delivers a blow to those who fear miscegenation and to all those who maintain the belief that race matters. Nor does Christmas fully own the passer's discourse. As long as his racial identity remains unknown to him, his suspected passing is only real in the minds of white racists. As McKinley and Bennett (among other critics) argue, the ultimate uncertainty about racial identity challenges all racial boundaries because it shows the precariousness of their basis in the racialization of behaviors and practices, which prove insufficient when the issue of miscegenation is raised. Uncertainty both dissolves racial boundaries and simultaneously serves as the very condition necessary for passing to succeed.

If the unsolved racial enigma in the novels constitutes the core of Faulkner's defiance of racial lines, the distance the novels assume in relation to the external determination of racial identity further emphasizes their arbitrariness. In *Absalom, Absalom!*, both Mr. Compson's first attempts at describing the enigmatic Charles Bon and Shreve's full disclosure of him are brought into question by the distance between the text and the narrators in relation to the available facts of Sutpen's story. Shreve's unreliable narration favors the ultimate negation of race as being the reason for Henry killing Charles, and of his construction of the latter as a mulatto passer. In a similar vein, the warnings in *Light in August* that "[m]an knows so little about his fellows" (433) and "most of what folks tells on other folks aint true" (438) serve as reminders that the town's beliefs might not correlate with the truth, because "memory believes before knowing remembers" (487).[30]

To conclude with Faulkner's challenge to fallacious racial classifications, *Light in August* seems to contain a subtle—yet major and hitherto overlooked—example of this challenge. It seems to me that the figure of Joe Brown/Lucas Burch

---

[30] Many critics have argued about the ultimate failure of narration provoked by the limited access to knowledge and the convenient turn to imagination. In this vein, Miller suggests that "[s]uch passages express the impossibility either of finishing the story or of continuing it in one's own life except as the repetition, once again, of the failure to make it come out right" (155). For major studies on the questioning form of the narrative, see both Rimmon-Kenan and Flores.

functions as a counterpart to Joe Christmas and could ultimately be speculated to be the real passer in the novel, once again enhancing both the indispensability of the fear of miscegenation and the blurring of racial lines. Indeed, for the town this fear is essential for perpetuating existing racial lines when they are perceived to be in danger of being blurred, but this fear becomes paranoia when the lines of separation are shown to be nonexistent or false. Byron Bunch thus brings out the striking parallels between Christmas and Brown, as noted by Martin Kreiswirth (64-66). In addition, the portrayals of the characters embrace several features that work as signposts of blackness in interracial literature: they are both "stranger[s]" (421, 424); Christmas's skin color is like parchment (423), while Brown is "dark complected" (439); they share Joanna Burden's cabin; their names are evocative of mulatto sacrifice and skin color (422, 425, 437); they are bootleggers; they are lazy (426-27); and they behave alike. The novel plays with this confusion of the characters several times, as when, for example, Lena has her child, whose father may be Joe Brown. Lena talks about Mrs. Hines' confusion:

> 'She keeps on talking about—She is mixed up someway. And sometimes I get mixed up too, listening, having to . . . .' Her eyes, her words, grope, fumble. 'Mixed up?'
> 'She keeps on talking about him like his pa was that—the one in jail, that Mr Christmas. She keeps on, and then I get mixed up and it's like sometimes I cant —like I am mixed up too and I think that his pa is that Mr—Mr Christmas too—' . . . . But I am afraid . . . .'
> 'Of what?'
> 'I don't like to get mixed up. And I am afraid she might get me mixed up, like they say how you might cross your eyes and then you cant uncross [them] . . . .' (701)

This precious passage summons the ghosts of miscegenated offspring by reinforcing the suggestion of Brown's passing.[31] These parallelisms are, however, constructed only in the imagination, left as diffuse as the fears they produce. Brown's reproach to the sheriff about Christmas—"the folks in this town is so smart. Fooled for three years. Calling him a foreigner for three years, when soon as I watched him for three days I knew he wasn't no more a foreigner than I am. I knew before he even told me himself" (470)—invites an ironic reading already kindled by Byron's depiction, and by Brown's inconsistencies in his interview, when he is at pains to distinguish himself from Christmas.

Ironically, Brown is prefigured as either the man who really does pass in the novel so as to avoid being blamed for murdering Joana Burden, or as the man who reinforces the absurdity of racial distinctions. Brown is thus Faulkner's joke played on Jefferson, a town that is conclusive in its judgments, but which might be fooled by the racial distinctions of its own invention simply because there is no reliable way to discern them. In the end, with Brown suspected of being a mulatto and/or a murderer, the resolution of Christmas's assassination of Joanna could be a mistake entirely, and Christmas's story could be merely a brutal way of establishing social order through bigotry, as noted by Duvall. As a 1932 article in *The Philadelphia Tribune* warned bigots: "Careful Lyncher! He May Be Your

---

[31] Though not focusing on miscegenation, Arnold Weinstein builds up from this passage an insightful interpretation of the way in which the novel establishes a fusion of the stories of Joe Christmas and Lena Grove through confusion.

Brother!" (qtd. in Larsen 124). Again, it is in the embodiment of racial threat and the challenge condensed both in the same character and in the practice of passing itself that we encounter the paradox or the ambivalence that so startlingly shapes Faulkner's novels.

Thus, Faulkner explores the pertinent theme of the mulatto—who suffers contradictions, confusion, isolation, and pain—by combining and drawing out the stereotypes of this figure to the ultimate conclusions, which find a dramatic extreme in the passer. His narrative strategy splendidly enriches the treatment of passing in literature by means of locating the social secrecy characteristic of the practice at the core of his narrative, and by retaining its mystery until it is passed on to the reader. Furthermore, as Piglia has observed, this sagacious employment of the narrative enigma enables the development of multiple narrative perspectives that cause the telling to revolve around it, creating an intense effect of ambiguity. The prevailing cluster of external white perspectives of the mulatto encircles the narrative enigma, dominating its reading, and even going so far as to attempt to violate the secret itself. Precisely because of the overbearing external perspective—that of pertaining to a town and a country entrenched in racial discourse—Faulkner can portray the internal conflict of the mulatto figure as a threat of miscegenation promoted in a society that establishes inequality upon a biracial structure, especially that of the postbellum South and—remarkably—that of the segregated South in the 1930s. This threat finds its culminating provocation in the social practice of passing, and it is so potent because of the presence of an individual whose racial identity is unknown. It is only under this circumstance that he or she can hide away and produce the offspring of miscegenation, which allows the threat to be activated. In other words, it is precisely because the passing requires an unresolved racial mystery to succeed that racial uncertainty disrupts the white supremacists' external perspective that constructs both Christmas's and Bon's stories.

Faulkner's works present a development of features common in novels of passing, turning the point of interest toward the white fear of miscegenation and of the practice itself, rather than toward the fear of discovery. His work also furthers the genre by embracing an oppressive external narrative perspective of the passer instead of reinforcing a crisis of identity that would water the seed of black pride in the mulatto—especially during the interwar period during which Faulkner was writing—and encourage the character's return to the race. Faulkner thus inscribes a shift that delves into white rather than African American concerns, exploring in a simultaneous challenge and endorsement the underpinnings of the Jim Crow system. Consequently, it is Benet's intuition that in the irresolution of the mystery lies the force of the ambivalent and impenetrable conflict of the hearts as lived in the United States during the Jim Crow period. This allows the talented Faulkner to envision in the practice of passing—with all of its contradictions, dramatic effects, and secrecy—both a strikingly effective narrative theme and an optimum, multilayered device for molding his modern social and political narratives.

Works Cited

Bal, Mieke. *Narratology: Introduction to the Theory of Narrative*. 1980. Toronto: U of Toronto P, 1985. Print.

Banta, Martha. "Razor, Pistol, and Ideology of Race Etiquette." *Faulkner and Ideology*. Ed. Donald M. Kartiganer and Ann J. Abadie. Jackson: U of Mississippi P, 1995. 172-216. Print.

Bassett, John E. *Vision and Revisions: Essays on Faulkner*. West Cornwall, CT: Locust Hill P, 1989. Print.

Batty, Nancy E. "The Riddle of *Absalom, Absalom!*: Looking at the Wrong Blackbird?" *Mississippi Quarterly* 47.3 (1994): 460-88. Print.

Benet, Juan. *La inspiración y el estilo*. Madrid: Alfaguara, 1999. Print.

Bennett, Juda. *The Passing Figure: Racial Confusion in Modern American Literature*. New York: Lang, 1996. Print.

Berland, Alwyn. Light in August: *A Study in Black and White*. New York: Twayne, 1992. Print.

Berzon, Judith. *Neither White Nor Black: The Mulatto Character in American Fiction*. New York: New York UP, 1978. Print.

Bluestein, Gene. "Faulkner and Miscegenation." *Arizona Quarterly* 43.2 (1987): 151-64. Print.

Brodsky, Claudia. "The Working Narrative in *Absalom, Absalom!*: A Textual Analysis." *Amerikastudien / American Studies* 23.2 (1978): 240-59. Print.

Brooks, Peter. "Incredulous Narration: *Absalom, Absalom!*" *Comparative Literature* 34.3 (1982): 247-68. Print.

Caughie, Pamela L. "Passing as Modernism." *Modernism/modernity* 12.3 (2005): 385-406. Print.

Crist, Robert. *Language & Being in Faulkner*. Athens, GA: Giannikos, 1989. Print.

Davis, James F. *Who Is Black? One Nation's Definition*. University Park: Pennsylvania State UP, 1991. Print.

Davis, Thadious M. *Faulkner's 'Negro': Art in the Southern Context*. Baton Rouge: Louisiana State UP, 1983. Print.

Domínguez, Virginia R. *White by Definition: Social Classification in Creole Louisiana*. New Brunswick, NJ: Rutgers UP, 1997. Print.

Doneskey, Renard. "'that pebble's watery echo': The Five Narrators of *Absalom, Absalom!*" *Heir and Prototype: Original and Derived Characterizations in Faulkner*. Ed. Dan Ford. Conway: U of Central Arkansas P, 1987. 13-32. Print.

Doody, Terrence. *Confession and Community in the Novel*. Baton Rouge: Louisiana State UP, 1980. Print.

Duvall, John N. "Murder and the Communities: Ideology in and around *Light in August*." *William Faulkner's* Light in August. Ed. Harold Bloom. New York: Chelsea, 1988. 135-57. Print.

---. *Race and White Identity in Southern Fiction: From Faulkner to Morrison*. New York: MacMillan, 2008. Print.

Entzminger, Betina. "Passing as Miscegenation: Whiteness and Homoeroticism in Faulkner's *Absalom, Absalom!*" *The Faulkner Journal* 22.1/2 (2006): 90-105. Print.

Fabi, M. Giulia. *Passing and the Rise of the African American Novel.* Urbana: U of Illinois P, 2001. Print.
Faulkner, William. *Novels 1930-1935: As I Lay Daying; Sanctuary; Light in August; Pylon.* Ed. Joseph Blotner and Noel Polk. New York: Library of America, 1985. Print.
---. *Novels 1936-1940: Absalom, Absalom!, The Unvanquished, If I Forget Thee, Jerusalem [The Wild Palms], The Hamlet.* Ed. Joseph Blotner and Noel Polk. New York: Library of America, 1990. Print.
Flores, Ralph. *The Rhetoric of Doubtful Authority: Deconstructive Readings of Self-Questioning Narratives, St. Augustine to Faulkner.* Ithaca, NY: Cornell UP, 1984. Print.
Genette, Gérard. *Figures III.* Paris: Seuil, 1972. Print.
Ginsberg, Elaine K., ed. *Passing and the Fictions of Identity.* Durham, NC: Duke UP, 1996. Print.
Guerard, Albert J. *The Triumph of the Novel: Dickens, Dostoevsky, Faulkner.* New York: Oxford UP, 1976. Print.
Hale, Grace Elizabeth. *Making Whiteness: The Culture of Segregation in the South, 1890-1940.* New York: Vintage, 1998. Print.
Huggins, Nathan. *Revelations: American History, American Myths.* Ed. Brenda Smith Huggins. New York: Oxford UP, 1995. Print.
Ickstadt, Heinz. "The Discourse of Race and the 'Passing' Text: Faulkner's *Light in August*." *Amerikastudien / American Studies* 42.4 (1997): 529-36. Print.
Jerng, Mark C. "The Character of Race: Adoption and Individuation in William Faulkner's *Light in August* and Charles Chesnutt's *The Quarry*." *Arizona Quarterly* 64.4 (2008): 69-102. Print.
Jones, Suzanne W. *Race Mixing: Southern Fiction since the Sixties.* Baltimore, MA: Johns Hopkins UP, 2004. Print.
Kartiganer, Donald M. "The Meaning of Form in *Light in August*." *William Faulkner's* Light in August. Ed. Harold Bloom. New York: Chelsea, 1988. 9-41. Print.
---. *The Fragile Thread: The Meaning of Form in Faulkner's Novels.* Amherst: U of Massachusetts P, 1979. Print.
Kaup, Monika, and Debra J. Rosenthal. *Mixing Race, Mixing Culture: Inter-American Literary Dialogues.* Austin: U of Texas P, 2002. Print.
Kennedy, Randall. *Interracial Intimacies: Sex, Marriage, Identity, and Adoption.* New York: Vintage, 2004. Print.
Kinney, James. *Amalgamation! Race, Sex, and Rhetoric in the Nineteenth-Century American Novel.* Westport, CT: Greenwood, 1985. Print.
Krause, Daniel. "Reading Shreve's Letters and Faulkner's *Absalom, Absalom!*" *Studies in American Fiction* II (1983): 153-69. Print.
Kreiswirth, Martin. "Plots and Counterplots: The Structure of *Light in August*." *New Essays on* Light in August. Ed. Michael Millgate. Cambridge: Cambridge UP, 1987. 55-79. Print.
Kutzinski, Vera M. "Borders and Bodies: The United States, America, and the Caribbean." *The New Centennial Review* 1.2 (2001): 55-88. Print.

Ladd, Barbara. *Nationalism and the Color Line in George W. Cable, Mark Twain, and William Faulkner.* Baton Rouge: Louisiana State UP, 1996. Print.
Lalonde, Christopher A. *William Faulkner and the Rites of Passage.* Macon, GA: Mercer UP, 1996. Print.
Lam, Bethany L. "*Light in August* in Light of Foucault: Reexamining the Biracial Experience." *Arizona Quarterly* 64.4 (2008): 49-68. Print.
Larsen, Nella. *Passing.* Ed. Carla Kaplan. New York: Norton, 2007. Print.
Lemire, Elise. *"Miscegenation": Making Race in America.* Philadelphia: U of Pennsylvania P, 2002. Print.
Matthews, John T. *The Play of Faulkner's Language.* Ithaca, NY: Cornell UP, 1982. Print.
---. *William Faulkner: Seeing Through the South.* West Sussex: Wiley-Blackwell, 2009. Print.
McKee, Patricia. *Producing American Races: Henry James, William Faulkner, Toni Morrison.* Durham, NC: Duke UP, 1999. Print.
McKinley, Gena. "*Light in August*: A Novel of Passing?" *Faulkner in Cultural Context.* Ed. Donald M. Kartiganer and Ann J. Abadie. Jackson: UP of Mississippi, 1997. 148-65. Print.
Mencke, John G. *Mulattoes and Race Mixture: American Attitudes and Images, 1865-1918.* Ann Arbor, MI: UMI Research, 1979. Print.
Michaels, Walter Benn. *Our America: Nativism, Modernism, and Pluralism.* Durham, NC: Duke UP, 1995. Print.
Miller, J. Hillis. "Two Relativisms: Point of View and Indeterminacy in the Novel *Absalom, Absalom!*" *Relativism in the Arts.* Ed. Betty Jean Craige. Athens: U of Georgia P, 1983. 148-70. Print.
Moreland, Richard C. *Faulkner and Modernism: Rereading and Rewriting.* Madison: U of Wisconsin P, 1990. Print.
Morrison, Toni. *Playing in the Dark: Whiteness and the Literary Imagination.* New York: Vintage, 1993. Print.
Murray, Pauli. *States Laws on Race and Color.* 1951. Athens: U of Georgia P, 1997. Print.
Novak, Philip. "Signifying Silences: Morrison's Soundings in the Faulknerian Void." *Unflinching Gaze.* Ed. Carol A. Kolmerten, Stephen M. Ross, and Judith Bryant Wittenberg. Jackson: UP of Mississippi, 1997. 199-215. Print.
Novkov, Julie. *Racial Union: Law, Intimacy, and the White State in Alabama, 1865-1954.* Ann Arbor: U of Michigan P, 2008. Print.
Parker, Robert Dale. Absalom, Absalom! *The Questioning of Fictions.* Boston, MA: Twayne, 1991. Print.
Peterson, Christopher. "The Haunted House of Kinship: Miscegenation, Homosexuality, and Faulkner's *Absalom, Absalom!*" *The New Centennial Review* 4.1 (2004): 227-65. Print.
Piglia, Ricardo. "Secreto y narración: Tesis sobre la *nouvelle.*" *El arquero inmóvil: Nuevas poéticas sobre el cuento.* Ed. Eduardo Becerra. Madrid: Páginas de Espuma, 2006. 187-205. Print.
Pitavy, François L. "The Narrative Voice and Function of Shreve: Remarks on the Production of *Absalom, Absalom!*" *William Faulkner's* Absalom, Absalom!:

A Critical Casebook. Ed. Elisabeth Muhlenfeld. New York: Garland, 1984. 88-109. Print.

---. *William Faulkner's* Light in August: *A Critical Casebook*. New York: Garland, 1982. Print.

Polk, Noel. *Faulkner and Welty and the Southern Literary Tradition*. Jackson: UP of Mississippi, 2008. Print.

Porter, Carolyn. *Seeing and Being: The Plight of the Participant Observer in Emerson, James, Adams, and Faulkner*. Middletown, CT: Wesleyan UP, 1981. 241-75. Print.

Price, Steve. "Shreve's Bon in *Absalom, Absalom!*" *Mississippi Quarterly* 39.3 (1986): 325-35. Print.

Puxan, Marta. "Narrative Strategies on the Color Line: The Unreliable Narrator Shreve and Racial Ambiguity in Faulkner's *Absalom, Absalom!*" *Mississippi Quarterly* 60.3 (2007): 529-59. Print.

Rimmon-Kenan, Shlomith. *A Glance Beyond Doubt: Narration, Representation, Subjectivity*. Columbus: Ohio State UP, 1996. Print.

Robinson, Owen. *Creating Yoknapatawpha: Readers and Writers in Faulkner's Fiction*. New York: Routledge, 2006. Print.

Romine, Scott. *The Narrative Forms of Southern Community*. Baton Rouge: Louisiana State UP, 1999. Print.

Ross, Stephen M. *Faulkner's Inexhaustible Voice: Speech and Writing in Faulkner*. Athens: U of Georgia P, 1989. Print.

Ruppersburg, Hugh M. *Voice and Eye in Faulkner's Fiction*. Athens: U of Georgia P, 1983. Print.

Smith, John David, ed. *Racial Determinism and the Fear of Miscegenation Pre-1900 and Racial Determinism and the Fear of Miscegenation Post-1900*. New York: Garland, 1993. Print.

Snead, James A. "*Light in August* and the Rhetorics of Racial Division." *Faulkner and Race*. Ed. Doreen Fowler and Ann J. Abadie. Jackson: UP of Mississippi, 1987. 152-69. Print.

Sollors, Werner. *Neither Black nor White yet Both: Thematic Explorations of Interracial Literature*. Cambridge, MA: Harvard UP, 1999. Print.

Stonequist, Evett V. *The Marginal Man: A Study in Personality and Culture Conflict*. 1937. New York: Russell, 1965. Print.

Sugimori, Masami. "Racial Mixture, Racial Passing, and White Subjectivity in *Absalom, Absalom!*" *The Faulkner Journal* 23.2 (2008): 3-22. Print.

Sundquist, Eric J. *Faulkner: The House Divided*. Baltimore, MA: Johns Hopkins UP, 1983. Print.

Towner, Theresa M. *Faulkner on the Color Line: The Later Novels*. Jackson: UP of Mississippi, 2000. Print.

Wald, Gayle. *Crossing the Line: Racial Passing in US Literature and Culture*. Durham, NC: Duke UP, 2000. Print.

Watson, Jay, ed. *Faulkner and Whiteness*. Spec. issue of *The Faulkner Journal* 22.1/2 (2006/2007). Print.

Weinstein, Arnold. "Fusion and Confusion in *Light in August*." *The Faulkner Journal* 1.2 (1986): 2-14. Print.

Weinstein, Philip M. *Faulkner's Subject: A Cosmos No One Owns*. Cambridge: Cambridge UP, 1992. Print.

Williamson, Joel. *New People: Miscegenation and Mulattoes in the United States*. Baton Rouge: Louisiana State UP, 1980. Print.

Wittenberg, Judith Bryant. "Race in *Light in August*: Wordsymbols and Obverse Reflections." *The Cambridge Companion to William Faulkner*. Ed. Philip M. Weinstein. Cambridge: Cambridge UP, 1995. 146-67. Print.

"Not White, Not Quite": Irish American Identities in the U.S. Census and in Ann Patchett's Novel *Run*

SARAH HEINZ

ABSTRACT

In most (post)colonial and intercultural systems, white skin has acquired the role of a normative model that has profoundly shaped hierarchies and identities. This paper will assess the role of white identity as the norm by analyzing the ambivalent position of the Irish in America as both white and non-white. Underpinned by findings from whiteness studies, this article will look at data from the U.S. Censuses of 2010, 2000, and 1990 with respect to the categories race, ethnicity, and ancestry. The analysis will then be related to Ann Patchett's novel *Run* (2007), in which an Irish American family that adopted two black boys is faced with internal conflicts. The thesis is that in contemporary America, Irishness has become an attractive identity that is white and, at the same time, ethnically specific, an ambivalence that makes it possible to be different and special and to deal with trauma and guilt while enjoying the safety and privilege of whiteness. Irishness and whiteness are therefore flexible categories or self-identifications that are detached from notions of genetics, biology, and heritage and are free to be appropriated by everyone.

In one of the episodes of the Irish-British television comedy *Father Ted*, set on the fictitious Irish Craggy Island, a black priest comes to visit Father Ted for a funeral. Sister Monica enthuses about the commitment of the African church, a comment to which the black priest answers: "Sure I wouldn't know, I'm from Donegal" ("Grant Unto Him"). While the sister's words first establish the whiteness of Irish people, thus excluding the priest from Irishness, the priest's reply serves to destroy this notion. The humor thus created exposes our concept of Irishness as white and substitutes it for a more inclusive notion, which is that skin color has no inherent meaning in itself and assigns no reliable identity to the self or to the other.

This ambivalence between inclusion and exclusion and self and other in the construction and performance of Irishness and whiteness forms the underlying logic of the following argumentation. For that reason, the question of the truthfulness or legitimacy of self-reported ancestries or races in the U.S. Census or the validity of pejorative terms such as 'Plastic Paddy' and their implicit claim to authenticity will not be the focus of this analysis.[1] More interesting than asking

---

[1] The slang term 'Plastic Paddy' is applied to people who claim to be Irish or of Irish ancestry without having actual ancestral connections to Ireland or who know little or nothing of Irish culture. In Ireland, the term is also used to refer to outdated images of Irish culture as promoted by the commercialised celebrations of 'Irish traditions' abroad. The term implies an opposition between 'authentic' Irish culture and the fabricated notions of Irishness that are mostly connected with the Irish diaspora. It is the goal of this paper to question these seemingly clear-cut dichotomies of the authenticity or inauthenticity of a national culture. See Scully; Arrowsmith.

whether people who claim to be Irish in the United States today really are Irish is the question why and how Irishness has come to be attractive to white people. Therefore my emphasis will be on people's self-identification as Irish and the accompanying performance of Irishness and whiteness. Here, I follow Richard Dyer's approach, who states:

> My focus is representation. Thus, on the one hand, what follows is not directly about how white people really are, how we feel about ourselves, how others perceive us. [...] This is about how white people are represented, how we represent ourselves—images of white people, or the cultural construction of white people [...]. On the other hand, how anything is represented is the means by which we think and feel about that thing, by which we apprehend it. (xiii)

My argumentation is therefore based on an approach which claims that neither national nor racial identities are a natural, territorial, or historical fact. Using the terms of the U.S. Census, identities are self-identifications and self-classifications, i.e., they are changing images of the self and therefore implicitly also images of the other which are fabricated and chosen, both deliberately and unconsciously. The content of this paper is comprised of sources from the social sciences and the humanities because both disciplines and their material focus on processes of self-identification and the individual's strategies and needs of belonging to a cultural, national, or ethnic group. Data from the U.S. Censuses of 1990, 2000, and 2010, and the American Community Surveys (ACS) of 2002 to 2009 will be used in conjunction with the contemporary American novel *Run* by Ann Patchett. The analyses of census and ACS data combined with my interpretation of Patchett's novel show that the feeling of belonging to a nation as an 'imagined community,' as introduced by Benedict Anderson, is grounded in a society's imagined sense of self rather than in a genetic or factual link.

This imagined sense of self, identity, and community can then take the shape of self-reported data from a survey like the census, or it can take the shape of a contemporary novel like *Run*, which is concerned with the protagonists' experiences of belonging to a nation, an ethnic group, or a family. The surveys and the novel therefore shed light on the same questions that Dyer has outlined in the quotation above: "This is about how white people are represented, how we represent ourselves—images of white people, or the cultural construction of white people [...]. On the other hand, how anything is represented is the means by which we think and feel about that thing, by which we apprehend it" (xiii).

In this manner, the different acts of reading these images in surveys like the census and in contemporary literature create our modern sense of the nation in the first place, as Anderson has suggested: "fiction seeps quietly and continuously into reality, creating that remarkable confidence of community in anonymity which is the hallmark of modern nations" (36). In a second step then, all our experiences of community are, according to this paper's basic assumption, created, shaped, and framed by the individual's skin color and the social evaluations and categorizations attached to this color.[2] Nationality, ethnicity, and skin color

---

[2] For a discussion of the conjoined hierarchies and systems of difference in terms of nationality, ethnicity, and skin color, see the essays in Nakano Glenn. See also the specific American focus of the essays in Higginbotham and Andersen.

thus merge in the ambivalent positions of Irish Americans in the past and today. Such identities, in turn, create and shape the smaller communities, families, and individuals that are represented in the census and in Patchett's novel. Processes of self-identification are therefore the central focus of both the census and *Run*.

A fictional narrative like *Run* takes a qualitative approach towards an individual's life, identity, and experience—an approach that has been termed "experientiality" or the "communication of anthropocentric experience" in narrative (Fludernik 59). In a novel like *Run*, we can live and think with the protagonists, we can have an emotional encounter with them, and we can enter their most private and intimate spaces and memories. A census, on the other hand, takes a radically quantitative approach towards human experience. While replies are obtained from individuals, these replies are collected only to enable the compilation of general statistics. Thus, every citizen in the United States is included in the census, yet his or her individual experience is aggregated into a percentage point that cannot be tracked back to the respondent as an individual.[3] Where the census is legally bound to keep each respondent's privacy, a novel is allowed, or perhaps even expected, to give the reader insight into the protagonist's privacy, including their self-identifications and the images they have of themselves and others. The census categorizes and generalizes, while the novel particularizes and shows that individual responses to the question of identity might often exceed the categories created for its analysis. Thus, the combined examination of statistical data and a literary text makes it possible to assess the necessity, effects, and dangers of categorizations from two complementary perspectives; both kinds of material speak of the relevance of human experience and self-identifications in larger communities.

The social construction of self and the question of whiteness is considered by Daniel Bernardi when he suggests: "Who passes [as white] at what moment and in what place are historical and discursive questions, and the performance is not necessarily conscious and is almost never conscientious, inasmuch as those who count as white emerge, transform, and re-emerge with space, time, and method" (xxii).[4] This comment can be equally applied to Irishness or any other kind of identity, be it gendered, classed, or raced. Consequently, the analysis of data from the census and the interpretation of Patchett's novel *Run* will investigate the performance, function, and oscillation of Irishness between whiteness and its other.[5]

---

[3] Of course, this is not a question of ignoring individual people's experiences or selves but an issue of confidentiality. By law, neither the census takers nor any other Census Bureau employees are permitted to reveal identifiable information about any person, household, or business taking part in the census. This legal measure ensures the privacy and security of personal data obtained by Census Bureau employees. The Census Bureau states: "The U.S. Census Bureau has an obligation to produce accurate, relevant statistics about the nation's economy and people, but we recognize that it is your information that we collect to produce these statistics" (*Data Protection*).

[4] See also Noel Ignatiev and John Garvey's analysis of the white race as "a historically constructed social formation" (1).

[5] In this context, it has to be stressed that the terms white and non-white, white and black, self and other are not used in the sense of evaluative judgments but should always be thought of as cultural constructs. The reader should therefore think of all designations and labels for skin color, race, and ethnicity used in the paper as if in quotation marks. For a discussion of the dif-

White skin is more than a biological fact or an ontological category: whiteness is relative because it only turns into an identity through comparison, difference, and interchange.

The census categories of race, ethnicity, and ancestry and the inclusive American Irishness that *Run* proposes are not issues of essential selves and genetic origins that can be objectively proven or tracked down via family trees. Rather, whiteness and Irishness are a question of passing or, in the sense of the census and this paper, self-identifications. The notion of passing, the attempt at or successful act of being accepted as the member of a different group, is interesting in the context of whiteness and Irishness as self-identifications and social formations: if one can pass for white and/or Irish, identities as well as bodies are not bound to racial, ethnic, or ancestral essences. The term passing has often implied that such a passing is wrong or illegal, that you pass for what you are not. At the same time, passing seems to make it impossible to be who you 'really' are (see Kroeger). In her article "Whiteness as Property," legal scholar Cheryl Harris describes how her grandmother, a fair-skinned black woman who worked in a Chicago department store in the 1930s, suffered from passing as white: "Each evening, my grandmother, tired and worn, retraced her steps home, laid aside her mask, and reentered herself" (1711).

Passing has recently been re-interpreted, however, as a means to deconstruct binary oppositions: "passing wreaks havoc with accepted systems of social recognition and cultural intelligibility" and "blurs the carefully marked lines of race, gender, and class, calling attention to the ways in which identity categories intersect, overlap, construct, and deconstruct one [an]other" (Schlossberg 2). The following analysis of the ways in which whiteness and Irishness are strategically deployed as identity markers highlights the changing social contexts and the individual and collective needs that are served by claiming specific identities. In that sense, the putative visibility of whiteness turns into a case of passing and, therefore, into a question of constructing and deconstructing the common discourse of knowledge and cognition in terms of vision. What such an analysis amounts to is a disruption of the connection between the visual and the known, or the "logic of visibility" and the "certain degree of epistemological certainty" that this logic seems to entail (Schlossberg 1).

In this context I will look at the relative whiteness of the Irish in America who occupy an ambivalent position between white and black. On the one hand, the Irish have always been seen as the darker race compared with their English colonizers or Americans of Anglo-Saxon ancestry. Indeed, the Irish have themselves often "sought analogies between Ireland's experiences of colonial oppression and the experiences of black people in slavery and subjugation" (Brannigan, "Ireland" 230). On the other hand, Irishness has become an increasingly popular means for white Americans to enrich their whiteness with a specifically ethnic but nonetheless white and familiar identity. Analyzing these shifting constructions

---

ferent meanings of race, ethnicity, and ancestry, see the paper's section on the U.S. Census. For a discussion of the problematic terms attached to an analysis of whiteness and its others (e.g., non-white, black, people of color, or colored) see Dyer 11.

of American Irishness reveals the blind spots of whiteness and its strategic use in contemporary America.

Ambivalent Whiteness: Embodying Irish American Identities

Common assumptions about the human skin and the way we talk about skin and skin color are a useful first approach to the fashion in which we perceive ourselves and others. At first glance, our skin seems to be a simple biological fact; it is our largest organ and it has a specific color, depending on our environment and our genetic makeup. Next to categorizing people as either male or female, skin color is usually one of the first things we notice. It is therefore "putatively self-evident to the naked eye" (Nishikawa 1725). This self-evidence is connected to the logic of visibility outlined above, a logic that seems to ground our perceptions in essential, bodily truths. We talk about skin as an external marker which can connote superficiality, but we also interpret the skin as a transparent screen or sign of inner qualities: "we still believe that something is true if it is naked, the absence of makeup is still seen as a mode of authenticity, and nakedness is still the ideal of the natural. 'Only skin deep' connotes superficiality, and only that which gets under one's skin can truly touch or arouse a person" (Benthien ix). Skin is therefore interpreted as a sign of personal and collective identities, and it becomes what Benthien calls "a place where boundary negotiations take place" (ix). In a similar vein, Serres posits that skin is the place "where the ego is decided" (qtd. in Benthien 1).

And yet, skin is by no means as natural as it seems, nor is it a merely transparent sign of an internal essence: "Rather, it is a relationship subject to a great many strategies of interpretation and staging" (Benthien ix). This relational aspect ties in with research in postcolonial studies that questions concepts of race, nature, and the ensuing essentialist hierarchies (see JanMohamed; Bhabha, *Location*). It also connects with a new focus in gender studies. In this field, seemingly unmarked norms of masculinity have been reassessed as relational and dependent upon notions of the female as the stigmatized and deficient other (see Brod; Connell). What these approaches share is the basic assumption that the self always needs an other to define itself, and that we can find ambivalence, relativity, and (inter)dependence at the heart of all hierarchies (see Hall; Bhabha, "Other Question").

In this vein, one of the main aims of whiteness studies is to show that the point of view from which we assess the skin of the other is by no means as absolute, immutable, objective, and neutral as science, theory, and traditional historiography try to make us believe. Instead, it is a legal, political, economic, and cultural construct that profoundly shapes individuals and societies.[6] The central problem is what Dyer calls the invisibility of whiteness as a specific, raced position. The point of whiteness studies, therefore, is to make whiteness visible through making it strange. The final goal is to reveal that its invisibility has turned whiteness into a

---

[6] For the legal construction of whiteness see López. For the role of wages and the economy see Roediger, *Wages* and Roediger, *Working*. For the connection of whiteness and gender see Oyewùmí.

position of power whose contingency must be revealed: "As long as race is something only applied to non-white people, as long as white people are not racially seen and named, they/we function as a human norm. Other people are raced, we are just people" (Dyer 1). This discourse of whiteness as the human norm then entails radical consequences for concepts of the non-white skin as an additional layer of dirt on the tabula rasa of whiteness, or as a deviation, degeneration, or genetic aberration (cf. Benthien 145-53).

This seemingly neutral 'scientific' description of non-white skin is indebted to the logic of visibility and connected to evaluations and hierarchies. The black skin of the other is linked to savagery, barbarism, backwardness, and emotionality. It is therefore linked to an irrevocable inferiority. In contrast, the white skin of the self signalizes rationality and intelligence, and therefore superiority and supremacy. In such essentialist logic, whiteness thus ceases to be a color and becomes the invisible norm; however, the logic of visibility is still applied to whiteness because it turns into an outward sign of power.

The point of whiteness studies is to reveal that roles are assigned to both white and black people according to images and evaluations of their skin, a contingency that is then masked via discourses of nature, evolution, and radicalization. Binary thinking creates not only an other, but also a self which is dependent on and afraid of that which it seemingly dominates. The ideal ego thus created is presented as "white and whole," as Bhabha formulates (*Location* 76). Yet in spite of its status as non-racial and normal, this ego is as raced, dependent, and colored as its counterpart. A focus on the relativity of the human skin furthers the goal of whiteness studies, which is to make the contingency and constructedness of whiteness visible. To be white is not a natural fact, but an act of passing: "There are no white people, only people who pass as white" (Bernardi xxii).

With regard to white skin as a relative skin, the Irish and their racial position is central and interesting because the Irish can be positioned in-between white colonizer and black colonized as they have taken up both roles in history, often at the same time. Due to Ireland's proximity to Great Britain and its at least partial complicity in Britain's colonial project, e.g., as soldiers, missionaries, sailors, and captains of slave ships, Ireland's status as a postcolonial nation is far from unambiguous.[7] Ireland can thus be interpreted as "both subject and object of forms of imperial hegemony" (16) in Flannery's discussion of "the relative 'position' of 'Irish' postcolonial debates" (15). Matthew Frye Jacobson illustrates this relative position of the Irish with an example from U.S. history, and explains how, incongruously,

> it is one of the compelling circumstances of American cultural history that an Irish immigrant in 1877 could be a despised Celt in Boston—a threat to the republic—and yet a solid member of The Order of Caucasians for the Extermination of the Chinaman in San Francisco, gallantly defending U.S. shores from an invasion of "Mongolians." (5)

In this equation of whiter vs. darker groups coming to America, Irish people thus took up a flexible and shifting position that always depended on the places

---

[7] See the discussion of Ireland's status in postcolonial studies in Flannery and in Lloyd. For a historical overview over the Irish complicity in, as well as the often simultaneous resistance to, British colonization, see Akenson 454-56.

and times of their arrival and the proportions of white people who were already there (see Dyer 53-54). Nevertheless, the Irish were often deemed white enough to be included in white societies and were keen on aligning themselves with the white majorities in America. This whitening of the Irish also extended to the Irish immigrants' sense of self, their religious and class affiliations, and their aspired social and economic success: "For Catholic Irish immigrants, becoming American meant becoming white: and proximity to African-Americans, whether spatial, cultural, or political, was inimical to such a process" (Garner 121). Much in the sense of passing as a form of upward mobility, Irish Catholics in particular attempted to get rid of their status as a 'race apart.'[8]

This racialization of the Irish had already started in the eighteenth and nineteenth centuries and was dominated by the idea of the 'missing link' between ape and Anglo-Saxon, a depiction which intensified with the rise of the Fenian movement and the arrival in 1860 of the first chimpanzees and gorillas in London (see Curtis; Dyer 52). The so-called 'Celt' was described with characteristics also attributed to African Americans: wild look and childish manner, barbarity and violence, rampant sexuality, lack of control and intelligence, superstition, tribal organization, and immoral character. Noel Ignatiev notes: "In the early years [of Irish immigration to the United States] Irish were frequently referred to as 'niggers turned inside out'; the Negroes, for their part, were sometimes called 'smoked Irish'" (41). This analogy with uncivilized peoples was extended to any ethnic group perceived as other and non-white, and comparisons between Native Americans and Irish Catholic immigrants illustrate that "some among the Protestant clergy openly displayed condescension for both Irish Catholic immigrants and Red Indians, demanding that they be 'civilized' by means of education and conversion" (Lenz 304). But this parallel between African or Native Americans and Irish Americans was not only drawn by those who wanted to point out the negative, backward characteristics of both. Often enough, the link between, for example, African slave and Irish colonized or immigrant was made to point out the injustice of both their conditions (see Brannigan, "Ireland"; Brannigan, *Race*).

The history of Irish-American whiteness and its flexible status in a system of epidermal hierarchies that overlap with class, religion, and education therefore outline the 'everything and nothing' quality of such categorizations. It is precisely this mercurial quality of Irishness that has turned it into an attractive self-identification in recent years. Especially since the 1990s, Irishness in the United States has been used to refer back to an assumed authenticity and rootedness that the white mainstream of America feels to have lost, thus creating an easy-to-consume

---

[8] For Irish Catholics, such acts of passing included not only a transgression of religious but also of class boundaries because Irish Catholics were seen as being from the lower, uneducated classes and as influenced by a foreign religion that kept them dependent, childish, and primitive. By many Protestant Americans, Catholicism was judged as anti-democratic. American nativists thus evaluated Catholicism as tyrannical and dangerous (see McGreevey on nativism and Catholics). Steve Garner remarks of the nineteenth century: "Indeed, the incompatibility of the Irish with modernity became a cliché in American commentary" (122). Class and religion were therefore combined into a seemingly natural racial category that effectively excluded Irish Catholics from many jobs, public positions, educational facilities, and neighborhoods.

Irishness as a "powerful origin myth" for Americans (Negra, "Introduction" 4). At the same time, this seemingly exclusive identity of having Irish roots has been used as what Diane Negra terms "the ideal guilt-free white ethnicity of choice, subject to a predominantly (and peculiarly) ecumenical vision" ("Introduction" 11). Irishness thus has turned into a category "for every taste and purpose, offering a means of being both white and ethnically different" ("Introduction" 10) and a possibility to enjoy "the pleasures of white ethnic heritage" (Negra, "Consuming Ireland" 76).

This oscillation between otherness and whiteness has made it possible for the Irish to be included in a white mainstream, enjoying all the social capital of whiteness.[9] Yet it grounds the Irish American self in an identifiable cultural context that lives up to the expectations of an ethnically diverse America in which to be white increasingly means to have no ethnically specific background. To be 'just white' thus indicates a perceived lack at the heart of mainstream America that can be remedied by a simplified version of Irishness as a specific, yet unsuspicious ethnicity. Negra therefore talks about Irishness as a form of "enriched whiteness" ("Introduction" 1) while Vincent J. Cheng contends that "in the United States today, Irishness may be both popular and comfortable precisely because it remains an identifiable (and presumably authentic) ethnicity that is nonetheless unthreatening and familiar" (32). Irishness as generic otherness thus can be consumed, as Regina Bendix aptly puts it, in a global but comfortably white "market of identifiable authenticities" that is available for everyone who wants to be white and ethnically specific at the same time (qtd. in Cheng 32). The ever more global phenomenon of the increasingly popular St Patrick's Day celebrations is one case in point for Irishness as an enrichment of a white self that can gain a guilt-free ethnicity without losing its social capital.

Enriching Whiteness in America: Irish Americans in the U.S. Census

In the following pages I want to illustrate my findings on whiteness and Irishness with data from the U.S. Census and an interpretation of the novel *Run*. In addition to data from the U.S. Censuses of 1990, 2000, and 2010, I will include data compiled by the ACS between 2002 to 2009 to focus on three categories: race, ethnicity, and ancestry.

The terms ancestry, ethnicity, and race invoke overlapping connotations of belonging to an exclusive group along blood lines and genealogies that assign a specific biological identity to the individual. Yet the U.S. Census stresses that its definitions are inclusive and contingent, and defines ancestry as "a person's ethnic origin, heritage, descent, or 'roots,' which may reflect their place of birth, place of birth of parents or ancestors, and ethnic identities that have evolved within the United States" (Brittingham and de la Cruz 1). Ethnicity is connected to origin and defined as "the heritage, nationality group, lineage, or country of birth of

---

[9] For a discussion of whiteness as social capital see Garner 48-62. In the same vein, Ruth Frankenberg defines whiteness as "a location of structural advantage" (1).

the person or the person's parents or ancestors before their arrival in the United States" (*Questions and Answers*). This concept must be amended by the category of race, which is not defined according to "biological, anthropological or genetic criteria" but rather "reflect[s] a social definition of race recognized in this country" (*Questions and Answers*). The census thus takes a constructivist stance towards race, ethnicity, and ancestry, turning them into social rather than biological categories: "These categories are socio-political constructs and should not be interpreted as being scientific or anthropological in nature. Furthermore, the race categories include both racial and national-origin groups" (Hoffmeyer-Zlotnik and Warner 120). Consequently, all three categories are very close to each other, asking about the group, culture, and tradition that the respondent feels he or she belongs to or self-identifies with.[10]

Nevertheless, the terms race and ancestry at least imply a biological, genetic, or familial link to the group with which people identify themselves. This sense of belonging is strengthened by the census definition of the term 'White' which "refers to people having origins in any of the original peoples of Europe, the Middle East, or North Africa. It includes people who reported 'White' or wrote in entries such as Irish, German, Italian, Lebanese, Near Easterners, Arab, or Polish" (Grieco 1). Interestingly, the Irish are the first example of groups that are unproblematically included in the category of whiteness, even if they wrote in an extra entry to specify "Irish." The Census 2010 Brief on the white population again took the entry 'Irish' as their first example for groups categorized as white (see Hixson, Hepler, and Kim 2). In the U.S. Census, the Irish are categorized as white.

In this context, it is important to stress again that responses in the census reflect self-identification: "Respondents were asked to report the race or races they considered themselves and other members of their household to be" (Grieco 2). As outlined above, my goal is not to question the validity or legitimacy of these self-identifications but rather to make some conjectures about the reasons why they may have been chosen. More than objectively reporting about racial diversity in the United States, the census can give hints at the desirability of being a member of a racial, ethnic, or ancestral group. The answers to the questions on race, ethnicity, and ancestry from the census can therefore indicate both the desirability of being white and the coexistent need to belong to an ethnic group.

The ambivalent status of whiteness in the United States becomes visible in its treatment by the census. On the one hand, 'white' is a privileged category because ever since the first U.S. decennial census in 1790, whites have been enumerated in every census. Other groups, e. g., Native Americans, who were first included in the 1870 census, were added in the options given for the race question at a later date, the most recent addition being the option to identify more than one race that was available in the Census 2000 for the first time. Also, white is the most prevalent race: In the Census 2000, of the total population (which was then estimated at 281,421,906), 211.5 million people (75.1 %) reported to be white, while an addi-

---

[10] On the question of the categories race, ethnicity, and the related notion of nationality and their complex and often interchangeably used meanings, see Glazer and Moynihan; see also Hobsbawm and the essays in Delanty and Kumar.

tional 5.5 million people (2 %) reported white and at least one other race. Thus, 77.1 % of the total population self-identified as white alone or in combination with other races (Grieco 3). The previous census of 1990 showed a very similar picture, when 80.3 % of the population self-identified as white. The 2010 census continues this prevalence of whiteness as the primary racial self-identification, but it also continues the decreasing tendency of the white population as a percentage of the total population. Of the total population in 2010 (which was estimated at 308,745,538), 72.4 % self-identified as white alone while 2.4 % self-identified as white and at least one other race. Thus, 74.8 % made up the category of white alone or in combination with other races. As in the 2000 census, the white population had the lowest growth rate compared to other racial groups in the United States (see Hixson, Hepler and Kim 3).[11] Despite this continuing decrease, whiteness is still the prevalent race found in the United States, but it is decidedly categorized as a race. This seems to contradict Dyer's thesis that "other people are raced, we are just people" (1). However, both the census procedure and its internal organization implicitly reify the status of whiteness as an unraced norm. All ethnic and racial groups, plus the 'Two or More Races' population are presented in reports from the 2000 census that are entitled *We The People*, and these groups each have their own census advisory committee. White people are the only exception to this.[12] Reviewing the dominant and persisting status of the race category of whiteness from the beginning of the census until today, and adding the fact that the majority of Americans still self-identify as white, this exceptional status of white people can strengthen the assumption of whiteness studies, which posits that white people are so universal that they represent humanity as a whole in spite of their treatment as a race in the census. The attempt at mirroring America's diversity in the census as the diversity of non-white or mixed people reflects an increasing awareness of white guilt while inconsistently maintaining white privilege via an ethnically and racially emptied notion of whiteness.

A look at the reported ancestries can add to these results. Question number ten of the 'long form' census of 2000 asks: "What is this person's ancestry or ethnic origin?" (*Long-Form Questionnaire*).[13] Again, the close association between

---

[11] A comparison of the Census 2000 and 2010 shows that the white alone population has one of the lowest growth rates within the white population (6.5 %), while within the white alone category, the Not Hispanic or Latino population has grown by a mere 1.2 % (Hixson, Hepler and Kim 3). The Census Brief comments: "The total U.S. population grew by 9.7 percent, from 281.4 million in 2000 to 308.7 million in 2010. In comparison, the White alone population grew by 6 percent from 211.5 million to 223.6 million. But while the White alone population increased numerically over the 10-year period, its proportion of the total population declined from 75 percent to 72 percent. The White alone-or-in-combination population experienced slightly more growth than the White alone population, growing by 7 percent. However, both groups grew at a slower rate than the total population, as well as all other major race and ethnic groups in the country" (Hixson, Hepler and Kim 4).

[12] See information provided by the *Online Gateway to Census 2000*.

[13] Beginning with the 2010 Census, the question on ancestry was no longer included because only the shorter version of the questionnaire, which asks only ten questions, was distributed. The long form, which still includes the question on ancestry, is now only used for ACS data collection. In the 2000 census, approximately one of every six households received the long form.

ancestry and ethnicity becomes obvious, underlined by the examples that the questionnaire provides for the respondents. The first three examples for ancestries are Italian, Jamaican, and African American (the latter also being one of the five official race categories), while the empirically most common two ancestries are not given: German and Irish. The three largest ancestries reported in 1990 were German, Irish, and English. With respect to Irishness, we can add the large group of people indicating Scotch-Irish ancestry, which also ranks among the fifteen largest ancestries today (Brittingham and de la Cruz 4-5). In 2000, German, Irish, and English were still the largest European ancestries, but each had decreased in size by at least 8 million (more than 20 %). As a proportion of the population, Irish ancestry decreased from 15.6 % to 10.8 %, while Scotch-Irish decreased from 2.3 to 1.5 % (cf. Brittingham and de la Cruz 3). This decrease is primarily due to the European ancestries' lower growth rates when compared to other groups, e.g., Mexican, Chinese, or Filipino, whose percentage in the total population increased between 1990 and 2000.[14] Therefore, Irish ancestry still was the second-largest group, yet the proportion of Irish people in the population was decreasing. However, if we track the development of Irish and Scotch-Irish ancestries from the Census 1990 through the Census 2000 to the American Community Surveys of 2002 to 2009, we can see an interesting twist to this downward tendency.[15]

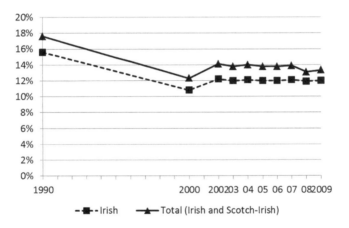

Fig. 1: Percentage of Irish and Scotch-Irish ancestries of the total population. Both the censuses and the ACS asked people to write in their "ancestry or ethnic origin." All results reflect self-identification.

---

[14] Brittingham and de la Cruz explain: "The population of many ancestries, such as Mexican, Chinese, Filipino, and Asian Indian, increased during the decade, reflecting sizable immigration, especially from Latin America and Asia. Several small ancestry populations, including Brazilian, Pakistani, Albanian, Honduran, and Trinidadian and Tobagonian, at least doubled" (3).

[15] Comparable ACS data for the years 2000 and 2001 is not available because the public files for these two years only provide data for areas of 65,000 or more people of some counties and geographical places.

After the continuing decrease of Irish and Scotch-Irish ancestries in the Censuses of 1990 and 2000, the ACS of 2002 shows an increase of 1.8 % in the number of people claiming Irish or Scotch-Irish ancestry. Compared with the decrease of 5.3 % between 1990 and 2000 (which equals more than eight million people), this might not seem a significant upward movement, but in total numbers this is an increase of nearly five million people in only two years who self-identify as Irish or Scotch-Irish. One explanation for this tendency could be an accelerating growth rate of Irish or Scotch-Irish people through immigration or birth rates. Yet as outlined above, the growth rate of respondents self-identifying as white in the Census 2010 has decreased, and it experiences the slowest growth rate of all race groups in the United States today.[16]

And yet, in spite of this decrease of white people in the proportion of the American population since 2000, the American Community Surveys of 2002 to 2009 show that the percentage of people indicating Irish ancestry remains fairly stable since the considerable increase between 2000 and 2002. Cross-tabulated with data on race, all respondents of the ACS who claimed an Irish or Scotch-Irish ancestry were categorized as white.[17] This cross-tabulation corroborates that Irish Americans are part of the group identifying as white, the group with the lowest growth rates in the U.S. It therefore also shows that the increase of people of Irish and Scotch-Irish ethnicity must have other causes. An important additional development connected to the stable increase of Americans indicating an Irish or Scotch-Irish ancestry is the doubling of applications for Irish citizenship from the United States around 2000 (cf. Negra, "Irishness" 369). These two developments can be interpreted as a further indication of the desirability of Irishness and its potential to enrich whiteness.

In this context, Negra's thoughts on Irishness after 9/11 are interesting because she explicitly connects Irishness to a feeling of lacking 'ethnic content' and therefore being culturally empty in white mainstream America. Negra suggests that one explanation for the re-evaluation of Irishness after 2000 is the collective trauma and guilt experienced after September 11. She argues that notions of whiteness, identity, and masculinity that had formed the center of the American mainstream were critically contested before 9/11 but regained currency after the shock of the attacks. Here, the white, male Irishness of the New York fire fighters and policemen functioned as a means to identify with America and face up to terror without being ideologically suspect—a strategy that Negra calls "political decontamination" ("Irishness" 367). She explains:

---

[16] See the Census Brief on race and Hispanic origin which comments: "Between 2000 and 2010, the Hispanic population grew by 43 percent—rising from 35.3 million in 2000, when this group made up 13 percent of the total population. The Hispanic population increased by 15.2 million between 2000 and 2010, accounting for over half of the 27.3 million increase in the total population of the United States. The non-Hispanic population grew relatively slower over the decade, about 5 percent. Within the non-Hispanic population, the number of people who reported their race as White alone grew even slower between 2000 and 2010 (1 percent). While the non-Hispanic White alone population increased numerically from 194.6 million to 196.8 million over the 10-year period, its proportion of the total population declined from 69 percent to 64 percent" (Humes, Jones, and Ramirez 3).

[17] ACS data can be found online at http://www.census.gov/acs/www/, 18 February 2012.

> If before September 11 Irishness was most often invoked to negotiate the traumas of deficient family values or to assuage a sense of capitalism run amok, its flexibility is such that after this seminal event, it could be differently mobilized to stave off an anxious, traumatized perception of American identity. (365)

Summing up, one can say that the United States is indeed becoming more diverse, as the census indicates. While the majority of Americans still self-identify as white, this whiteness is enriched by the notion of Irishness as a specific ancestry, cultural tradition, and ethnic group. In spite of decreasing growth rates of the white population, the decade after the Census 2000 saw a disproportionally higher increase in people claiming an Irish ancestry. Irishness can therefore be interpreted as a desirable identity for mainstream America, making it possible to deal with the trauma of 9/11 and white guilt, and to be both different and special while enjoying the safety and privilege of whiteness. Irishness and whiteness are therefore flexible categories that are detached from notions of genetics, biology, and heritage and are free to be appropriated by everyone.

The Ambivalences of Irish American Whiteness in Ann Patchett's *Run*

The tendency to use Irishness to enrich whiteness with notions of innocence, community, and origins, and the fundamental constructedness of racial, ethnic, and ancestral identities and categories can be illustrated by Ann Patchett's novel *Run*. The novel is set in contemporary Boston, an area traditionally dominated by Americans with Irish ancestry. The focus of the novel is the Doyle family, a hybrid mixture of white and black people, of African and Irish Americans, of three generations, and of men and women. The development of this family illustrates how the meanings that Irishness and whiteness can acquire are constructed and flexible. They are identities that can include and exclude people, an inclusion or exclusion that says more about the strategies and needs of people than about biology or genetics.

Without falling into a culturalist trap however, the novel also shows that skin color is something that is genetically given, but has no inherent meaning when it comes to social status, class, living conditions, intelligence, emotions, or character. In this vein, one protagonist in the novel says: "Sometimes I feel like my entire life has been some sort of study in genetics" (196). What is nature and what is nurture remains unclear throughout the novel. Thus, one of the story's central questions remains unanswered, i.e., that of the meaning of being a family in spite of adoption, differences in skin color, or internal conflicts and strife. In her review for the *New York Times*, Janet Maslin comments that *Run* is about a family that is "as united by nurture as they are different in nature." Consequently, *Run* can also be described as a novel about relations and how they make up our selves, as well as our past, present, and future. John Updike calls *Run* "a stylized fable of families" and the German translation of the novel's title is *Familienangelegenheiten* (family matters). It is indeed a family story about relatives and relations, and how our immediate and extended family shapes us into the relative beings that we are. It is also a novel about the society in which we and our families are situated, shaping

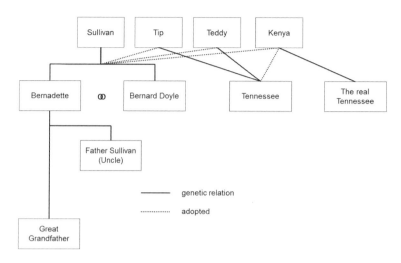

Fig. 2: The Doyle Family Tree

these families and their futures in turn. In this relative and relational world, color is one of the central categories that enables orientation, and it is no coincidence that the novel's central events take place in a huge, white snowstorm that makes orientation difficult by blurring boundaries: "Snow like this took away all the familiar markings. It erased the environment, the place where Tip and Teddy and Doyle had all grown up. [...] They could have been anywhere in the world where snow fell in endless repetition, the three of them having this very conversation" (38). And later on, the snow painfully foregrounds contrasts—the color of red blood and black skin, or the contrast between rich and poor: "There was blood beneath her head, a bright and shocking soak of red against the white" (42).

With the exception of the first and last chapters, the plot of the novel spans about twenty-four hours and includes many memories and retrospections which explain the present situation of the Doyle family. It is the story of a Catholic Irish American couple in Boston, Bernadette and Bernard Doyle, who have one natural-born son, Sullivan. Because they remain childless after their first son, they adopt two black boys, Tip and Teddy, brothers who are given up for adoption in quick succession. While Sullivan, the white Irish American boy, is the black sheep of the family, ruining his father's career and illegally selling diluted medication, Tip and Teddy are well-behaved, nice children: "As children, both Teddy and Tip had been so good. They were practically legends of patience in certain circles, sitting quietly in their white shirts at dinner tables full of adults, occasionally offering up a single insightful, and utterly charming question" (34). This inversion is made clear by Sullivan when citing a speech by Martin Luther King: "It's King, of course. Pretty good that I remembered that much. Except that the white brother part doesn't work exactly. It should be our black brothers. 'We have sometimes given our black brothers the feeling that we like the way we were being treated'" (257). Teddy, on the other hand, wants to be a Catholic priest like his adoptive uncle. While Sullivan lives apart from his family, helping the poor in Africa and drifting around the world without staying in contact with his parents, Tip and Teddy feel love and responsibility for their adoptive relations, especially their father. This inversion illustrates the constructedness of Irishness and whiteness. Passing for white and Irish is not based on genetic links, biology, or skin color, but rather depends on self-identification and adopted traditions.

A second theme of the novel that draws attention to this constructedness of ancestral and racial identities is the recurring motif of labeling and categorizing. *Run* constantly underlines how these two activities create our world and ourselves. Tip's passion is ichthyology, and he is happiest in the warmth of his lab among his fish specimens which he labels and sorts. His favorite authors include Carl Linnaeus and especially Charles Darwin, whose book, *Voyage of the Beagle*, is one of Tip and Teddy's dearest childhood memories. Beyond this obvious activity of categorization, every protagonist is also named and labeled by the people surrounding them; for example: "Tip was smarter and Teddy was sweeter. They had heard it since a time before memory. Sweet and Smart or Smart and Sweet" (73).[18] Teddy tries to categorize the world according to his Catholic belief as good or evil, Doyle's world of politics is all about being active or passive, and Kenya, the black girl that the Doyles adopt after her mother dies in a car accident, lives in a world which is about being white and black, an insider or outsider. Binary oppositions thus structure most of the protagonists' lives. They look for labels and categories in order to reduce complexity and deal with overwhelming situations. Many of these categories have to do with colors and skin color. When Kenya's natural mother Tennessee is run over by a car, Kenya reacts to this traumatic situation by categorizing the strangers around her by the color of their skin:

> The ambulance driver was a black man with some island accent. Of the two men who worked on her mother, one was white and one was black. All three of the policemen were white men. The white ambulance attendant snapped a white plastic collar around her mother's neck while the black ambulance attendant belted her legs. (46)

The excessively repetitive use of the two adjectives white and black in this passage reflects the binary world view of Kenya and the society in which she has grown up. People, their bodies, their personalities, and their social places are assessed according to a categorization into white and black as the primary two features of humanity. Kenya's act of seeing and her subsequent acts of categorization and labeling reproduce the hierarchy of which she herself is a victim: "Looking, and being looked upon, produces relations of power, the premise of the politics of identity" (Sen 151). Due to this logic of visibility, Tip, Teddy, and Kenya are taken for a family after the accident because they are black, while Doyle is excluded due to his whiteness: "No one asked Doyle if he belonged anywhere in this group. In fact there was a moment when a policeman tried to shoo him away" (46). Exclusion and inclusion are based on a seemingly biological and visible fact, while the inclusiveness of the adopted, mixed-race Irish, and

---

[18] Doyle himself has already labeled his adopted sons in terms of the future he has in mind for them, as Tip and Teddy are the names of two famous Irish American politicians from Massachusetts: Tip O'Neill and Ted Kennedy.

African American Doyle family is denied because it is contrary to the visual categorization and labeling that seems to underlie American daily life. This is stressed again when the ambulance leaves: "They had left the black girl with the two young black men who didn't know her. After all, they looked like they belonged together" (48). The whole novel is about questioning the certainty of such categorizations without denying the human need to categorize and label the world and the people in it. Consequently, the family that is established at the end of the novel is a patchwork family of white, black, Irish, and African American people of three different generations.

These people are biologically related to each other as Tennessee turns out to be Tip and Teddy's mother. Nevertheless, their sense of family exceeds a narrow, merely biological notion of a common mother or ancestry. The central symbol for this excess is Kenya. Tip, Teddy, Sullivan, and Doyle think that she is Tip and Teddy's biological sister, and only the reader comes to know that she is not. Her adoption into the family emphasizes that the act of integrating Tip and Teddy's assumed sister into the Doyle family undermines the main goal of her adoption. Instead of creating a more homogenous family unit through the reunion of the three supposed siblings, the adoption adds heterogeneity into the Doyle family by integrating a girl with no genetic ties to any of the family's members. Thus, the Doyles are a family first and foremost in the sense of emotional, adopted, and cultural ties, with love being the strongest tie between them. This becomes clear in the end when old Father Sullivan and Teddy meet the rest of the Doyles in the hospital: "There in the waiting room sat his entire immediate family: Doyle and Tip, Sullivan and Kenya, all together. [...] He loved them, each of them, for being themselves and for being part of his favorite niece and for being the family of Teddy, whom he loved above all others" (269). The novel therefore acknowledges the protagonists' yearning for biological mothers, fathers, and siblings, yet it is aware of the impossibility of this yearning. To underline this non-biological notion of family, the novel shows that people who are not related are often closest to one another, while those who are related do not understand or even like each other. Doyle is distant with his only natural child, Sullivan, while Sullivan has an instant close relationship to Kenya, a complete stranger. Tennessee, whom Kenya thinks is her mother and whom she loves fiercely, is not her real mother, and Tennessee's closest relationship is not with her biological sons, but with her friend, the real Tennessee and Kenya's real mother. Finally, Father Sullivan has a distant relationship with Sullivan and Doyle, who are related to him biologically, while there is an intense relationship with Teddy, for whom his adopted uncle is, in turn, the center of his family.

The metaphor that this discussion of genetics, family, and relationship revolve around is motherhood. In the novel it represents origins and identity and the quest for your individual self, something which Kenya expresses in a telling enumeration: "Home, bed, sleep, mother—who knew more beautiful words than these?" (80). Fathers are not relevant, and the only father in the novel, Doyle, has taken on a motherly, hen-like quality after his wife Bernadette's death (see 27, 95). When the characters in the novel think about their identities, they always turn to memories and imaginations of mothers.

Benadette, Tip and Teddy's adoptive mother, is an Irish American, red-headed girl who resembles the family's beloved statue of the Virgin and Mother Mary and is the lost center of the Doyle family. Having died when Teddy and Tip were five and six years old, she is remembered in crucial situations when people are trying to think about their future and their past. This adoptive and then lost mother has completely replaced Tip and Teddy's unknown genetic mother, which is made clear when Doyle ponders the possibility that Tennessee might be his sons' biological mother: "The mother was or she wasn't, and as far as Doyle was concerned, even if she was, she wasn't. His boys had a mother, and their mother was in the Old Calvary Cemetery in Roslindale" (79). Despite their skin color and their genes, the boys have become white Irish Americans—even whiter and more Irish than Bernadette's natural son, Sullivan.

For Kenya, her 'real' mother is the Tennessee who raised her, and Kenya does not know that the woman who raised her is not her biological mother and that Tennessee is not her real name. Therefore Tip and Teddy have to be her brothers. Only the reader is aware of the irony when everybody seems to find physical evidence for Kenya's non-existent genetic connection to Tip and Teddy. The similarities that people detect between themselves and others therefore say more about self-identification than about genetic links with an objective truth value. Tip and Teddy often look like their adoptive father Doyle; to Doyle, Sullivan looks like his natural mother Bernadette, while Teddy thinks that Sullivan looks more like Doyle. In the same way that notions of family, relationship, and identity are interrogated by the novel's intricate staging of interconnections, identifications, and more or less accurate acts of labeling and naming, the notion of the mother and motherhood as biological markers of belonging, roots, and origins is questioned. It is therefore no coincidence that all of the mothers in the novel die when their children are young and survive only in people's memories.

The novel ends with a trinity of deceased mothers for Kenya and therefore also for the Doyle family: "The three of them watched over her now, her mother and the woman she didn't know and Bernadette, who was both a photograph and a saint carved out of rosewood" (259). Thus, Kenya is linked to Ireland, where the carved statue of Mary (who looks like Bernadette) comes from; she is also linked to Africa, first and foremost by her own first name; and she is linked to America by the name that both of her black mothers bear, Tennessee. By including Tip, Teddy, and Kenya into the family, Doyle can deal with the loss of Bernadette, while the re-integration of Sullivan is only made possible by losing Tennessee and including Kenya. Whiteness is enriched by blackness, and Irishness is enriched by Africanness. By these inclusions, all of the characters are able to deal with guilt and loss because they can come to terms with their role in a family that is extended and yet closely linked, giving support and identification to all its members, no matter whether they are genetically or emotionally connected. At the same time, notions of whiteness, blackness, Ireland, America, and Africa are de-essentialized, as such categories do not consist of genes or clearly separated ethnic groups.

This constructivist notion of racial, gendered, or national identities centers on the negotiation of the Irish American identity of the Doyle family, with each member having one characteristic often seen as typically Irish. Consequently, only the combination of all the Doyles and the people to whom they are connected form an ideal, or even a stereotype, of Irishness. Yet this stereotype is simultaneously deconstructed by the family's internal hybridity. The traits seen as essentially Irish are the Catholicism of Father Sullivan and Teddy; the values of family, children, and tradition that play a central role for Doyle and Tennessee; the hospitality and good humor of Sullivan and the real Tennessee; Teddy's naive but endearing sweetness ; Tip's and Doyle's fervent belief in a cause; the sacrifice and martyrdom of Bernadette, Tennessee, Tip, and Teddy; and the violence of the mad Irish boy Sullivan. The drinking problem of the maternal great grandfather, with whom the novel starts, rounds off this panorama of stereotypical Irishness.[19] Each of these characteristics seems to be exclusive to an essential notion of Irishness. But much in the way of the joke from *Father Ted*, with which I began this essay, Irishness as a cultural tradition and an identity is seen as inclusive and open to everyone who wants to adopt it, very much like the U.S. census defines race, ancestry, and ethnicity.

The adoption of Tip and Teddy, and later of Kenya, is therefore more than a simple plot device. It is an overarching metaphor for contemporary America and a comment on the nature versus nurture debate. Only the Doyle family as a whole can embody Irish America, each single member being only one aspect of it. At the same time, the fact that the family consists of men and women, white and black, old and young, spiritual and scientific minds, politicians, and sportswomen points to the heterogeneity and hybridity of notions like roots, race, ethnicity, ancestry, skin color, or identity, thus emptying them of an exclusive, genetic essence and visible truth. In the end, identities are much like Tennessee's face after the accident in which she saves her son Tip's life: "sliced and stitched, undone and reassembled" (142). Thus, the diversity of the Doyles not only mirrors the diversity of America, but it also symbolizes that which exceeds categorization. We cannot *not* categorize, as the novel and its constant processes of naming and labeling show. But we also have to be aware of that which exceeds statistics, categories, and labels.

Again, Kenya is at the center of this excess. She is the 'runner' of the title, whose vitality, speed, and movement demonstrate that the particular and the individual will always exceed our need to contain and narrow our world by creating categories and reducing individuals to percentages in a statistic. The novel can therefore be read as a comment on statistical approaches as those taken by the census or the ACS. Where the census attempts to fit all respondents into a set of given categories, the novel illustrates the impossibility of containing the diversity of the individual within such categories. The fact that the Census 2000 allowed respondents to specify more than one race for the first time in the history of the census indicates an awareness of the reductive consequences of categorization that form the core of *Run*.

---

[19] This stereotype complies with Irish character types that could be found on English, Irish, and American stages from the seventeenth century onward, and lives on in caricatures, novels, and magazines of the eighteenth century to the present day. George Bernard Shaw's play *John Bull's Other Island*, first staged in London in 1904, is one of the best-known and most critical engagements with this Irish stereotype. For a discussion of the stage Irishman and his functions and effects on both auto- and heterostereotypes of Ireland, see Cheng 28-61; Heininge. See also the caricatures in Curtis.

Conclusion

Summing up, this paper's point of departure was that skin, its color, and the ethnic and ancestral identities that are mapped onto both are relative and contingent constructions that are open to acts of passing and self-identification. In contemporary America, Irishness has thus become an attractive identity that is white and ethnically specific at the same time, an ambivalence that makes it possible to be both different and special and to deal with a trauma like 9/11 and the experience of white guilt while enjoying the safety and privilege of whiteness. Irishness and whiteness are therefore detached from notions of genetics, biology, and heritage and are free to be appropriated by everyone. Through a combined interrogation of white skin as a colored skin, and the shifting Irish position as more or less white, we can effectively question the cultural capital of white privilege by making whiteness strange: "Power is established in exercising control or maintaining a hierarchy of power, relationally. Whiteness is then a trope for the negotiation of power within a relationship" (Sen 163).

This focus on relational identities in terms of skin and skin color—but also in terms of family, ancestry, the adoption of traditions, or our needs and strategies of self-identification as documented in the census, the ACS, and *Run*—can help us question essentialist notions of identity without ignoring our need to ask one of the most burning and recurring questions of humankind: Who am I? The fact that we will never be able to answer this question conclusively, neither in terms of genetics, biology, nor culture, is one of the issues that an interrogation of white identities can demonstrate.

The census and the ACS attempt to answer the question of identity by statistically representing the whole nation and enabling their respondents to have their personal self-identifications reflected as a percentage of the total population. Patchett's novel, on the other hand, enables the reader to gain access to individual processes of self-identification by describing the thoughts and feelings of individual characters, thus taking the perspective of the individual and his or her personal history. Both approaches are needed to fully assess the necessity, effects, and dangers of identifications, categories, and acts of naming and labeling. The ambivalent and changing whiteness of the Irish, its recent use in contemporary America, and the evaluations and assumptions connected with it, are only one instance of these dangers, effects, and necessities. Making whiteness strange thus opens the space of Bhabha's "not white/not quite" for the overarching issue of identity (*Location* 92).

Works Cited

Akenson, Don. *An Irish History of Civilization*. Vol. 1. Ithaca, NY: McGill-Queen's UP, 2005. Print.

Anderson, Benedict. *Imagined Communities: Reflections on the Origin and Spread of Nationalism*. 2nd ed. London: Verso, 2006. Print.

Arrowsmith, Aidan. "Plastic Paddies vs. Master Racers: 'Soccer' and Irish Identity." *The International Journal of Cultural Studies* 7 (2004): 460-79. Print.

Benthien, Claudia. *Skin: On the Cultural Border Between Self and the World*. New York: Columbia UP, 2002. Print.

Bernardi, Daniel. "Introduction: Race and the Hollywood Style." *Classic Hollywood, Classic Whiteness*. Ed. Daniel Bernardi. Minneapolis: U of Minnesota P, 2001. xiii-xxvi. Print.

Bhabha, Homi K. "The Other Question: Difference, Discrimination, and the Discourse of Colonialism." *Black British Cultural Studies: A Reader*. Ed. Houston A. Baker, Manthia Diawara, and Ruth H. Lindeborg. Chicago, IL: U of Chicago P, 1996. 87-106. Print.

---. *The Location of Culture*. London: Routledge, 1994. Print.

Brannigan, John. "Ireland, and Black!: Minstrelsy, Racism, and Black Cultural Production in 1970s Ireland." *Textual Practice* 22.2 (2008): 229-48. Print.

---. *Race in Modern Irish Literature and Culture*. Edinburgh: Edinburgh UP, 2009. Print.

Brittingham, Angela, and G. Patricia de la Cruz. *Ancestry 2000: Census 2000 Brief*. U.S. Census Bureau, June 2004. Web. 31 May 2011.

Brod, Harry S., ed. *The Making of Masculinities: The New Men's Studies*. Boston; MA: Allen, 1987. Print.

Cheng, Vincent J. *Inauthentic: The Anxiety over Culture and Identity*. New Brunswick, NJ: Rutgers UP, 2004. Print.

Connell, Robert W. *Masculinities*. Cambridge: Polity, 1995. Print.

Curtis, L. Perry, Jr. *Apes and Angels: The Irishman in Victorian Caricature*. Newton Abbot, Devon: David & Charles, 1971. Print.

Data Protection and Privacy Policy. U.S. Dept. of Commerce, 16 Feb. 2011. Web. 18 Feb. 2012. <http://www.census.gov/privacy/data_protection/>.

Delanty, Gerard, and Krishan Kumar, eds. *Handbook of Nations and Nationalism*. London: Sage, 2005. Print.

Dyer, Richard. *White*. London: Routledge, 1997. Print.

Flannery, Eóin. *Ireland and Postcolonial Studies: Theory, Discourse, Utopia*. Basingstoke: Palgrave Macmillan, 2009. Print.

Fludernik, Monika. *An Introduction to Narratology*. London: Routledge, 2009. Print.

Frankenberg, Ruth. *White Women, Race Matters: The Social Construction of Whiteness*. Minneapolis: U of Minnesota P, 1993. Print.

Garner, Steve. *Whiteness: An Introduction*. London: Routledge, 2007. Print.

Glazer, Nathan, and Daniel P. Moynihan. *Ethnicity: Theory and Experience*. Cambridge, MA: Harvard UP, 1975. Print.

"Grant Unto Him Eternal Rest." *Father Ted*. Hat Trick Productions. London. 26 May 1995. Television.

Grieco, Elizabeth M. *The White Population 2000: Census 2000 Brief*. U.S. Census Bureau, Mar. 2001. Web. 31 May 2011.

Hall, Stuart. "The Spectacle of the Other." *Representation: Cultural Representations and Signifying Practices*. Ed. Stuart Hall. London: Sage, 1997. 223-79. Print.

Harris, Cheryl I. "Whiteness as Property." *Harvard Law Review* 106.8 (1993): 1707-91. Print.

Heininge, Kathleen. *Buffoonery in Irish Drama: Staging Twentieth-Century Post-Colonial Stereotypes.* New York: Lang, 2009. Print.
Higginbotham, Elizabeth, and Margaret L. Andersen, eds. *Race and Ethnicity in Society: The Changing Landscape.* Belmont, CA: Thomson and Wadsworth, 2006. Print.
Hixson, Lindsay, Bradford B. Hepler, and Myoung Ouk Kim. *The White Population 2010: Census 2010 Brief.* U.S. Census Bureau, Sept. 2011. Web. 1 Feb. 2012.
Hobsbawm, Eric. *The Invention of Tradition.* Cambridge: Cambridge UP, 1983. Print.
Hoffmeyer-Zlotnik, Jürgen H. P., and Uwe Warner. *Die Abfrage von 'Ethnizität' in der international vergleichenden Survey-Forschung.* Mannheim: Forschung Raum und Gesellschaft e. V., 2009.
Humes, Karen R., Nicholas A. Jones, and Roberto R. Ramirez. *Overview of Race and Hispanic Origin 2010: 2010 Census Briefs.* U.S. Census Bureau, Mar. 2011. Web. 6 Feb. 2012.
Ignatiev, Noel. *How the Irish Became White.* New York: Routledge, 1995. Print.
Ignatiev, Noel, and John Garvey. "Introduction." *Race Traitor.* Ed. Noel Ignatiev and John Garvey. New York: Routledge, 1996. 1-5. Print.
Jacobson, Matthew Frye. *Whiteness of a Different Color: European Immigrants and the Alchemy of Race.* Cambridge, MA: Harvard UP, 1998. Print.
JanMohamed, Abdul. "The Economy of Manichean Allegory: The Function of Racial Difference in Colonialist Literature." *"Race," Writing, and Difference.* Ed. Henry Louis Gates, Jr. Chicago: U of Chicago P, 1989. 78-106. Print.
Kroeger, Brooke. *Passing: When People Can't Be Who They Are.* New York: Public Affairs, 2003. Print.
Lenz, Peter. "'Not All of Them are Paddies': Irish-Americans and the (Un-/Re-) Embracing of Irish Identity." *Anglia* 128.2 (2010): 298-314. Print.
Lloyd, David. *Anomalous States: Irish Writing and the Post-Colonial Moment.* Dublin: Lilliput, 1993. Print.
Long-Form Questionnaire. United States Census 2000. U.S. Dept. of Commerce, n. d. Web. 24 July 2013.
López, Ian Haney. *White by Law: The Legal Construction of Race.* New York: New York UP, 2006. Print.
Maslin, Janet. "For Ex-Mayor's Family, Everything is Political." *New York Times.* New York Times, 20 Sep. 2007. Web. 6 Feb. 2012.
McGreevey, John T. *Catholicism and American Freedom: A History.* New York: Norton, 2003. Print.
Nakano Glenn, Evelyn, ed. *Shades of Difference: Why Skin Color Matters.* Stanford, CA: Stanford UP, 2009. Print.
Negra, Diane. "Consuming Ireland: Lucky Charms Cereal, Irish Spring Soap, and 1-800 Shamrock." *Cultural Studies* 15.1 (2001): 76-97. Print.
---. "Introduction." *The Irish in Us: Irishness, Performativity and Popular Culture.* Ed. Diane Negra. Durham, NC: Duke UP, 2006. 1-19. Print.
---. "Irishness, Innocence, and American Identity Politics before and after September 11." *The Irish in Us: Irishness, Performativity and Popular Culture.* Ed. Diane Negra. Durham, NC: Duke UP, 2006. 354-71. Print.

Nishikawa, Kinohi. "White." *The Greenwood Encyclopedia of African American Literature*. Ed. Hans Ostrom and J. David Macey, Jr. Westport, CT: Greenwood, 2005. 1725-26. Print.

Online Gateway to Census 2000. U.S. Dept. of Commerce, n. d. Web. 6 Feb. 2012.

Oyewùmí, Oyèrónké. *The Invention of Women: Making an African Sense of Western Gender Discourses*. Minneapolis: U of Minnesota P, 1997. Print.

Patchett, Ann. *Run*. London: Bloomsbury, 2008. Print.

Questions and Answers for Census 2000 Data on Race. U.S. Dept. of Commerce, 14 Mar. 2001. Web. 18 February 2012.

Roediger, David R. *The Wages of Whiteness: Race and the Making of the American Working Class*. New York: Verso, 1991. Print.

---. *Working Towards Whiteness: How America's Immigrants Became White*. New York: Basic, 2005. Print.

Schlossberg, Ruth. "Introduction: Rites of Passing." *Passing: Identity and Interpretation in Sexuality, Race, and Religion*. Ed. María Carla Sánchez and Linda Schlossberg. New York: New York UP, 2001. 1-12. Print.

Scully, Marc. "'Plastic and Proud?' Discourses of Authenticity Among the Second-Generation Irish in England." *Psychology & Society* 2.2 (2009): 124-35. Print.

Sen, Ruma. "Locating Whiteness: History, Power, Identity and the Postcolonial Framework." *Atenea* 27.1 (2007): 149-66. Print.

Updike, John. "A Boston Fable." *The New Yorker*. The New Yorker, 1 Oct. 2007. Web. 6 Feb. 2012.

Taking Fire from the Bucolic:
The Pastoral Tradition in Seven American War Poems

ANDREW MILLER

ABSTRACT

    This article examines the role that the pastoral mode plays in seven American war poems: Herman Melville's "The Scout toward Aldie," Wallace Stevens's "The Death of a Soldier," Robert Frost's "Range Finding," James Dickey's "Firebombing," Walt Whitman's "When Lilacs Last in the Dooryard Bloom'd," Bruce Weigl's "The Song of Napalm," and Brain Turner's "Eulogy." The essay observes that, contrary to the way in which it is often presented in the European tradition, the pastoral in the American tradition is not invoked as a means of taking cover from the horrors of war, but is instead described as being in league with war. Thus, the pastoral often takes the form of the counter-pastoral and reflects the negotiation that Leo Marx observes occurring between American depictions of nature and depictions of industrial urban life.

I.

    In his discussion of the pastoral tradition and its relationship to English poetry of the First World War, Paul Fussell writes "if the opposite of peace is war, the opposite of experiencing moments of war is proposing moments of pastoral. Since war takes place outdoors and always within nature, its symbolic status is that of ultimate anti-pastoral" (Fussell 231). Fussell's observation fits well with the role that the pastoral has come to play in much of the war poetry of Western literature. From the epics of Homer to the work of Ivor Gurney, the pastoral has become a means of taking cover from the bellicose. Often, the opposition between pastoral descriptions and the descriptions of war occurs at close quarters. In many poems, at the very moment when the poet is about to describe the visceral consequences of a fight, he or she seemingly looks away, changing the focus from the gore of battle to the calm of a bucolic landscape. More often still, the shift is made for the purpose of the elegy, which traditionally uses pastoral imagery as a symbolic figuration of rebirth. However, while the opposition between the pastoral and the bellicose continues well into the twentieth century, in many of the best American war poems it is muddied, even undermined. From the poems of Herman Melville to those of Brian Turner, pastoral symbols are invoked not as sources of shelter from the horrors of war, but as means for describing these horrors and their consequences. The bucolic images invoked in such poems as Melville's "The Scout toward Aldie" and Turner's "Eulogy" become the camouflage for war itself. Beginning with Melville's "Scout," then, this essay will trace the course of this alliance between the pastoral and the bellicose in seven American poems: Melville's "Scout," Wallace Stevens's "The Death of a Soldier," Robert Frost's

"Range Finding," James Dickey's "The Fire Bomber," Walt Whitman's "When Lilacs Last in the Dooryard Bloom'd," Bruce Weigl's "The Song of Napalm," and Brian Turner's "Eulogy."

II.

The traditional opposition between pastoral descriptions and the descriptions of war finds its origin in the fourteenth book of the *Iliad* in which Homer interrupts his description of the Trojan assault on the Grecian ships with the story of Hera's seduction of Zeus (named Juno and Jupiter in Alexander Pope's translation):

> Gazing he spoke, and, kindling at the view,
> His eager arms around the goddess threw.
> Glad Earth perceives, and from her bosom pours
> Unbidden herbs and voluntary flowers:
> Thick new-born violets a soft carpet spread,
> And clustering lotos swell'd the rising bed,
> And sudden hyacinths the turf bestrow,
> And flamy crocus made the mountain glow
> There golden clouds conceal the heavenly pair,
> Steep'd in soft joys and circumfused with air;
> Celestial dews, descending o'er the ground,
> Perfume the mount, and breathe ambrosia round:
> At length, with love and sleep's soft power oppress'd,
> The panting thunderer nods, and sinks to rest. (393-406)

Anyone familiar with the passage knows that it is not an arbitrary digression. Juno's motive for seducing her husband at this time and at this place (the top of Mount Ida) entails a flanking action, so to speak. For the Trojan attackers, Jupiter serves as something equivalent to air-cover. His presence on the mountain top ensures that no other deity from the Pantheon can assist the Greeks. Distracting Jupiter from his watch and drugging him with sleep, then, Juno effectively cuts off the Trojans, leaving them in the hands of Neptune, a god who favors the Greeks. Beyond the goddess's own tactical objectives, however, there remain the poet's. In his description of the gods' embrace, Homer takes his time to elaborate the effects that their love-making has on the natural world. Their procreation is magnified in the flora around them, and this magnification reflects one of the poem's themes: that love is the natural state of being, while war is an abomination. At least, this is the interpretation that E. R. Curtius offers us when he describes Homer's shift from the bellicose to the pastoral as being symptomatic of the poet's refusal to accept the tragic as "the basic element of existence" (185). According to Curtius, regardless of its military consequences, the union of the gods and the ensuing botanical procreation act as counters to the horrors of war, for they are the symbolic manifestations of the natural order.

We have but to reflect on the pastoral tradition as it manifests itself in Virgil's *Aeneid* or in the poetry of the Renaissance to recognize how these later traditions reiterate Homer's attitude. Time and again, the pastoral is employed as a means of soothing war's 'wrinkled front' or taking cover from it. Thus, the refuge that

Homer seeks on Mount Ida becomes one of the major conventions of war poetry in the West: a convention that manifests itself in the poetry of the twentieth century as well. Here, for example, is Ivor Gurney's "To His Love" (1916):

> He's gone, and all our plans
> Are useless indeed.
> We'll walk no more on Cotswolds
> Where the sheep feed
> Quietly and take no heed.
>
> His body that was so quick
> Is not as you
> Knew it, on Severn River
> Under the blue
> Driving our small boat through.
>
> You would not know him now...
> But still he died
> Nobly, so cover him over
> With violets of pride
> Purple from Severn side.
>
> Cover him, cover him soon!
> And with thick-set
> Masses of memoried flowers-
> Hide that red wet
> Thing I must somehow forget. (7)

Gurney's poem is clearly divided between the pastoral state of peace and the visceral effects of war. The first three stanzas revisit some of the most traditional pastoral themes. Invoking the idyllic scenery of the English countryside, the sheep and the River Severn, the poem begins as a résumé of Milton's "Lycidas." With his "quick" body, the beloved is even described in a manner that calls to mind Milton's shepherd, a parallel further justified by Gurney's use of floral images, which are deployed in accordance with the standard operating procedures of the pastoral elegy. If there is a distinction to be made between Homer's description of Mount Ida and Gurney's description of the Cotswolds, it exists in how Gurney's poem calls into question the potency of its own pastoral symbolism. Whereas Homer might be said to use pastoral description as a symbolic means of deflecting the horrors of war, Gurney's speaker cannot achieve this effect. Beautiful as they are, the river, the sheep and the small boat are useless in that they afford the speaker no fortification against the onslaught of grief and the ghastly reality of "the red wet thing [he] must somehow forget." Beginning with the traditional pastoral, then, Gurney's speaker discovers that the tradition is exhausted, and this realization is reflected in the way he finally falls prey to a traumatized sort of panic at the beginning of the poem's last stanza. Such a line as "Cover him, cover him soon!" is uttered by a man who can find no cover at all.

Gurney's speaker is what Jahan Ramazani describes as the 'melancholic mourner': a mourner distinct from those one finds in traditional elegies such as Milton's "Lycidas" because, "unlike their literary forebears or the 'normal mourners' of psychoanalysis, [melancholic mourners] refuse such orthodox consolations as the rebirth of the dead in nature, in God, in poetry itself" (4). As Ramazani argues at length, for these mourners, there is only the heart-breaking memory of dying and death. However, while we might describe Gurney's speaker in this way, and thus describe him as someone who finds no relief in the pastoral tradition, it must also be said that the pastoral remains structurally intact. Faced with its obsolescence, the speaker does not shy away from employing it; instead alluding to its failure becomes only another aspect of the poem.

The failure of the pastoral to stave off the speaker's grief does not spell an end to the opposition between the pastoral and description of war. Rather, it reiterates it, in that Gurney's poem is effectively divided between the bucolic Cotswolds and the grisly body of the beloved. The former seemingly belongs to the realm of sanity; the latter to the realm of trauma and melancholia. According to Paul Fussell, the reason such an opposition is maintained in the English poetry of the First World War is because of the overall importance English culture and literature had come to place on the idea of nature as a place of sanity. As Fussell describes it, from the nineteenth century onward, the English countryside becomes portrayed as "a 'stay' against the chaos of industrial life" (235). Confronted with the congestion of modern cities and the erosion of traditional morality—commonly regarded as an element of rural life—the English came to see nature as an opposition to the grim realities of the city. It is only logical, then, that when confronted with a conflict such as World War I, a poet such as Gurney would intensify this opposition in his verse. After all, what greater industrial chaos could there have been than the modern, mechanized warfare seen at the Battles of the Somme and Verdun? Confronted with the memory of the war-machine and its brutal efficiency, Gurney's speaker may be said to retreat to the high ground of English poetic sanity—the pastoral.

However, the cover Gurney's speaker takes in the pastoral is not to be found in many of the war poems of the United States as the American relationship with landscape is less embroiled in conceptions of idealization than in those of utility. From the poems of Herman Melville through the poems of Brian Turner, nature is often described in American verse as an ally of war, not as its antagonist. The American attitude toward the pastoral mode is well described by Robert Hughes, who in his discussion of the landscape painting of Thomas Cole, recognizes how the traditional views of Americans toward the land were founded in utility, not aesthetic satisfaction. Hughes writes:

> Landscape wasn't landscape to the average American eye: it was territory, property, raw materials. Its qualities were practical—the fertility of the soil and the ores it might contain, the availability of water, the kind of trees it bore, the hundred questions that all converged toward one: "How can I exploit this?" The idea that wild terrain might be, in of itself, a "spiritual" resource occurred to very few white Americans—in fact their main spiritual tradition, that of Puritanism, had argued vehemently against it—treating uncultivated land as "wilderness," a place of biblical trial and the abode of demons. (142)

As we will see, the American notions of exploiting the land will figure prominently in many American war poems, in which the notions of the protective pastoral canopy become synonymous with the idea of 'good cover' in the strictest military sense.

This exploitation can be seen by examining two stanzas from Melville's "The Scout toward Aldie" (1866). The narrative of the poem describes an episode from the American Civil War, in which a troop of Federal soldiers search for the Confederate raider Lieutenant Colonel John S. Mosby and his band of partisan rangers. In these stanzas, the narrative describes an ambush performed by Mosby on the Federals:

> As restive they turn, how sore they feel,
>   And cross, and sleepy, and full of spleen,
> And curse the war. "Fools, North and South"
> Said one right out. "O for a bed!
>   O now to drop in this woodland green"
>   He drops as the syllables leave his mouth—
>   Mosby speaks from the undergrowth—
>
> Speaks in a volley! out jets the flame!
>   Men fall from their saddles like plums from trees;
> Horses take fright, reins tangle and bind;
> "Steady—Dismount—form—and into the wood"
>   They go, but find what scarce can please:
>   Their steeds have been tied in the field behind,
>   And Mosby's men are off like the wind. (666)

Although they invoke the symbolic imagery of the pastoral, Melville's lines deploy this imagery in an entirely different manner than we find in Homer and Gurney. Longing to "drop in this woodland green" as a passionate shepherd would, the Federal soldiers find that the 'green' is the site of a deadly ambush. Part of the power of this passage comes, then, from Melville's allusion to one of the pastoral tradition's central *tableaux*: the bucolic repose. This repose finds its origins in the opening lines of Virgil's "First Eclogue" in which the shepherd Tityrus "lolls" about, "serenading / the woodland spirit beneath a spread of sheltering beech" (1-2). For Tityrus, the pastoral world is not only the site in which contemplation occurs and from which poetry is born; it is also the location in which he can find 'shelter.' In Latin, Virgil's phrase for this is *"sub tegmine fagi,"* which translates as "beneath the shield." In short, the shepherd is protected by the canopy of leaves above him, finding cover in the 'green.' In these lines, then, Virgil founded the idea that the pastoral provides safety for those who seek it, and it is this notion of safety that Melville perverts with a savage irony: the soldiers' desire to find bucolic repose in the 'green' becomes fulfilled in the violent death that the 'green' holds in store for them.

But the bucolic repose is not the only aspect of the pastoral that Melville perverts. His Federal soldiers also find themselves in the traditional place of the youths or nymphs of Arcadia: youths or nymphs who, as the convention generally has it, are spied upon by hidden admirers. In the English tradition, one of the the best manifestations of this conventional narrative can be found in Andrew Marvell's poem "The Picture of Little T.C. in a Prospect of Flowers," in which Marvell's speaker remains concealed to enjoy the beauty of the nymph, Little T.C., as she gathers various kinds of flowers in an idyllic setting. In Melville's version of the narrative convention, however, the beloved is replaced by a sniper.

I have used to the word 'pervert' to describe Melville's alterations to these pastoral *tableaux*, but, in many respects, the word is inaccurate. It suggests that Melville's portrayal of the pastoral corresponds solely to his own ironic sensibilities and that it does not represent an overall American attitude toward the tradition. I do not believe this to be the case. Certainly, Melville is aware of the irony of transforming Arcadia into an ambush. However, the matter does not only entail his perverse sensibilities. "The Scout toward Aldie" reflects an entirely different and—I would argue—uniquely American attitude toward the pastoral: an attitude that figures the American pastoral as inherently counter-pastoral.

The distinction between the pastoral and the counter-pastoral is clearly defined by Charles Lock, who identifies the pastoral mode as convention which we see through:

> In the pastoral we are enabled to see through conventions as in themselves they really and beatifically are: yet 'to see through' in two senses, as seeing the convention for what it is, and, despite that, allowing the convention to be that through which we see. At which point we can simply observe that all 'serious' literature must partake of the counter-pastoral, must solicit resistance to its own seductions. Pastoral, we might venture, comes to life—to life as literature, and in literature—only when it fails to seduce: when it is felt to be cold. Better, perhaps: when it is felt to be colluding in the reader's own act of resistance, when it would forbid its readers to ignore or 'see through' its conventions. (100)

The pastoral comes to life, in Lock's sense of the phrase, when it becomes a counter to its own conventions—when it becomes an agent of the counter-pastoral. In this role, the mode functions to obstruct the line-of-sight by which the reader becomes seduced. This obstruction occurs when nature is described as resisting conventionalization. Melville's perversions of the *tableaux* correspond to this sort of obstruction, in that they introduce the Latin tradition while simultaneously booby-trapping it with the realities of war.

This resistance is best seen in the way that the bellicose is integrated—even fused into the natural world. Notice, for example, Melville's refusal to describe Mosby's men. Although the narrative clearly states that the shots come from the raiders, the raiders are, in fact, identified by nothing more than aspects of the natural world. When they speak, they speak in "jets of flame"; when they retreat, they are "off like the wind." Such descriptions do not merely entail a mere perversion of the pastoral tradition; they involve a complete departure from one of the traditions rhetorical figures: the *argumentum a loco*. In classical rhetoric, this topos describes a landscape as a site that reflects the narrative themes of a literary plot. In the *argumentum a loco*, the realities of nature are effectively neutralized or, at the very least, transformed into stage props for the narrative action. Thus, it is always spring in Arcadia because the story that is told there entails young love and procreation. In modern critical parlance, we disdain such a figure as it gives rise to the pathetic fallacy. Certainly, Melville holds such ideas in a similar sort of disdain, suggesting that to conceive of nature in this way is ludicrous. Melville toured many of the Civil War battlefields just weeks and sometimes even days after the hostilities had ended. He understood only too well that the 'green' is not merely a background to the killing.

The participation of nature in battle is, however, not limited to its role as a killer, though. Melville is also keen to use nature as the model of how men die.

Consider the comparison the poet makes between the falling soldiers and the falling plums: when shot, the troopers "fall from their saddles like plums from trees." In one respect, we might ascribe such a line to being on a par with the traditional pastoral in that it does *cover* a grisly element of war. We have only to imagine the physical consequences of being hit by a Minié ball (an American Civil-War-era bullet) to conceive of what Melville is *not* describing in such a line. However, the comparison entails another integration of the pastoral and war. Once the shots are fired from the 'green,' their effect is to transform the dead soldiers into objects of nature. Such a descriptive move extends the general attitude of this poem: death in battle is not an abomination to the natural order. Instead, it reflects this order, suggesting that this sort of death has a procreative effect, for the soldiers become overripe fruits to be harvested.

One is tempted to believe that Wallace Stevens had Melville's description in mind when he wrote the following lines:

> Life contracts and death is expected,
> as in a season of autumn.
> the soldier falls.
>
> He does not become a three-days personage,
> imposing his separation,
> calling for pomp.
>
> Death is absolute and without memorial,
> as in a season of autumn,
> when the wind stops,
>
> when the wind stops and, over the heavens,
> the clouds go, nevertheless,
> in their direction. (97)

Stevens's splendid poem "The Death of a Soldier" (1923) may be said to surpass Melville's in its vivid simplicity and imagistic grace, but the gesture made in the poem closely resembles that made by "The Scout toward Aldie." The central piece of rhetoric in the poem is the comparison between a falling leaf and a falling soldier; in this way, the poem enacts a similar kind of union between war and nature. Stevens's soldier falls in a manner that parallels Melville's soldiers, a parallel is further strengthened by the poem's final image of the wind, which is portrayed as the principal force behind the falling leaf. Like Mosby's raiders, who "are off like wind," the wind in Stevens's poem is a force that cannot be stopped, diminished, or even fully comprehended.

If there is a significant difference between the two poems' treatment of war and pastoral, that difference may be found in the comparison the two poets draw between the falling soldiers and those falling elements of the natural world. Like Christ's mustard seed, which, after it falls, "groweth up, and becometh greater than all herbs" (Mark 4.32, Authorized Vers.), Melville's soldiers fall like fruits and so may be said to achieve some sort of rebirth. However ironic it may seem, the image of the plums also parallels the portrayal of death that Whitman offers us in "When Lilacs Last in the Dooryard Bloom'd" (discussed below). Melville's fruits also anticipate the role that the poppy will play in the British and Commonwealth poetry of the Great War. Like John McCrae's poppies, which "blow" "between the crosses" in "Flanders fields," Melville's fruits ripen due to war (McCrae 85). Stevens's falling leaves, however, do not suggest such a rebirth. Rather, their death is "absolute and without memorial."

Such poems as Melville's "Scout" and Stevens's "Soldier" would seem to reflect a pervasive tendency in the American pastoral tradition. In his classic study of this tradition, *The Machine in the Garden* (1964), Leo Marx characterizes the American pastoral as being filled with "the ominous sounds of machines" (16). Unlike Fussell's characterization of the English consciousness, which looks for sanity in the natural world, and thus regards nature as being separate from 'the chaos' of industrial life and, by consequence, from war, Marx suggests that, for the American consciousness, the natural world does not provide such a clear-cut source of sanity. Rather, nature is inherently integrated with and/or interrupted by the presence of machines. The description of this interruption, Marx argues, is one of reoccurring themes of American literature. Marx writes:

> The ominous sounds of machines, like the sound of the steamboat bearing down on [Huck and Jim's] raft or of the train breaking upon the idyll at Walden, reverberate endlessly in our literature. We hear such a sound, or see the sight which accompanies it, in *The Octopus, The Education of Henry Adams, The Great Gatsby, The Grapes of Wrath*, "The Bear"—and one could go on. (16)

Applied to such poems as Melville's "Scout" at least, Marx's insights allow us to see how the integration of nature and war is yet another manifestation of the interruption of nature by the machine. Like the horns of the steamboat or the train, the gunshot breaks in on the idyll, until this breaking-in becomes a convention.

No American war poem better expresses this interruption than Robert Frost's poem "Range Finding" (1916):

> The battle rent a cobweb diamond-strung
> And cut a flower beside a ground bird's nest
> Before it stained a single human breast.
> The stricken flower bent double and so hung.
> And still the bird revisited her young.
> A butterfly its fall had dispossessed
> A moment sought in air his flower of rest,
> Then lightly stooped to it and fluttering clung.
> On the bare upland pasture there had spread
> O'ernight 'twixt mullein stalks a wheel of thread
> And straining cables wet with silver dew.
> A sudden passing bullet shook it dry.
> The indwelling spider ran to greet the fly,
> But finding nothing, sullenly withdrew. (126)

One is tempted to compare the narrative action of the poem to the concluding scene of Lewis Milestone's 1930 film adaptation of *All Quiet on the Western Front*, in which the protagonist, Paul Bäumer, is killed after exposing himself to sniper fire in order to get a better look at a butterfly just beyond the lip of his trench. Frost's sonnet depicts a similar scene, in that it focuses on a small patch of grass in a manner that calls to mind the close-ups of Milestone's last sequence.

However, while the comparison with the film is tempting, to make too much of it would have the effect of hindering the real potency of the poem and would also limit our ability to recognize the more likely source of Frost's inspiration: Thomas Hardy's drama *The Dynasts*, in which Hardy offers the following description of Waterloo:

> Yea, the coneys are scared by the thud of hoofs,
> And their white scuts flash at their vanishing heels,
> And swallows abandon the hamlet-roofs.
>
> The mole's tunnelled chambers are crushed by wheels,
> The lark's eggs scattered, their owners fled;
> And the hedgehog's household the sapper unseals.
>
> The snail draws in at the terrible tread,
> But in vain; he is crushed by the felloe-rim
> The worm asks what can be overhead,
>
> And wriggles deep from a scene so grim,
> And guesses him safe; for he does not know
> What a foul red flood will be soaking him!
>
> Beaten about by the heel and toe
> Are butterflies, sick of the day's long rheum,
> To die of a worse than the weather-foe.
>
> Trodden and bruised to a miry tomb
> Are ears that have greened but will never be gold,
> And flowers in the bud that will never bloom. (505-06)

Comparing Hardy's passage with Frost's poem affords us a striking contrast between the two poets' visions of the pastoral. Doing so also fortifies the distinction I argue exists between the British and American pastoral traditions. For Hardy, war is the nemesis of the pastoral. Armed with the most powerful verbs of destruction, Hardy's passage is a blitz of crushing, scattering, feeling, treading, beating, flooding and soaking—all of which is perpetrated on the minute and otherwise meek universe of the fields. Frost rejects this vision and, in doing so, his poem resists Hardy's pastoral mode in a manner that corresponds to Melville's resistance to Virgil's. Instead, "Range Finding" is exemplar of how the imagery of war interrupts the pastoral calm—as does the machine in the garden—and of how this interruption leads to a fusion of the pastoral and the bellicose. Like the interruption by the war in Melville's poem, the bullets in Frost's have seemingly little effect on the doings of nature. The flower is cut, but the butterfly still lands on it.

This extremely unsentimental portrayal of the pastoral classifies war not as a uniquely human activity, but as one of the principal demons of nature itself. To illustrate this idea, Frost employs what we might regard as the least bellicose of poetic forms—the sonnet. The effect of the sonnet form on this theme is that it places the violence of the battle and the tranquility of the pasture into a carefully balanced musical structure. Unlike what one would expect to find in the work of Frost's contemporaries, the Futurists, who employ radical free-verse forms to typographically illustrate the violence of battle on the page, Frost opts for a poetic form that reflects a pristine sort of order, in which the actions of a mother bird tending her "nest" do not contradict the effects of bullet "staining a breast." In the work of a lesser poet, such an easy rhyme would be the stuff of convenience, but for Frost it relates a bitter truth: nature and war are at peace with one another. The bullet that shakes the cobweb dry interrupts the natural calm. But this interruption has little effect on the life of the spider. For the spider, it is a meaningless vibration and noise. The gunshot is only a meaningful in the human world where it signifies a uniquely manmade sort of death.

For Frost, then, nature is loaded with a sublime sort of terror, a terror which one senses in the sullenness of the spider, for, while the poem does not address such bellicose realities as artillery bombardment, the sulking spider who figures so prominently in its final lines in no way contradicts this sort of devastation. Instead, the spider takes a tenor's part in a savage opera in which the bullet (that metonym of war) sings baritone. What "Range Finding" leaves us with, then, is a sense of awe at the microscopic interplay between two sorts of death.

If Frost's poem describes war in the microscopic, James Dickey's "Firebombing" (1966) describes it with no less awe in the macroscopic:

> —when those on earth
> Die, there is not even sound;
> One is cool and enthralled in the cockpit,
> Turned blue by the power of beauty,
> In the pale treasure-hole of soft light
> Deep in aesthetic contemplation,
> Seeing the ponds catch fire
> And cast it through ring after ring
> Of land: O death in the middle
> Of acres of inch-deep water! (17)

This passage from "Firebombing" calls our attention to the way in which new weapons give rise to new themes in war poetry. The awe that Dickey's bombardier-speaker expresses about the mass destruction he sees occurring below him would be inconceivable before the advent of high-altitude strategic bombing. Experienced on the ground, the speaker's fire bombs would be devastating, and one could not conceive of using a word such as 'pastoral' to describe their effects. Seen from the speaker's vantage point, however, the fire bombs fabricate an entirely new landscape, one which, if it does not include the symbols of the traditional pastoral, at least gives rise to a new sort of bucolic: the landscape of aesthetic terror.

To contemplate this landscape as the speaker does may be said to reinvigorate the pastoral elegy not in the sense of breathing new life into age-old floral conceits, but in the sense of portraying the deaths of "those on earth" as becoming part of "the power of beauty." Such a transformation renews Ovid's idea of 'bodies changing.' In fact, so potent is the sort of metamorphosis that Dickey describes that his own term "aesthetic contemplation" seems a feeble one, for the idea of aesthetic contemplation calls to mind the careful judgments of the discerning connoisseur— one whose realm of investigation is that of the beautiful. But what the speaker sees is not a manifestation of the beautiful alone, for, as Kant instructs us, the beautiful "cultivates [...] finality in the feeling of pleasure" (66). But the general sentiments that Dickey's fire bomber describes do not correspond to such cultivation. Rather, the death that Dickey's speaker regards— "cast" in the rice paddies—confronts him with the sublime, that other agent that Kant sets in opposition to the beautiful and that Edmund Burke describes as finding its source in "terror" (36). In a great many respects, a speaker such as Dickey's finds in war the terrible augmentation of the sublime as it emerges "in the middle / of acres of inch-deep water." The poem may also be said to both allude to Hardy's *The Dynamist* and to reject that its pathos, for, like Frost's speaker, Dickey's is inspired with awe.

The amoral attitudes of Frost's and Dickey's speakers preclude, of course, one of the principal themes of war poetry: that of loss. However, loss has been a major theme of American war poems, and, beginning with Walt Whitman's *Drum-Taps*, the pastoral has figured prominently in the descriptions of it. Best known for "When Lilacs Last in the Dooryard Bloom'd," the post-war section of *Leaves of Grass* does not shy away from incorporating nature into its description of war. Certainly, the lush floral imagery of "Lilacs" makes Whitman's elegy for President Lincoln one of finest examples of the pastoral in American letters. The poem is also another example of the integration of the pastoral and the bellicose. In the poem's 1892 version, at least, "Lilacs" connects its descriptions of combat with its descriptions of the "death carol" of the "gray-brown bird," described in the poem's fourteenth section. The song of the bird anticipates the panoramic descriptions of battle that are described in the fifteenth section. Thus, the bird sings the "carol of death" as an introduction to the dead.

> To the tally of my soul,
> Loud and strong kept up the gray-brown bird,
> With pure deliberate notes spreading filling the night.
>
> Loud in the pines and cedars dim,
> Clear in the freshness moist and the swamp-perfume,
> And I with my comrades there in the night.
>
> While my sight that was bound in my eyes unclosed,
> As to long panoramas of visions.
>
> And I saw askant the armies,
> I saw as in noiseless dreams hundreds of battle-flags,
> Borne through the smoke of the battles and pierc'd with missiles I
>   saw them,
> And carried hither and yon through the smoke, and torn and bloody,
> And at last but a few shreds left on the staffs, (and all in silence,)
> And the staffs all splinter'd and broken.
>
> I saw battle-corpses, myriads of them,
> And the white skeletons of young men, I saw them,
> I saw the debris and debris of all the slain soldiers of the war,
> But I saw they were not as was thought,
> They themselves were fully at rest, they suffer'd not,
> The living remain'd and suffer'd, the mother suffer'd,
> And the wife and the child and the musing comrade suffer'd,
> And the armies that remain'd suffer'd. (270)

The descriptions and the ghastly consequences of battle do not figure as memories for this speaker. Instead, they are the collateral effects of the bird's song, which, in the previous section of the poem, is both celebration of death and an invocation of the muscularity of the natural world. That the song should inspire the vision that Whitman relates here calls attention to the poem's own metaphysical theme, which involves describing nature not as an ally of war, but as a "deliveress" (269), who emancipates the soul by way of war's greatest product: death. The bird's carol, then, serves as an apology for this emancipation and thus re-classifies the war dead: they are not lost, but, thanks to war itself, are returned into the cosmological engine of creation.

Whitman's optimistic portrayal, however, is not shared by other American poets, many of whom relate personal war experiences in which both death and horror figure as permanent losses. Especially since the poems written during or after the Confessionalist movement in the middle part of the twentieth century, many American war poems have come to reflect the melancholic mourning we observed in Gurney's "To His Love." This is particularly true of the poetry that comes out of the Vietnam War, a body of work which is more often than not written by actual combat veterans and which is generally steeped in deeply personal experiences. Here is a passage from Bruce Weigl's "The Song of Napalm" (1988):

> But still the branches are wire
> and thunder is the pounding mortar,
> still I close my eyes and see the girl
> running from her village, napalm
> stuck to her dress like jelly,
> her hands reaching for the no one
> who waits in waves of heat before her. (34)

Like Dickey's speaker, Weigl frames the narrative of his poem in a memory. The speaker begins with a description of the natural world of the present and then proceeds to relate how this world is constantly integrated with or even invaded by his memories of war. Thus, the poem functions in a similar way as Gurney's, and its speaker has similar motivations for invoking the pastoral tradition as Gurney's does: Nature would seem to afford him a vision of peace. However, Weigl's speaker (again like Gurney's) finds that the pastoral world is finally too frail to shelter him from the incursions of memory. This is reflected in the passage above, in which the branches of the trees the speaker has been describing become "wire" and the "thunder is the pounding of mortars." Such sudden declarations call to mind the panicky words that end Gurney's poem. Like the world of the Cotswolds whose beauty cannot 'cover' the beloved—at least not enough—the natural world that Weigl's speaker encounters only serves to reveal the memories that he seeks to escape.

However, the parallel between Gurney's "To His Love" and Weigl's "The Song of Napalm" does not extend as far as the opposition of nature and war. Weigl always writes from a decidedly American perspective of the pastoral tradition, in that, like Melville, Stevens, Frost, Dickey, and Whitman, his vision of nature is infiltrated by world of the bellicose. Lacking the celebratory aspects we encounter in Dickey's and Whitman's poems, Weigl's "Song" still engages in descriptions of a sublime instant in which conflagration of war gives rise to a terrible beauty. This beauty centers on the girl in the flames: a figure who calls to mind Nick Ut's famous photograph of a child running from a napalm strike. However, unlike Ut's photograph, which shows the child naked and burned, Weigl's description of the girl does not call attention to the horror of napalm. At least in this stanza, Weigl does not subject us to the gore of burns or the photographic exactitudes of documentary description (although these realities are depicted at the end of the poem). In the stanza quoted above at least, such descriptions would have the effect of diminishing the sublime reality that Weigl's sets out to describe. In this reality, the girl remains seemingly frozen with her arms outstretched in a way that calls to mind love's embrace. The sublime terror that the speaker describes to us is, then, is paralleled by the notion of love and youth—notions which the poem—written as an address to the speaker's lover—places in to a pastoral context by alluding to the natural world in the beginning of this stanza.

The effect of this mixture of sublime terror and pastoral love gives the poem its psychological tension. Presented as an address to the speaker's lover, "The Song" attempts to relate how war annihilates the temporal, spatial, and emotional barriers that characterize modern, adult life and its relationship with nature. The fact that the poem begins with the lines

> After the storm, after the rain stopped pounding,
> we stood in the doorway watching horses
> walk off lazily across the pasture's hill (33)

calls our attention to how—for Weigl's speaker—the pastoral functions as what Cathy Caruth would term 'a traumatic parable,' a parable in which the circumstances of a traumatic experience can only be related through a prosthetic literary narrative. Exploring literary texts by way of Freud's work on traumatic neurosis, Caruth postulates that certain experiences can only be related by way of parables, because one can only claim the lost experience of a trauma by creating a narrative structure that bears witness "in a language that is always somehow literary: a language that defies, even as it claims, our understanding" (5). Weigl's invocation of the pastoral setting with its horses and hills functions as such a parable in that these natural elements become the staging area for the return of the traumatic memory. Turning with his lover to the pasture, the speaker employs the pastoral to narrate his war experiences for her. In short, one landscape informs another. He uses what she can see in the landscape and realities of peace to inform her about the landscape and realities of war. In this way, the speaker uses the one geography to describe the other.

The important role that nature has played in the formation and description of American identity in American literature cannot be underestimated. In his seminal discussion of the historical relationships between Americans and the American landscape, Perry Miller famously describes America as "a nation that was, above all other nations, embedded in Nature" (209). It is not surprising, then, that American descriptions of war are equally embedded in nature and that, like the pervasive ambiguities that exist throughout the American pastoral tradition, these descriptions should also relate a vast array of ambiguities. If these ambiguities have found new manifestations in the American war poems of the first decade of the twenty-first century, they show a shift away from the sublime and/or traumatic descriptions of the natural world and war and instead move toward more staid and cynical descriptions.

These early twenty-first-century attitudes are best expressed in a recent collection of war poems: Brian Turner's *Here, Bullet* (2005), which features Turner's poem, "Eulogy", an elegy written *in memoriam* one of Turner's fellow soldiers, Private First Class B. Miller.

> It happens on a
> Monday, at 11:20
> A.M.,
>
> as tower guards eat
> sandwiches
>
> and seagulls drift by
> on the Tigris River.
>
> Prisoners tilt their
> heads to the west
>
> though burlap sacks
> and duct tape blind
> them.
>
> The sound
> reverberates down
> concertina coils
>
> the way piano wire
> thrums when given
> slack.
>
> And it happens like this,
> on a blue day of
> sun,
>
> when Private Miller
> pulls the trigger
>
> to take brass and fire
> into his mouth:
>
> the sound lifts the
> birds up off the water,
>
> a mongoose pauses
> under the orange
> trees,
>
> and nothing can stop
> it now, no matter what
>
> blur of motion
> surrounds him, no
> matter what voices

           crackle over the radio
           in static confusion,

           because if only for
           this moment the earth
           is stilled,

           and Private Miller has
           found what low hush
           there is

           down in the
           eucalyptus shade,
           there by the river. (31-33)

The overall tone of this poem is one of a summary. Absent are the dramatic tensions that one finds in earlier poetic descriptions of war. Even Stevens's generalizations and Frost's matter-of-factness convey greater levels of dramatic tension than this poem. In place of such tension, Turner's speaker relates the events that surround Private Miller's death with a torpid poignancy. Consider, for example, the poem's first stanza: "It happens on a / Monday, at 11:20 / A.M." This statement does more to lay bare the commonplace nature of death than to describe a particular instant of it. While the day and time are specified, the use of the simple present tense calls our attention to the regularity of deaths such as Private Miller's.

One of the factors that supports Turner's approach is his obvious awareness of his reader's familiarity with the wars in Iraq and Afghanistan by way of television news. The various elements described in the first five stanzas of the poem include objects that the average viewer of CNN would know only too well: "tower guards," "the Tigris River," "prisoners" blinded with "burlap sacks and duct tape." These things function more as a series of synecdoches of the reader's larger preconceptions than any attempt on the poet's part to introduce fresh material. Even the description of the Private's death seems referential: "when Private Miller / pulls the trigger / to take brass and fire / into his mouth: / the sound lifts the / birds up off the water." The line break between "fire" and "into his mouth" is the only place where the poem thwarts our general expectations, in that it gestures toward to sudden convulsions of combat and/or the moment of suicide. Here is a place of turmoil in the poem. It is a place of ambiguity. However, even this ambiguity is not unique to the reader's preconceptions of these conflicts, as the suddenness of death in Iraq and Afghanistan (either at the hands of enemy combatants or by suicide) has come to be understood as another element of the commonplace. As NBC News correspondent Jim Miklaszewski reports in an article from July 2010, in 2009 alone, 386 American soldiers, marines, sailors and members of the air force took their lives either while stationed abroad or on leave from Iraq or Afghanistan in the United States (Miklaszewski).

What Turner's poem relates, then, is the psychological consequences of stalemate and occupation, such as these conditions have given rise to the kind of death that the poem describes. Out of the blankness of routine comes a moment of violence, a moment that, like any other ambush, recedes as soon as death occurs.

The role that nature plays in this constellation of boredom, frustration, and death is one that parallels the role it plays in Melville's "Scout": death comes suddenly out of the dullness of the desert landscape. That the Private's death might have been at his own hand does not change this relationship. Instead, it allows us to understand the way this landscape and its routines have become integrated into the psychology of both the speaker and the Private. The "fire" that the Private takes "into his mouth" may be said to be the result of an ambush from *within*. Suicide (if we can conclude that this is what Turner's speaker describes) speaks like Mosby from the undergrowth of thought, and thus the mind of the Private corresponds to the landscape in which he finds himself, for, as the poem suggests, death does not begin with "giving fire," but with a "sound" that "reverberates," lifting "the birds / up off of water" and that causes "a mongoose" to "pause." What this sound is is not clear. Certainly, like the "fire" "spoken" by Mosby's raiders, the sound signals the death of the Private, but nothing more is specified. The relative vagueness of the sound, however, does not delimit its greater meaning in the natural world. In fact, the natural world would seem to define the sound, giving it exactness even. The actions of the animals are done in the response to it. The flight of the birds and the pause of the mongoose—these are nature's registration of the death.

In this poem, nature performs a series of symbolic gestures. In fact, it becomes a vast pantomime for the Private's death. In psychological terms, one could describe this pantomime as a displacement: Turner's speaker does not approach the subject of the Private's death directly; instead, he projects this death upon the natural world, characterizing it by way of a series of symbolic gestures: the flight of the birds, the shadow of the eucalyptus, etc. Thus, his poem may be described as another kind of traumatic parable, in which nature is invoked in order to relate about combat that which cannot be related. But even more than functioning as such a parable, "Eulogy" would seem to return to the notions expressed in "Range Finding," in that the sound that causes the death negotiates a place for itself in the natural world.

What is curious about Turner's poem, however, is that it reinstates the opposition between war and nature, if only in the way the sound that brings the death contrasts with the "low hush" that the Private finds in death. This hush corresponds to peace the traditional elegist seeks to assign to the dead. As the poem relates, the hush might even be said to correspond to the essential state of things: the standard condition of *this* war, for as the speaker relates, the hush is something that comes before and after the sound, and thus it is a constant in this drab world of the tower guards. The sound of death is an eruption, then, into the middle of this hush.

However, if Turner reinstates the opposition between war and the pastoral in this way, he does so in a manner that radically redefines war, at least as it was described by the other poets dealt with in this essay. From the Trojan assault on the Grecian ships to the all-consuming fire of napalm, in these other poems war is presented as state of affairs equally balanced with the state of peace. In Homer, this balance is further illustrated by the depictions on the Shield of Achilles, in which a city at war and a city at peace are contrasted and found to be equal. In Weigl, a similar contrast occurs; the peaceful night in which the speaker addresses his lover is juxtaposed with the day on which he witnessed the napalm strike. But in Turner's poem, the suggestion is that what happens in war consists of isolated acts of violence that are both preceded by and proceed from lengthy periods of dull calm. This depiction of war blurs the distinction between war and peace, and this blurred distinction is carried into Turner's version of the pastoral elegy, which symbolically manifests itself in the shadows of the eucalyptus. Thus, in the reality of the tower guards, war happens in an instant and then it is erased by the tense peace that saturates all with its long hush until war's instant return. When we consider the possibility of the Private's suicide, this relationship between peace and war, of course, suggests that it is peace that brings death—the psychology of clinical depression and Post-Traumatic Stress Disorder is the element of war that materializes in peace and that resolves itself by creating a war-like event: the violent destruction of the self.

In any event, "Eulogy" entails a return to the pastoral tradition that Gurney describes in his poem. The peace of the Cotswolds with the river and its little boat are revisited in the shade of a eucalyptus. One might even go so far as to claim that Turner's speaker achieves the state of peace that Gurney's does not, for he allows the Private to lie covered by the tree's shadow. At the very least, whether the Private died by his own hand or not, his body does not evoke the same ghastly transfiguration of the speaker's memory as the body of Gurney's beloved.

However, if Turner's poem reinvests itself in the traditional pastoral, it equally shares with the other American War poems a vision of the pastoral in which nature has become either an enemy combatant or a profiteer in death. Earlier, I argued that the reason why the pastoral has changed sides in this way can be fruitfully connected to Leo Marx's observation that the American pastoral is a literary site in which the American consciousness must negotiate the tranquility afforded it by nature and modern industrial realities. However, to delimit the relationship to this rivalry between pastoral nature and the machine alone ignores the degree to which the realities and concepts of the wilderness have figured as subjects of American literature. In short, understanding and appreciating American attitudes toward the wilderness (not the pastoral) may afford us an understanding of American attitudes toward war.

III.

The traditional European pastoral has always been constructed by way of a spectrum of sorts. This spectrum runs from the city to the wilderness, allotting the realms of the pastoral a place between these extremes. As Marx relates, Virgil's "ideal pasture has two vulnerable borders: one separates it from Rome, the other from the encroaching marshland. It is a place where Tityrus is spared the deprivations and anxieties associated with both the city and the wilderness" (22). As the pastoral tradition developed in Europe, one of these borders became increasingly distant. Century after century, the encroaching marshlands of Europe have been transformed from a reality of wilderness into a mere idea. While a similar transformation is occurring in North America, the vastness of its territory and the powerful myths that reconstruct this vastness in the American imagination keep the border of the marshlands (i.e., the wilderness) closer. One might even argue that in the North American consciousness, Virgil's ideal pasture has never existed in any real sense. Instead, the pastoral manifests itself as an unstable admixture of civilization and wildness. Thus, as a term or ideal, the pastoral comes to the American continent enfeebled, a part of those European aspirations that originally set out to tame the American wilderness. However, the possibility of such a taming is limited by the fact that the American experience, rather than rejecting the wilderness, has turned toward it both as a source of identity and as a recognition of threat.

Certainly, this American attitude is what the poet and naturalist Gary Snyder means when he writes: "The depths of mind, the unconscious, are our inner wilderness areas, and that is where the bobcat is *right now*. I do not mean personal bobcats in personal psyches, but the bobcat that roams from dream to dream" (16). Although Snyder would here address an overall human consciousness, not a uniquely American one, his notion of a universal bobcat—an untamed and untamable animal that prowls not one but any number of unconscious minds—is a decidedly American notion of the mind, if only because the metaphor that facilitates it takes the form of a decidedly American animal: The bobcat is indigenous to the western United States. By placing this animal into the unconscious of all men, Snyder (an American) effectively transforms the Sierra Nevada Mountains of California into universal unconsciousness: in this way, America becomes the human mind. If this notion is problematic in a general sense, it at least facilitates the understanding that, in an American sense, the spectrum between the city and the wilderness may not include a pastoral space, for the city neighbors the marshland from which the bobcat may be said to come. Accepting this reality may mean accepting the idea that the American pastoral poem amounts to a problematic idyll: a text that invokes an ideal landscape only to find it at odds with the men and women who occupy it. The war poems addressed in this essay uphold a similar suggestion, as each, in its own way, invokes the pastoral tradition, but also denies the facile peace of the pastoral world. Instead they hail nature as a force in which no satisfaction can be achieved without taking fire from the bucolic.

Works Cited

Burke, Edmund. *A Philosophical Enquiry into the Origin of Our Ideas of the Sublime and Beautiful*. 1757. Oxford: Oxford UP, 2009. Print.

Caruth, Cathy. *Unclaimed Experience: Trauma, Narrative, and History*. Baltimore, MA: Johns Hopkins UP, 1996. Print.

Curtius, Ernst Robert. *European Literature and the Latin Middle Ages*. Translated by Willard R. Trask. Princeton, NJ: Princeton UP, 1953. Print.

Dickey, James. *Buckdancer's Choice*. Middletown, CT: Wesleyan UP, 1968. Print.

Frost, Robert. *Collected Poems*. New York: Henry Holt, 1969. Print.

Fussell, Paul. *The Great War and Modern Memory*. Oxford: Oxford UP, 1975. Print.

Gurney, Ivor. *Selected Poems*. Ed. P.J. Kavanagh. Oxford: Oxford UP, 1990. Print.
Hardy, Thomas. *The Dynasts: An Epic-Drama of the War with Napoleon*. Fairford: Echo Library, 2010. Print.
Homer. *Iliad*. Translated by Alexander Pope. London: B.L., 1719. Print.
Hughes, Robert. *American Visions: The Epic History of American Art*. London: Marvell, 1997. Print.
Kant, Emmanuel. *Critique of Critical Judgment, Part One*. 1790. Translated by James Creed Meredith. Stilwell, KS: Digireads, 2005. Print.
Lock, Charles. "The Pastoral and the Prophetic: Making an Approach to Geoffrey Hill." *Salt* 17.1 (2003): 92-115. Print.
Marx, Leo. *The Machine in the Garden: Technology and the Pastoral Ideal of America*. 1964. Oxford: Oxford UP, 1978. Print.
McCrae, John. "In Flanders Fields." *The Penguin Book of First World War Poetry*. London: Penguin, 1996. 85. Print.
Melville, Herman. *Complete Works*. Ed. Raymond W. Weaver. London: Constable, 1924. Print.
Miklaszewski, Jim. "Record Number of Army Suicides in June." NBC NEWS. com. MSN. 15 July 2010. Web. 27 Sept. 2013.
Miller, Perry. *Errand into the Wilderness*. Cambridge, MA: Belknap Press of Harvard UP, 1956. Print.
Ramazani, Jahan. *Poetry of Mourning: The Modern Elegy from Hardy to Heaney*. Chicago, IL: U of Chicago P, 1994. Print.
Snyder, Gary. *The Practice of the Wild*. San Francisco: North Point, 1990. Print.
Stevens, Wallace. *Collected Poems*. New York: Vintage, 1990. Print.
Turner, Brian. *Here, Bullet*. Farmington, ME: Alice James, 2005. Print.
Virgil. *The Eclogues, The Georgics*. 1966. Translated by C. Day Lewis. Oxford: Oxford UP,1983. Print.
Weigl, Bruce. *The Song of Napalm*. New York: Atlantic Monthly, 1988. Print.
Whitman, Walt. *Leaves of Grass*. 1892. New York: Bantam, 1983. Print.

Nature's Nation on the Screen: Discursive Functions of the Natural Landscape in Early American Film[*]

DIMITRIOS LATSIS

ABSTRACT

Although several cultural historians have tried to grapple with the discursive relationship between nature and technology during the ascent of modernity in America at the turn of the nineteenth century, and the issue has even been addressed in terms of its impact on contemporaneous visual culture, this contradiction remains unanswered with respect to cinema, the artistic form *par excellence* of the period. In this paper I address the issue by examining the variety of functions that natural landscape and its celluloid incarnations served in early American cinema. By considering potent actuality and fiction films of the period between 1895-1910, as well as nineteenth-century aesthetic constructs like 'transcendence,' the sublime (both natural and technological), and nature's role in the representation of the nation, I focus on the landscape's iterations in political, cultural, and narrative contexts, as well as the part it played in expressing anxieties and 'mastery' narratives attendant to the emergent modernity. This account bears out a concrete and apt explanation of the reasons why cinema occupies a privileged position in modern technological culture that has "inherited the alchemical dreams of the past" (Bryant 105). It is in this 'alchemy' that I propose the transposition of the natural into the visually reproducible takes place.

> The photograph has this advantage: it lets nature have its way.
>
> Walt Whitman

Introduction

In the foreword to the 1979 edition of his influential work of film theory, *The World Viewed*, philosopher Stanley Cavell reflects on cinematic ontology and the rapport of the projected image with its 'natural source.' For him, one impetus in the development of the medium is "the confidence that [one's] capacity for extracting beauty from nature and from the photographic projection or displacement of nature is inexhaustible, which is of course a confidence at the same time in nature's and in film's capacity to provide it" (xiv). Cavell thus posits that a guiding principle in artistic creation through film is the latter's power to 'arrest' the immanence of nature in movement and then 'offer it up' to the spectator for the

---

[*] This article is dedicated to Iris Cahn, Scott MacDonald, Charles Musser and Tom Gunning: for initiating and sustaining the scholarly conversation on early cinematic landscapes. I wish to thank Profs Lauren Rabinovitz, Joni Kinsey, and Gigi Durham at the University of Iowa for their consistent counsel and support during the writing and revision of this piece and of the larger project to which it belongs. I am additionally grateful to the Journal's reviewers for their insightful and precise comments.

meaning-making process that ensues when the image is projected on screen. One issue, however, that has troubled cinema and its practitioners since its advent is film's capacity as an innately technological art form to convey the natural sublime in its fullness. To put it differently, how does the aesthetic experience of a landscape 'pass' through celluloid, intermittent mechanisms, and the white fabric of a projection screen? As Leo Marx stated in his famous treatise, "[the machine in the garden] is a distinctive industrial-era feature of the pastoral mode, [...] which exposes the illusory character of the retreat to nature as a way of coping with the ineluctable advance of modernity" (*Machine* 378). It is then truly surprising that cinema, the techno-artistic medium *par excellence* of the 'Age of Mechanical Reproduction,' has not received more attention in terms of its plurivalent and diachronic interface with the natural, especially during its period of emergence and increased interaction with other forms of visual culture around the turn of the twentieth century.

This paucity of relevant scholarship is all the more surprising if one considers the fact that some of the earliest observations made by specialists and laypeople of the period on the then-new invention pointed—as had Walt Whitman—precisely to this ontological bond that the *cinématographe* manifested to nature. Henri de Parville, the technical and scientific correspondent for *Les Annales Politiques et Litéraires*, was one of the earliest, if not the first, to refer to this early fascination with nature when he reported on the Lumières public demonstrations that had taken place in December of 1895: "The animated photographs are small miracles. We can make out all the details, the plumes of smoke that ascend, the sea waves that only just broke on the shore, the rustling of the leaves in the wind" (de Parville 270). This remark directly parallels one made in 1860 by the inventors of one of the many devices that anticipated the advent of cinema (in this case, the proto-bioscope) who announced that it would bring about "a complete revolution of the photographic art. [...] We will see landscapes in which the trees bow to the whims of the wind, the leaves ripple and glitter in the rays of the sun" (qtd. in Sadoul 38). Is it mere coincidence that the earliest observers of the new medium intuitively referred to natural landscapes when they wanted to describe its privileged relationship to the real? Similarly, is it without significance that one of its foremost innovators, D. W. Griffith, declared just before his death in 1948, half a century into cinematic history, that "what the motion picture lacks [today] is beauty—the beauty of the moving wind in the trees. [...] That they have forgotten entirely" (qtd. in Goodman).

Although several cultural historians and theorists have occasionally referred to these concerns and have indeed tried to grapple with the uneasy push and pull between nature and technology experienced during the ascent of modernity at the turn of the twentieth century in America, the issue has mostly been addressed in terms of its impact on contemporaneous visual culture.[1] The contradiction looms large and unanswered, however, with respect to cinema, the rapidly emerging visual narrative form of the period. It is thus important that any research into the

---

[1] Many scholars have ably addressed this particular dynamic in their work. See, for example, Nye and, of course, Marx's *The Machine in the Garden*.

use of landscape in motion pictures begin by examining the variety of functions that nature and its celluloid incarnations served in early American cinema. By looking into potent actuality and fiction samples from American filmography between 1895-1910, as well as into such nineteenth-century aesthetic constructs as transcendence, the sublime (natural and technological), and nature's historical role in the (self-)representation of the nation, the significance of landscape's iterations in political, cultural, and narrative contexts, and the part it played in expressing anxieties and 'mastery' narratives attendant to modernity becomes clear. It is thus arguable that the reasons for why cinema occupies a "privileged position in modern technological culture that has inherited the alchemical dreams of the past" are partly to be found in the 'alchemy' that takes place when the natural is transposed into the visually reproducible (Bryant 105).

The 'Dual Sublime': Origins and American Context

The first acknowledgement of the split between a natural and a technological sublime as it later came to be manifest in art can be found in the original Longinian treatise. There already, the first (or third) century scholar discerns two classes of the sublime in his theorization on grandeur (*peri hypsous*) in literature: the natural (to which he attributes the first two characteristics—conception of great thoughts and strong and inspired emotion) and one pertaining more to artifice. Longinus goes on to say that "natural greatness is the most important of all" (par. 9.1), and in the subsequent analysis he elaborates on the divide by referring to the natural sublimity of the dramatic and the exciting in *The Iliad* as compared to a "narrative" sublimity in *The Odyssey* (par. 9.13). Finally he refers to "image production" and visualization (par. 15.1) as the chief means of attaining aesthetic impact, grandeur, and energy, all necessary elements of the conceptual and sensorial elevation that the sublime entails.

Despite the fact that this foundational text cannot be said to have anticipated the emergence of visual media and current artistic practices as a field for the application of its ideas, it does address visuality (what is elsewhere called "rhetorical visualization" (par. 15.9) and its derivatives: concealment and amplification over argumentation and the narrative in the construction of the natural sublime. As Longinus notes, "Our attention is drawn from the reasoning to the enthralling effect of the imagination; and this effect on us is *natural* enough" (par. 15.11, emphasis mine); "accuracy is admired in art and grandeur in nature, impeccability in the former, erratic excellence in the latter" (par. 36.3-4).

With the revival of the sublime as an aesthetic object in the eighteenth century, the tension between categories of the sublime more aligned to the visual and those more pertinent to the locutory element also returned. Edmund Burke and other contemporaneous theorists began inquiring as to whether the sublime should be considered a fact of nature, of art (*techne* and therefore artificial), or of both. In analyzing the various ways in which the sublime can be manifest and experienced, for example, Burke states that "words seem to me to affect us in a manner very different from that in which we are affected by natural objects or by painting" (149). Here, the visual arts (and specifically painting) are identified with nature and, in the consideration of the sublime, are distinguished from the other category: that of words. Burke, of course, is defensive of words; he believes them to be generative of an equal degree of sublimity and declares poetry more dominant of the passions than painting in producing the sublime. This, however, still means that he maintains the aforementioned divide.

In his preface, Burke also posits that any excitement of the passions—on which the sublime hinges—is ultimately reliant upon nature (1-6). Such a conception of an elemental sublimity in nature that is then made manifest under various guises also occurs in Kant. According to Frances Ferguson, "Kant's treatment of the sublime [is articulated] with the production of duplicity, by finding aesthetic pleasure in nature—outside, that is, of the question of design or intention." Consequently, the sublime in nature is beyond any narrative or exposition, tropes that are assigned to it *a posteriori* in human perception: "The experience of pleasure in nature is, by definition, indifferent to your reactions" (130). If art is then to accurately convey the natural sublime, it must shun the particular, the humanly determined and expressed, shun *representation*, and engage the abstract (what Kant, as Donald Pease has pointed out, calls "confusion" [Pease 36]), that is *presentation*.

Indeed, when talking of the dynamical sublime, Kant positions empiricism (the anthropocentric approach) against transcendentalism (the nature-centric approach) and notes that the latter's implicit power to cause terror gives way to the human power to generate the idea of might in nature (cf. Budd 78-81). The progression in this dynamic model moves from an inherent, existing sublime, to one that is *interpreted*, conceded to nature, and appears after the introduction of the human point of view. Nature can thus be said to be sublime even before humans recognize it as such.

John Dennis (1657-1734), English dramatist and critic, was one of the first to recognize the resonance of the sublime in nature, seeing it in the concomitant sense of harmony and horror that stems from visually experiencing the natural world (30-39). But the first treatment of the natural sublime in the arts outside literature is arguably to be found in the work of such theorists as John Baillie, Lord Shaftesbury, and Joseph Addison. Latching onto the last part (par. 36) of Longinus's critique, in which he talks about the large rivers, the oceans, and the stars, the above-mentioned commentators established the 'great' in nature as a separate category of the aesthetic experience of it, and—crucially for Kant's conception—they separated the causative object from the experience itself. Thus, a fundamental non-unity exists between the experience of the appreciator and the aesthetic object per se. For instance, Joseph Addison speaks of a primary, experiential sublime stemming from nature and a secondary one that is summoned up indirectly through the work of art—to which category he also includes the sublime derived from "words" (cf. Walzer 66). Baillie would similarly say of landscape painting that "it may likewise partake of the sublime, representing Mountains; it can fill the Mind with nearly as great an Idea as the Mountain itself, inciting the Passions" (99). Arthur Schopenhauer also associates the highest three of his six degrees of beauty with the sublime in nature (202-03).

Observations like these anticipate pictorial treatments of the sublime scenery, ranging from the English Romantics such as James Ward's *Gordale Scar* (1812) to the expansive vistas of early film Westerns that Gilles Deleuze would classify under his category of 'image perception.' In such films the director can be seen as playing a game with nature through photography, as if trying to exorcise the apparatus and capture the being-there-ness of nature in its purity. These films suggest the notion of grandness in the commonplace, an everyday sublime that—in view of our explosive technological civilization and the awesomeness of the machine—might seem dated, a relic of the Enlightenment. Nonetheless, by looking to the nineteenth century and the sublime in American pastoral poetry and art, the existence of just such an outlook is confirmed; Walt Whitman's work is most enlightening in this respect.

The sublime in an American context has most often been associated with the outdoors and the gradually escalating dichotomy between nature, land, and wildlife on one hand, and the city, the machine, and technology on the other.[2] One of the most famous stanzas in Whitman's poetry attests to this interplay:

> I believe that a leaf of grass is no less than the journey-work of the stars [...]
> And the pismire is equally perfect, and a grain of sand
> And the narrowest hinge in my hand puts to scorn all machinery
> (55)

When E.M. Forster quoted these lines in *The Longest Journey* (1907) he emphasized Whitman's glorification of the commonplace by adding: "Ordinary people! Why, they're divine! They're forces of nature" (237-38). From Ralph Waldo Emerson onward, American artists in all forms would try to negotiate a twofold sublime: the transcendence in nature and the overwhelming power of an advancing technological civilization. Eminent examples of this can be found in Whitman's description of the power of steam locomotives ("To a Locomotive in Winter," 1876) and in Edward Weston's transition from the photographic sublime of the New Mexico desert to the grandeur of early industrial architecture. This latter "technological sublime," as Leo Marx first described it ("Machine" 27-42), has been associated by many with a narrative structure that contrasts with the abstractness and existential questioning that characterizes the natural/pictorial sublime. David Nye further specifies that "the historical narrative that was emerging with the technological sublime [was one leading] from discovery to conquest, the explorer giving way to the engineer" (83). The sublime allure of the machine in the American subconscious has always been tied to the narrative of empire and the narrative of the pioneer, as paintings by Thomas Cole (*The Course of Empire*, 1833-36) and Asher B. Durand (*Progress*, 1853) also attest.

With this ever-present duality, the advent of cinema has, since its 'attractions' phase (roughly 1895-1900) literally animated the natural sublime in light and shadows. This continuity of the cinematic sublime from earlier pictorial treatments has been acknowledged by such film scholars as Tom Gunning, who notes how early "panoramic travel films relied upon the experience of absorption in the

---

[2] On this issue see Arensberg; Nye; Den Tandt; see also the special issue of *Amerikastudien/ American Studies* 43.3 on the sublime, and the contribution by Robert Chianese in particular.

contemplation of nature," and sees them as a direct descendant of the "romantic sublime landscape painting which pictures nature as a sublime force" ("World" 32). Sergei Eisenstein himself spoke of landscape as "the freest element of film, the least burdened with servile, narrative tasks and the most flexible in conveying moods, emotional states and spiritual experiences" (217), all three of which are characteristic of the affective dimension of the natural sublime. To better understand how the natural/technological split in the sublime was carried forward into the new century through the intermediary of cinema, the above statements should be considered in tandem with the first narrative films (or 'story films' as they were called early on) such as the pioneering *Great Train Robbery* (1903), which summoned up images of Whitman's technological sublime of the railway, and the science fictions of Georges Méliès and his fascination with space travel, which Sean Cubitt sees as "pointing the sublime towards a post-modern time" (68).

Early Cinematic Landscapes: A Preliminary Taxonomy

For all landscape's importance as a discursive 'tool' within the nascent art's representational strategies, there can be no claim for its predominance over other, equally important cultural and aesthetic factors, such as spectacle, traffic, the machine, and motion.[3] Rather, what does emerge is that a plethora of early 'genres' (travel films, film panoramas, early Westerns, etc.) used nature as a dialectic focus, thus revealing some of the aesthetic nuances that a simple history of apparati, techniques, and filmmakers usually obscures. In this way, the argumentation of Jonathan Auerbach's body-driven paradigm, Lynne Kirby's spotlight on the railroad, and Livio Belloï's attention to 'looks' and visual relations can all serve as strong methodological antecedents.

Historians and commentators have repeatedly claimed that the preponderance of 'nature views,' 'landscape panoramas,' and 'natural attractions' (as they have variously been called) in early cinema can be seen as an attempt by the filmmakers to tap into a public yearning for the country's sublime natural heritage and the notion of 'the virginal land.'[4] A semiotic tension that arises in this context revolves around the presumed 'authenticity' with which the landscape is presented for the audience's contemplation, as Nanna Verhoeff has detected (188). This tension points back to the very debates waged around issues of ontology and the index that are foundational for film theory.

Indeed, it is particularly worth noting that theoreticians of cinematic realism—André Bazin chief among them—made frequent recourse to landscape as a picto-

---

[3] For insightful explorations of these aesthetic concepts in early film, see Rabinovitz, *For the Love*; Whissel; Rydel.

[4] See, in particular, Cahn, who also includes a very useful filmographic appendix; Verhoeff 188; Natali 81; Brunel; Mottet (Part I); Macdonald; Griffiths 41-42 and 66-67; Manthorne 55-60; Matthews 39-54. It must be said that the relative paucity of literature on the subject remains pronounced, despite the growing bibliography on the aesthetics of early cinema. Indeed, a lot of the most potent critical examinations of landscape in early American film have been thus far published by French cinema theorists and historians, as the list above testifies.

rial trope when referring to the grounding of the photographic in real life. In his discussion of neorealism, for instance, Bazin repeatedly refers to Italian landscape and the way it 'converses' with or 'corresponds' to the inner landscape of characters: "Every shot brings out one of the basic characteristics of this landscape. It is *the exact equivalent*, under *conditions imposed by the screen*, of the inner feeling men experience who are living between the sky and the water and whose lives are at the mercy of an infinitesimal shift of angle in relation to the horizon" (2: 37; emphasis mine). Similarly, in the case of American cinema, the mediated experience of the countryside has—since its earliest days—almost always been inextricably bound to an inner affective 'landscape' of nostalgia (a lost West; a simpler rural lifestyle, etc.), often a nostalgia for something that never actually existed. Such films continue and transpose into cinema the creative tactics of older media: the Great Pictures tradition in American art; the panorama format; the general aesthetics of the idyllic, pastoral, and sublime within public aesthetic consciousness; and as a distinctly American set of representational politics (cf. Griffiths 41-42; 66-67). As useful and important as these connections with other forms of visual culture of the same time might be, paying closer attention to the films and the context in which they were produced can offer more insight into cinema's multi-layered significatory process in its portrayal of nature.

One of the "films that featured the natural attractions of America [and] was routinely included in early film programs" was Biograph's 1902 travelogue *Down the Hudson* (Cahn 86).[5] The film is an ideal encapsulation of the changing aesthetic attitudes to the portrayal of 'the natural.' Rather than a still, serene, and awe-inspiring nature offered for the viewer's meditation, the film consciously approximates "a visually spectacular amusement park ride" (Macdonald 59) with the various angles and curves going in and out of coves and inlets, all shot from the deck of the boat. Gone is the sublime transcendence in color of Frederic Edwin Church and the Hudson River School's monumental paintings of that river and its shores. Instead, our ride along the water here approximates the time-lapse aesthetics of modern photography, and the spectator's perception of wooded banks and rocky slopes is filtered through multiple technological means: the boat that carries the camera and provides us with a continuously shifting viewpoint (much like the train did for a large number of other travel films); the locomotive forging through the shrubbery on the opposite shore; and finally, the city in which we arrive at the end and whose urban articulation refutes any hint of the natural that we have just experienced. Given the subtlety of these representational tactics, instead of hastily labeling films like *Down the Hudson* as instances of either a natural or a technological sublime, it would be preferable to regard them as early cinema's iterations of the hybrid schema of the "machine in the garden" that Leo Marx put forth as characteristic of this turn-of-the-century time span, an era that also contains the dawn of the motion picture.

---

[5] The film was copyrighted on October 6, 1903. According to the promotional description in the Edison catalogue, the "film was photographed from the deck of a boat that, indicated by the many changes of angle, was steering in and out of coves, inlets, etc. while journeying down the Hudson River. Many means of transportation are shown: paddle wheels, sailing vessels, steamers, and so on" (Niver and Bergsten 133).

Beyond the rise of modern tourism—the aesthetic reverberations of which have been pointed out by Jonathan Culler (164)—and beyond narratives of traffic in modernity as envisioned by Kristen Whissel, the speeding, viewing cruise captured in this visual ride fits well with a discourse of display and mastery. In order to assuage the rising anxieties of modernity (of either a technical or temporal nature), in *Down the Hudson*, technology and man-made incursions into the landscape (railway, quarries, housing) are rendered into a narrative of newly found mobility, mastery over natural forces, elimination of time in travel, and an impulse to contain, engulf, and regulate the landscape for the purposes of experience.[6] "Was the moving camera" in this juxtaposition or admixture of landscape and technology, Katherine Manthorne asks, "meant to be pressed into fulfilling the same service the Hudson painters had once performed [...] and if not, how were cameramen to redefine their role?" (57). Nature is not rendered as picturesque or ideal in the films, but rather as inducing sea-sickness and dizziness; it is a spatial obstacle of 'wilderness' to be overcome by technical intervention.[7] The painterly stillness of earlier representations has been replaced by frantic motion in this cinematic *perpetuum mobile*.

A lineage that can be traced for the progressive technological transformations of the natural, as portrayed in early cinema and the increasing interaction of the natural and the technological sublime on-screen, runs from the 'postcard-like' single shots of landscapes early on—usually waterfalls (Niagara in particular), mountains (often the Catskills), or waterways (the Hudson is an overused theme)—to proto-narratives where the man/machine duo 'cuts through' the landscape and makes its presence felt. Starting with the quaint *Waterfall in the Catskills* (1897), *Falls of Minnehaha* (1897), *Panoramic View of Niagara Falls* (1899), and *White Horse Rapids* (1900), early filmmakers of 'natural views' (Billy Bitzer, F.S. Armitage, and Robert Bonine prominent among them)[8] gradually transitioned to one-reel stories in which the natural is incorporated within a developing diegetic framework. These films include *Captain Nissen Going Through Whirlpool Rapids* (1901), *Trappers Crossing Bald Mountain* (1903), *Driving Cattle to Pasture* (1904), and, finally, more fully fleshed narratives (and early Westerns) such as *In the Haunts of Rip Van Winkle* (1906) and *A Round-up in Oklahoma* (1908). A tentative correlation that emerges is that a waning sublimity gives way to an increasingly anthropocentric technological sophistication. Thus it can be said that, in early films, the degree of contemplative spectatorship of the 'pastoral' in nature is inversely proportional to developments in transportation and photography, etc., that made pos-

---

[6] F.S. Armitage, the cameraman of the film (along with A.E. Weed), had used a time-lapse-like, time-condensing tactic before, taking single frames in four-minute intervals during the demolition of a building in Manhattan. The technique was meant to convey a sense of temporal disjunction and an "illusion of abruptness" in the image (Deutelbaum 45), thereby adopting a characteristically modern attitude toward the artistic rendering of temporality.

[7] On the discourse of wilderness within early film aesthetics, see chapters one and two in Mitman, and part three in Brownlow.

[8] See the entries in Niver and Bergsten for information on landscape and phantom ride films mentioned in this article.

sible a quasi-narrative depiction of 'the scenic' during early American cinema's period of transition to narratives.[9]

While actuality views and travelogues continued to be made and incorporated within the nickelodeon variety programs,[10] Iris Cahn argues that "the appeal of the landscape actuality film was short-lived, over-shadowed by the rise of the story film in the early 1900s" (86). Charles Musser nuances Cahn's position by arguing that the travel genre after 1903 was not eliminated due to the rise of story films, but rather played an important role in the move toward fictional narratives ("Travel Genre" 47-60). An effective case in point, in this respect, is certainly *The Hold-Up of the Rocky Mountain Express* (1906).[11] Shot as "a narrative example of a Hale's Tour" (Rabinovitz, "Bells" 176), it emphasizes the display of and movement through the landscape with a chase scene filmed from the front of the train, which additionally exemplifies the positioning of landscape "as an interstice to filmic narration, fragile and receding" (Natali 146; translation mine).[12]

In *Hold-Up* nature is framed both literally (the camera is fixed on the front of the train's engine car, providing a point-of-view shot) and metaphorically (the narrative is contained within scenes of the titular hold-up as well as shots within the train's interior and the passengers' abandonment on the rails at the end). Technology and storyline constantly condition our perception of the scenery, giving nature over to narrative 'consumption': the passing countryside comes to a halt to give way to the robbery and to the ubiquitous rails and bridges that reflexively point to the linearity of the voyage, recalling the progression of celluloid through a projector. Despite the persistent oscillation of the *fabula* "between a sometimes rather flimsy pretext of the fictionality as attraction and [...] a non-fictional genre" (Verhoeff 258), the film can easily be viewed as contributing to the tendency by means of which, as Verhoeff argues, "landscape is engineered [into] narration" (203-04).

The succession of 'phantom ride' vistas of landscape by the simplistic diegesis (one already bearing the marks of future Westerns) marks a mutual fragmentation. Nature is interspersed with the human, but the narrative is also 'invaded' by the natural, as for example when the bandits emerge from the hillside to surprise the train conductor or when the narrative assumes a 'dual' track, following the

---

[9] For more on the proto-narrative treatment of landscape during this transition, see Bowser, *Transformation* 150, 162; and Keil 131-32. Maurizia Natali also refers to this matter (86-87).

[10] For instance, Siegmund Lubin's *Glimpses of Yellowstone Park* (1909) and William Selig's *A Trip to Yosemite* (1909) can be seen as picturesque promotions of the burgeoning National Park Service.

[11] The film was copyrighted on April 12, 1906. The Edison catalogue summary runs: "The storyline is built around the mock hold-up of a train. The film ends as the bandits or train robbers are capture at a railroad crossing. Building up to the capture is a chase filmed from the front of the train following the four-wheeled pump car the fleeing train robbers are using. But, preceding the train hold-up is a scene filmed in a constructed set of the interior of a railroad car. There is a comedy sequence involving three women and two men, a Pullman porter, and a freeloading tramp. What relationship this scene has to the hold-up is not indicated. Nevertheless, it is the transition from the beginning locale of a railroad station to the hold-up. The film was photographed in Phoenicia, New York" (Niver and Bergsten 45).

[12] See the commentary in Rabinovitz (147-54) on this film and on the function of landscape (and narrative) in 'ride films' in general.

escaping rogues on two parallel levels, that of the railroad and the adjacent pathway. As a result, the story not only "authenticates the location," but "the location also makes the story happen" in a discursive exchange that features in many such 'transition films' (Verhoeff 204).[13] In contrast to the spectacle of nature with waterfalls and majestic panoramas in early actualities that hark back to their painterly counterparts and to transcendental ideals, from this point on, landscape will primarily signify only as part of a larger context, as the locus of the action, an *entr'acte* to it, or one extreme of the urban/rural, modern/quaint opposition that became a prevalent motif of the era (for example, *A Railway Tragedy* [1904]).

The mix of generic classifications—either perceived or imposed—in *The Hold-Up of the Rocky Mountain Express* is indicative of a larger transformation at play: namely, the changing perception of nature in public discourse of the time. The film has variously been seen as "two films in one: a travel/panoramic *strictu senso* and a fiction scenario, [...] it shows an unproblematic mixture of genres" (Kirby 41); as a "comedy" featuring chase scenes (Niver and Bergsten 45); as "combining a Western theme with the violent crime genre" (Hansen 47); it was promoted as "the greatest crowd drawer," offering "action [...] comedy [...] a race [...] and an exciting finish" (Niver 45). This hybridity is telling and marks a transition from display and single-tableau micro-stories, via chase films, to more fully fleshed-out narratives or, equally, from a natural/exhibitory to a technocultural/iterative conception of sublimity, from mimesis to diegesis. This transition, I would argue, had as one of its catalysts the assortment of expressive functions that landscape served at the turn of the century.

Nature: The 'Shifting Signifier'

If indeed "the importance of [the aforementioned] list [of genres] as a ground for characterization of narrativity in the establishment of generic conventions, cannot be overestimated" (Verhoeff 227), one of the facilitating factors was surely the status of nature as a shifting signifier. From a sociocultural perspective, Wolfgang Schivelbusch (partly echoing Walter Benjamin) confirms this dynamic relation between the proto-modern public's encounter with the 'natural' and the new artistic media (including film) through which it was represented:

> [...] remote regions were made available to the masses by means of tourism: this was merely a prelude, a preparation for making any unique thing available by means of reproduction. (46)

---

[13] See, for instance, the similar role of the railway in Edison's *A Romance of the Rail* (1903), the travails of the stock character Rip Van Winkle (also amidst the Catskill landscape) in *In the Haunts of Rip Van Winkle* (1906), or the way the "pastoral myth" and a "new rural utopia" are narrativized in early D.W. Griffith melodramas like *The Country Doctor* (1909) and *The Message* (1909) (see chapter II-1 in Mottet). Verhoeff provides a fuller account of narrativizing strategies of landscape in *Hold-Up of the Rocky Mountain Express*, but largely centers around the chase "genre" (226-29). Rabinovitz also refers to a "construction of nature [...] itself in opposition to civilization" and the identification of leisure with "spatial representation of nature and with tourist travel as opposed to urban civilization" (54, 141).

This perceptual montage of spaces (city-forest; local-exotic) came progressively to be matched by its cinematographic counterpart on-screen. Additionally, a new *Naturgeschichte* ('nature narrative/narrative within nature') certainly formed part of that transformation.[14]

Outside of a narratological valence, however, the natural and its figurations in early American film never ceased to carry a national and, more generally, a political undertone. As borne out by the epigraph above by Whitman, the photographic was—and still is, within an American context—also invested with a transcendental power due to its special ontological bond with natural reality. Cinema, as the ideal new form for an even more verisimilitudinous depiction of 'Nature's Nation,' only corroborated this notion. Thus, as Perry Miller has emphasized, discourse on scenery in an American context forms part of a continuum related to the self-conception of American nationhood and its identity as 'Nature's Nation.' Such a conception of the nation is evident, he argues, not only in the way in which Whitman, Thoreau, Melville and other intellectuals and artists "present us with the problem of American self-recognition as being essentially an irreconcilable opposition between Nature and civilization" (199), but also in the more general and popularly held belief that America was "a nation that was, above all nations, *embedded* in Nature" (211; emphasis mine). This 'ideological' use of a nature 'invested' with symbolic and patriotic value is on display in the early Westerns and wildlife films made at the end of the first decade of the 1900s. In fact, these efforts at capturing and rendering the landscape in a 'distinctly American style' can be contextualized both within developments in the industry as well as within the political arena.

Richard Abel has compellingly argued that the emergence of the Western can be linked to competition against so-called 'French quality' cinema and the increasing number of films produced by Pathé with specifically American subject matter (*A Western Hero* [1909], for example). In this contest between 'national myths' and their iconography onscreen, nature certainly held a point of pride; "scenic backgrounds out of doors are usually well selected," remarked one contemporary critic when trying to describe the disparity in style between French and American fare (qtd. in Abel 108). Pathé Films's status as the 'foreign other' served as a potent counterpoint against which to construct American aesthetic difference, especially as communicated through 'picturesque landscapes' and expanses of a mythologized West in films such as *The Girl from Montana* (1907) and *The Bandit King* (1907).

Among the first to shoot Westerns in authentic locations during the general move of the industry toward the Pacific coast was D. W. Griffith, whose 1911 film, *Fighting Blood*, has been called "a little lesson in paternalism and patriotism" (Simmon 49). Here the rural scenery of the San Fernando and Sierra Madre valleys plays host to the mobilization of pioneers against the 'not so vanishing Indian,' and the rollicking hills are enveloped in a gunpowder haze in which only American flags can occasionally be discerned. What is most striking is the transi-

---

[14] For a Benjaminian analysis of nature's role in the formation of modern narratives that can be applied across media, see Leahy 73.

tion of the characters from an agrarian mode of existence to a nationalistic fervor and the way this is tied to the landscape as a locus of confrontation. A little boy hoists the banner of the 'Grand Army of the Dakota Hills' (as explained in the intertitles) and the ensuing battles fill the diegetic space of the prairies that are being fought over. Two protracted panoramic overhead shots toward the end further emphasize the dichotomy between the disturbance of war and the surrounding scenery, which dwarfs everything. In this vein, a binary is also constructed between interiors—reserved for victims who are being attacked by the villainous natives—and exteriors where "husbands or lawmen race to the rescue within a natural landscape" (Cohen 85). The bucolic pastures become battle-fields for staging the superiority of both American military prowess and the patriots fighting for their manifest destiny.

To better grasp the strong confluence between the representational 'currency' of a virginal West with the developing jingoism of so-called 'properly American genres' within early cinema, it pays to consider contemporary politics and their relevance for visual culture. Scott Simmon has gestured to an association between Griffith's 'Plains Wars' narratives and the 'strenuous life' narrative most prominently propounded by Theodore Roosevelt (49). The figure of President Roosevelt as a national icon runs across a number of films from this period, jointly evoking both the national and the natural. The first adaptation of Jack London's *The Call of the Wild* made by Griffith in 1908 was "intimately connected to a back-to-nature movement in full force during Roosevelt's presidential years," and the documentary of his African safari, *Roosevelt in Africa* (1910) spawned a number of similar pre-World War I films in the years that can be said to have inaugurated America's 'romance' with wildlife in cinema.[15] In staging this travelogue for Selig in a California game preserve, the director, Cherry Kearton, effected a synergy of significations between the leader's persona, the figurative strength of untainted nature, and a narrative of conquest located squarely within the image-making strategies of its time. While acknowledging the undeniable tendency of natural narratives of the period to exoticize the 'other' (be they Native Americans, Africans, or countryside 'rubes'), a sociological approach of this kind is outside the scope of the present account. It is be more fruitful to ponder the political reverberations of Rooseveltian naturalism and its celluloid manifestations using a case in which the 'other' is not human, but rather a family of anthropomorphized stuffed animals.

Edwin S. Porter's *Teddy Bears* (1907) has often been analyzed in terms of its grim and unusual twist on a familiar fairytale ("Goldilocks and the Three Bears"), its mix of techniques (like stop motion animation with live action against painted backdrops), and its position at the nexus between display and an emergent form of cinematic storytelling.[16] However, the dialectic of spaces, the depiction of 'wilderness,' and the centrality of the hunter/Teddy Roosevelt character is just as

---

[15] Greg Mittman has drawn this parallel in considering actualities and early natural history films in *Reel Nature: America's Romance with Wildlife on Films*, 5-20. See also Brownlow 405-06.

[16] See Bowser 184-87, and in particular his assertion about the narrative progression as it relates to the setting (186); Musser, *Before* 349-51.

vital within the historical backdrop described above. To substantiate these claims, nature and landscape must serve here as the operative semiotic parameters.

The crucial shift within the film is the move from sets that represent the bears' home (where the majority of Goldilock's adventure takes place), to painted studio backdrops representing the surrounding forest, and finally to the authentic exterior locations at the end when the protracted chase through the snow begins. There seems to be a correlation between this move and the degree of mobility in the film as well as the departure from the familiar children's story into a proto-narrative in its own right. Of course, the final scene contains a further implicit reference to an already well-known tale, but this time it is a true one, with curious sociopolitical echoes. It is the anecdote of Roosevelt 'the hunter,' whose sparing of a little bear during an expedition captured America's imagination, sparked a craze for the eponymous stuffed toys (named after the president), and a 'return to nature' aesthetic in general. That this episode is encapsulated here in a pursuit through the wooded forest in the only truly out-of-doors, four-shot sequence of the film is revealing for the iconographic treatment of nature in Progressive Era American Art and for Roosevelt's public persona as an outdoorsman.[17]

Charles Musser points out that in a deviation from his usual tactics, the director Porter (for whom the film was one of his favorites) in *Teddy Bears* gestures toward a (still nascent) mimetic realism that, even though never realized, appears in a pre-Griffith guise in the landscape shots filmed in a city park (*Before* 351). Given the growing importance of 'realism' for the increasingly sophisticated spectators,[18] familiar and natural locales played a crucial role in the staging of these micro-narratives. According to Miriam Hansen, "*The Teddy Bears* takes part in this general tendency, both in its shift from artificial to natural settings, and in the way it associates them with competing modes of engaging the viewer" (55). Far from being a simplistic adaptation of a children's story, the film negotiates a complex balance between domesticity and the public sphere, fiction and realism, *techne* (guns, manufactured toys) and nature (animals, forest), violence and humanism, and between naiveté and political image-building, a balance that is often contingent on definitions of the natural and its dialectical relation to progress. Most of all, the growing emphasis on realism (on which Hansen so pointedly focuses) is revealed, by films like *The Teddy Bears*, to have been at least partially reliant upon the changing modes of making sense of and relating to 'the natural.'

Conclusion

What this summary account has revealed about cinema's first two decades—a time when landscape provided the analytical compass—is a complex picture of the stylistic and semantic factors that typified the new medium's fascinating rap-

---

[17] Brian Black has expanded on the function of nature in Roosevelt-era society and art, linking it—importantly in this context—to the push for the promotion of the burgeoning National Park system of which the president was a major proponent (27-42).

[18] A coded and perceived realism, to be sure (see Bowser, "Movies" 186-87).

port with nature, a rapport that is useful for analyzing the process of its evolution. Whether in denoting anxieties about technological modernity through narratives of mastery and mobility, providing a framing context for the emergence of narrative, serving political and societal ends, bringing concerns about ontology and realism in cinema to the fore, or linking up intertextually to representational tactics in turn-of-the-century visual culture, nature provides a strong vantage point from which to survey early American film. However, it should always be viewed within a larger matrix of related concerns (body, motion, history, society, spectacle), instead of being set apart as a specialized aesthetic niche. These interconnections become more apparent still when 'navigating' larger expanses of the (metaphoric) landscape of films that is not covered here: travelogues, illustrated lectures incorporating natural subjects, 'scenics,' and panoramas.

Within the first few years of the twentieth century, the output of (nature) actualities and narratives began to dwindle and a technological modernity came to dominate fiction films shot out of doors, many of which (just like the first studios) were now set in cities. Despite the common claim that "interest in nature [...] quickly moved into the background as film itself industrialized and developed increasingly popular narrative forms" (Macdonald 60), it does not seem to be the case that a total obliteration of landscape was necessarily tied to the development of a medium that eventually outgrew it. Rather, nature and its thematization in American moving image art 'survived'[19] through the appearance of the Western, through early Griffith melodramas made in a pastoral vein (see Mottet) and in various other films, albeit under different guises and serving different functions (for example, contrasting nature with a more complicated and advanced urban milieu). As Tom Gunning has recently asserted, "films presenting landscape 'views' formed a major genre of early cinema, gradually transforming into the travelogues of the classical cinema programme, lasting until the end of the studio system" ("Landscape" 52).

In any case, conceptualizing such a continuum is more helpful for a critical approach that wishes to relate the development of technocultural themes with the corresponding changes in the discursive uses of 'the natural.' Nature remained an important aesthetic and topical focus for cinema—at least as relevant as the city and the machine—and the interaction of the technological and the natural sublime extended well beyond this early period to films such as Pare Lorentz's WPA documentaries, Peter Hutton's experimental audiovisual 'portraits,' and Terrence Malick's narrative features *cum* nature poems, to name the works of but three artists who can be seen as prolonging and continuously reshaping this tradition. It is through the 'survival' and continuous reconfiguration of the natural landscape (as testified by the breadth of narrative and visual strategies in the films addressed above) that one can begin to negotiate the apparent paradox hinted at by Cavell; a paradox that perhaps no one has summarized more eloquently than Leo Marx in his theorization of the machine/garden duality as a mechanism to cope with the onset of modernity. The cinematographic apparatus can easily be envisaged

---

[19] Pierre Brunel has argued for a similar aesthetic survival of the 'idyllic' in twentieth-century literature and arts (151).

as one of these coping mechanisms, and landscape remains a dynamic and discursively rich element in the expressive palette of the seventh art.

Works Cited

Abel, Richard. *The Red Rooster Scare: Making Cinema American, 1900-1910*. Berkeley: U of California P, 1999. Print.
Arensberg, Mary. *The American Sublime*. Albany: SUNY P, 1986. Print.
Auerbach, Jonathan. *Body Shots: Early Cinema's Incarnations*. Berkeley: U of California P, 2007. Print.
Baille, John. "An Essay on the Sublime." *The Sublime: A Reader in British Eighteenth-Century Aesthetic Theory*. Ed. Andrew Ashfield and Peter De Bolla. Cambridge: Cambridge UP, 1996. 87-100. Print.
Bazin, André. *What is Cinema?* 2 vols. Berkeley: U of California P, 2004. Print.
Belloï, Livio. *Le regard retourné: Aspects du cinéma des premiers temps*. Québec: Éditions Nota Bene, 2001. Print.
Black, Brian. *Nature and the Environment in Nineteenth-Century American Life*. Westport, CT: Greenwood, 2006. Print.
Bowser, Eileen. "Movies and the Expansion of the Audience." *American Cinema 1890-1909: Themes and Variations*. Ed. André Gaudreault. New Brunswick, NJ: Rutgers UP, 2009. 179-201. Print.
---. *The Transformation of Cinema, 1907-1915*. Berkeley: U of California P, 1994. Print.
Brownlow, Kevin. *The War, the West, and the Wilderness*. New York: Knopf, 1979. Print.
Brunel, Pierre. *L'arcadie blessée: le monde de l'idylle dans la littérature et les arts de 1870 à nos jours*. Paris: Eurédit, 2005. Print.
Bryant, Daroll. "Cinema, Religion and Popular Culture." *Religion in Film*. Ed. John May and Michael Bird. Knoxville: U of Tennessee P, 1983. 101-14. Print.
Budd, Malcolm. *The Aesthetic Appreciation of Nature*. New York: Oxford UP, 2002. Print.
Burke, Edmund. *A Philosophical Enquiry into the Origins of Our Ideas of the Sublime and Beautiful*. Oxford: Oxford UP, 1998. Print.
Cahn, Iris. "The Changing Landscape of Modernity: Early Film and America's 'Great Picture' Tradition." *Wide Angle* 18.3 (1996): 85-100. Print.
Cavell, Stanley. *The World Viewed: Reflections on the Ontology of Film*. Cambridge: Harvard UP, 1979. Print.
Cohen, Paula Marantz. *Silent Film and the Triumph of the American Myth*. Oxford: Oxford UP, 2001. Print.
Cubitt, Sean. *The Cinema Effect*. Cambridge: MIT P, 2004. Print.
Culler, Jonathan D. *Framing the Sign: Criticism and its Institutions*. Norman: U of Oklahoma P, 1988. Print.
Dennis, John. "Remarks on a Book Entitled, Prince Arthur." *The Sublime: A Reader in British Eighteenth-Century Aesthetic Theory*. Ed. Andrew Ashfield and Peter De Bolla. Cambridge: Cambridge UP. 1996. 30-39. Print.

Den Tandt, Cristophe. *The Urban Sublime in American Literary Naturalism*. Urbana: U of Illinois P, 1998. Print.

Deutelbaum, Marshall. *"Image" on the Art and Evolution of the Film: Photographs and Articles from the Magazine of the International Museum of Photography*. New York: Dover, 1979. Print.

Eisenstein, Sergei. *Nonindifferent Nature*. Cambridge: Cambridge UP, 1987. Print.

Ferguson, Frances. *Solitude and Sublime: Romanticism and the Aesthetics of Individuation*. New York: Routledge, 1992. Print.

Forster, E. M. *The Longest Journey*. London: Penguin, 2006. Print.

Goodman, Ezra. "Flashback to Griffith." 1948. *The Fifty-Year Decline and Fall of Hollywood*. New York: Simon, 1961. 18. Print.

Gunning, Tom. "Landscape and the Fantasy of Moving Pictures: Early Cinema's Phantom Rides." *Cinema and Landscape*. Ed. Graeme Harper and Jonathan Rayner. London: Intellect, 2010. 31-70. Print.

---. "The World within Reach: Travel Images without Borders." *Travel Culture: Essays on What Makes Us Go*. Ed. Carol T. Williams. Westport, CT: Praeger, 1998. 24-36. Print.

Griffiths, Alison. *Shivers Down your Spine: Cinema, Museums, and the Immersive View*. New York: Columbia UP, 2008. Print.

Hansen, Miriam. *Babel and Babylon: Spectatorship in American Silent Film*. Cambridge, MA: Harvard UP, 1991. Print.

Keil, Charlie. *Early American Cinema in Transition: Story, Style, and Filmmaking, 1907-1913*. Madison: U of Wisconsin P, 2001. Print.

Kirby, Lynne. *Parallel Tracks: The Railroad and Silent Cinema*. Durham, NC: Duke UP, 1997. Print.

Leahy, Caitríona. *Der wahre Historiker: Ingeborg Bachmann and the Problem of Witnessing History*. Würzburg: Königshausen & Neumann. 2007. Print. Epistema 547.

Longinus. "On the Sublime." *Aristotle: The Poetics, "Longinus": On the Sublime, Demetrius: On Style*. Ed. T. E. Page et al. London: Heinemann, 1965. 122-256. Print.

Macdonald, Scott. "The Attractions of Nature in Early Cinema." *Unseen Cinema: Early American Avant-Garde Film 1893-1941*. Ed. Bruce Charles Posner. New York: Anthology Film Archives, 2005. 56-63. Print.

Manthorne, Katherine. "Experiencing Nature in Early Film: Dialogues with Church's Niagara and Homer's Seascapes." *Moving Pictures: American Art and Early Film, 1880-1910*. Ed. Nancy Mowll Matthews, Charles Musser, and Marta Braun. Manchester, VT: Hudson, 2005. 55-60. Print.

Marx, Leo. "The Machine in the Garden." *New England Quarterly* 29 (1956): 27-42. Print.

---. *The Machine in the Garden: Technology and the Pastoral Ideal in America*. 1964. New York: Oxford UP, 2000. Print.

Mathews, Nancy Mowll, ed. *Moving Pictures: American Art and Early Film, 1880-1910*. Manchester, VT: Hudson, 2005. Print.

Miller, Perry. *Nature's Nation*. Cambridge, MA: Belknap, 1967. Print.

Mitman, Gregg. *Reel Nature: America's Romance with Wildlife on Films*. Cambridge, MA: Harvard UP, 1999. Print.
Mohr, Hans-Ulrich, and Maria Moss, eds. *The American Sublime*. Spec. issue of *Amerikastudien / American Studies* 43.3 (1998). Print.
Mottet, Jean. *L'invention de la scène américaine: Cinéma et paysage*. Paris: L'Harmattan, 1998. Print.
Musser, Charles. *Before the Nickelodeon: Edwin S. Porter and the Edison Manufacturing Company*. Berkeley: U of California P, 1991. Print.
---. "The Travel Genre in 1903–04: Moving Toward Fictional Narratives." *Iris* 2.1 (1984): 56–57. Print.
Natali, Maurizia. *L'image-paysage: iconologie et cinéma*. Saint-Denis: UP de Vincennes, 1996. Print.
Niver, Kemp R. *Biograph Bulletins, 1896-1908*. Los Angeles: Locare, 1971. Print.
Niver, Kemp R., and Bebe Bergsten. *Motion Pictures from the Library of Congress Paper Print Collection, 1894-1912*. Berkeley: U of California P, 1967. Print.
Nye, David E. *American Technological Sublime*. Cambridge, MA: MIT P, 1996. Print.
Parville, Henri de. "Chronique." *Les Annales Politiques et Littéraires* 26 April 1896, 270. Print.
Pease, David. "Sublime Politics." *The American Sublime*. Ed. Mary Arensberg. Albany: SUNY P, 1986. 21-50. Print.
Rabinovitz, Lauren. "'Bells and Whistles': The Sound of Meaning in Train Travel Film Rides." *The Sounds of Early Cinema*. Ed. Richard Abel and Rick Altman. Bloomington: Indiana UP, 2001. 167-80. Print.
---. *For the Love of Pleasure: Women, Movies, and Culture in Turn-of-the-Century Chicago*. New Brunswick, NJ: Rutgers UP, 1998. Print.
Rydell, Robert W., and Rob Kroes. *Buffalo Bill in Bologna: The Americanization of the World, 1869-1922*. Chicago, IL: U of Chicago P, 2005. Print.
Sadoul, Georges. *Histoire générale du cinema, Vol 1: L'invention du cinéma, 1832-1897*. Paris: Denoel, 1948. Print.
Schivelbusch, Wolfgang. *The Railway Journey: The Industrialization of Time and Space in the 19th Century*. Berkeley: U of California P, 1986. Print.
Schopenhauer, Arthur. *The World as Will and Representation*. New York: Courier, 1966. Print.
Simmon, Scott. *The Invention of the Western Film: A Cultural History of the Genre's First Half-Century*. Cambridge: Cambridge UP, 2003. Print.
Verhoeff, Nanna. *The West in Early Cinema: After the Beginning*. Amsterdam: Amsterdam UP, 2006. Print.
Walzer, Arthur E. *George Campbell*. Albany: SUNY P, 2002. Print.
Whissel, Kristen. *Picturing American Modernity: Traffic, Technology, and the Silent Cinema*. Durham, NC: Duke UP, 2008. Print.
Whitman, Walt. *Leaves of Grass*. Ed. Sculley Bradley and Haold W. Blodgett. New York: Norton, 1973. Print.

# Forum

The 1946 Holocaust Interviews:
David Boder's Intermedia Project in the Digital Age

Alan Rosen, *The Wonder of Their Voices: The 1946 Holocaust Interviews of David Boder*. (Oxford: Oxford UP, 2010), 336 pp.
David. P. Boder, *Die Toten habe ich nicht befragt*. Ed. Julia Faisst, Alan Rosen, and Werner Sollors. (Heidelberg: Winter, 2011), 369 pp.

FRANK MEHRING

In the summer of 1946, Chicago-based psychologist David Boder undertook a remarkable interview project; today it represents the earliest acoustically recorded testimonies of the Holocaust. Boder went to shelter houses in and around Paris, Geneva, Munich, Wiesbaden, and Tradate to conduct 130 interviews. This archival treasure has been excavated and remediated (in the sense of Bolter and Grusin)[1] by the Illinois Institute of Technology. The remediation process has undergone several developmental stages from transcribing the original recordings, translating them into standard English, scanning the original transcripts, revising the transcripts, creating new translations, digitizing the original wire spool recordings, updating the audio quality, producing digital databases by interlinking the different media, and making them publically accessible via the Internet. Boder's remarkably rich archive of audio recordings has now been flanked by two book publications which help to critically approach, map, contextualize, and reframe the sources: Alan Rosen's comprehensive description and analysis of Boder's interview project *The Wonder of their Voices: The 1946 Holocaust Interviews of David Boder* (2010), and the first publication of Boder's interviews in German featuring literal transcriptions and detailed annotations entitled *Die Toten habe ich nicht befragt* ('I Did Not Interview the Dead'; 2011). Two questions loom over both books: Do these interviews change our perspective on the Holocaust? And if so, in what ways?

---

[1] Remediation refers to a process of translation or transformation of one medium into another. David Bolter and Richard Grusin describe media as "continually commenting upon, reproducing and replacing each other." Turning to Derrida's argument that there is nothing prior to writing, they claim correspondingly that for visual culture "there is nothing prior to mediation. Any act of mediation is dependent upon another, indeed many other, acts of mediation and is therefore remediation" (18). In Boder's case, the question arises on how far media determine our perspective on the Holocaust and whether the new public access to his audio archive can enhance or modify our understanding of trauma.

Rosen explains that "Boder has to be seen as exceptional, a renegade, even a prophet, whose vision of an archive of Holocaust testimony was years ahead of its time" (18). His account of Boder's project is, however, neither a celebratory appraisal of Boder's 'firsts,' nor does Rosen produce a smokescreen by pretending that he is excavating a forgotten chronicler of the Holocaust. Instead, Rosen frankly declares that Boder was not the first to interview displaced persons, his project was not unique, he did not work alone, he was not obscure or unknown, his project was not underfunded, and his major works were not hidden away in an obscure cellar or archive (23).

Rosen contextualizes Boder's approaches in the field of psychology, trauma research, and memory studies thereby avoiding the trap of isolating him from other interview projects conducted by institutes such as the Jewish Historical Institute in Poland (7200 interviews between 1944 and 1949), the Hungarian National Relief Committee for Deportees (3600 interviews between 1944 and 1948), or the German Central Historical Commission (2500 interviews).[2] As far as the displacement and trauma of World War II survivors are concerned, there is no shortage of recent studies that describe the visual dimension of the Holocaust (see, among others, Zelizer, Bathrick, and Ebbrecht). However, when it comes to early representations of the Holocaust and DP shelters, we soon encounter a gap between what is shown visually and how it is framed acoustically. International film crews closely followed the events leading to the liberation of concentration camps, producing moving images for Movietone newsreels shown in the United States and Great Britain that, until today, have become fundamental for memorialzing the Holocaust. Particularly striking film sequences have been remediated time and time again. How do they distort our perspective on the Holocaust? Rosen turns to the Buchenwald survivor Jorge Semprún, who recognized a crucial problem when he saw newsreel footage of one of the camps:

> Even though [the newsreel images] showed the naked obscenity, the physical deterioration, the grim destruction of death, the images, in fact, were silent. Not merely because they were filmed without live sound recording, which was standard practice at the time. They were silent above all because they said nothing precise about the reality they showed, because they delivered only confused scraps of meaning. (Semprún 200)

The commentary for these images, as Semprún argues, should be spoken by survivors in order to convey a sense of the actual experience. Rosen believes that such an observation could also come directly from one of Boder's notebooks. The conceived discrepancy between image and sound propelled Boder to give a new form of agency to those who are shown in film clips in extremely vulnerable situations and often in an undignified manner. Chronologically, Boder's interview project by

---

[2] Boder was, actually, a latecomer to interviewing displaced persons and survivors of concentration camps. After the liberation of the camps by Allied Forces and the complete surrender of Nazi Germany on 8 May 1945, there were eight to ten million displaced persons in Europe alone. At the beginning of various interview projects, understanding traumatic effects was less pressing than coping with the humanitarian challenge and the political problems these displaced persons posed for restructuring life in postwar Europe. When Boder arrived in France in late July of 1946, there were still more than one million people who had not returned to their countries of origin or did not know where to take refuge.

far transcends the actual trip to Europe in the summer of 1946; he used the audio sources as a basis for future research projects and publications.

Rosen approaches his subject from a very basic set of questions, which he answers with great analytical skill, care, and a remarkable sense of rhetorical refinement: "What, first of all, did Boder do? What led him to undertake his expedition to Europe to interview DPs? What then did he do with the material he gathered? And what happened to it in the aftermath of his death in 1961?" (21). It is crucial to understand that Boder's interviews were different from similar efforts in a number of ways. First, the interviews differed from an analytical perspective. Boder did not approach the socio-cultural conditions of displaced persons as a journalist but as a psychologist. He was among the first to understand that the suffering of displaced persons needs to be conceived under the framework of 'trauma.' In a letter from 19 June 1945, Boder explained:

> It seems to me to be the express desire of the Commander of the Army, General Eisenhower, that the proper organizations should be as completely informed through personal contact and their own specific methods of the human factors involved in the European tragedy and especially the tragedy of displaced persons. A group of motion picture producers have been flown to Europe only a few days ago. I think at least one psychologist should be entitled to facilities and cooperation for a survey with psychological methods and corresponding tools. (qtd. in Rosen 9)[3]

Second, the interviews differed from a technological perspective; they were recorded and archived via an early technical recording device—a recorder with wire spools—a somewhat cumbersome precursor to the technologically more advanced magnetic tape recorders. In the immediate years after World War II, the oral recordings of testimonies were new and differed greatly from the work of reporters in the news industry.[4] Third, the interviews were different in their scholarly trajectory. Despite the commercializing effects of visualizing the Holocaust in recent decades, Boder was the first to approach the testimonies from the perspective of trauma; this understanding has by now become widely accepted and has been productively put into practice by scholars such as Aleida Assmann, Jan Assmann, Jeffrey Alexander, Ann Kaplan, and many others too numerous to mention here. At the end of his introduction to *I Did Not Interview the Dead* (1949), Boder offers a 'traumatic index' which lists twelve entries to measure and better understand the loss and mental damage inflicted during the years of intern-

---

[3] Other projects include collections of testimonies of wartime writing and post-war interviews; oral and written accounts were surveyed by French historian Annette Wieviorka. Tony Kushner's survey shows how early testimonies were used and conducted to reveal Nazi crimes rather than investigate issues of personal trauma (276-78).

[4] The United States gained particular interest in the Holocaust with the publication of Anne Frank's diary in 1952. Media images of the telecast of the Eichmann trial in 1961 provided the ground for a massive production and proliferation of texts and audio-visual material related to the Holocaust. The airing of the television docudrama *The Holocaust* in 1978 exemplified how the Holocaust could be successfully marketed and used in popular media, walking a fine line between education and entertainment. The television series opened new pathways for future productions from Steven Spielberg's *Schindler's List* (1993) via Roberto Benigni's *Life is Beautiful* (1997) to Stephen Daldry's *The Reader* (2008), thereby shaping to a certain degree the image of the Holocaust in the minds of a global digital audience.

ment.[5] Ranging from "brutal and abrupt removal from the environmental stimuli" to "brutal punishment for trivial infringements of camp rules," it helps to assess traumatic conditions framed by brutality and injustice ("Traumatic Inventory"). Boder investigated the dynamics involved with the suppression of memory, negotiating the often violent rift between the traumatic wounds of the past and the desire to transcend them in order to cope with the challenges of the present. These are key elements in trauma studies, which Boder anticipated.

Rosen structures his book by offering four large parts subdivided into seven chapters. He covers biographical aspects of Boder's life, examines the central sources of *I Did Not Interview the Dead*, and discusses the context of Boder's interview projects. In chapter one, "I Could Not Help Wondering: On Boder's Biography and the Idea of Testimony," Rosen traces Boder's European life and education to address issues of cultural translation, transfer, and mobility after his arrival in the United States. This kind of framing allows Rosen to identify Boder both as a cultural insider and an outsider in his project in Europe. Chapters two and three, entitled "Summer, 1946, Part I and Part II" chronicle the two-month trip to Europe with precise information on the corresponding socio-political and cultural circumstances in the various DP camps. In chapters four and five, Rosen addresses issues of technology, focusing on the recording device and its impact on publication history in print media. Rosen analyzes the interviews by putting Boder's psychological training at the center of attention. In addition, he interprets the transcriptions as literary experiments, which enables him to understand the peculiar interdependence between aural recording, free speech, and literary text. In a three-part appendix Rosen offers a chronology of interviews, contextualizes the disputed number of Boder interviews, and reproduces the table of contents of Boder's *Topical Autobiographies of Displaced People* for researchers providing information on volumes, chapters, persons interviewed, pages, micro-cards, and the spools.

Boder's interviews with DPs took place during a fragile moment that Henry Greenspan describes as a "contradictory middle ground" ("Immediate," 112), a place betwixt and between. The displaced persons were able to tell their wartime stories at a point when their lives had not yet returned to some sort of normalcy at a new home within a well-structured social condition of work and family life. Boder is there with his recording device to capture this fleeting moment in time and space. Therefore, the audio recordings reveal an emotional quality found lacking in most other testimonies within the sphere of written transcriptions or descriptive reports.

Media, however, are neither neutral nor transparent. Rather, it is crucial to understand that the medium itself, in the sense of Marshall McLuhan, impacts the human experience in a more thorough way than the content that it mediates. What does this shift imply for our understanding of trauma, displacement, and

---

[5] This condensed version of the traumatic index was originally divided into eight categories (socio-economical, geographical, cultural affects, medical, work, direct physical violence, appearance, hygiene, clothes, transportation, and nutrition) with forty-six entries overall, spreading over eighteen pages. As Alan Rosen points out, Boder published the longer expanded version called "Traumatic Inventory" in the final volume of *Topical Autobiographies*.

belonging? In the following section I will assess what is gained and what is lost if we put the perspective of media at the center of our analysis. Memory and the production of memory become key issues in understanding the nexus of technology, aesthetics, and society. The first German edition of eight interviews, edited by Julia Faisst, Alan Rosen, and Werner Sollors, represents a remarkable case study to address the question of media. The precise transcriptions of the interviews in *Die Toten habe ich nicht befragt* in the original German language in which Boder conducted them, offer a revealing link between the recordings in the digital archive and Rosen's theoretical approach to Boder's interview project. Here we can trace what Rosen describes as a rawness of the testimonies, which is remarkably different from survivors who tell their stories from a perspective of hindsight after having worked through the experience in countless conversations over a long period of time. Here, as Rosen explains, we are able to recognize the "continued lack of mastery of one's own story at this early stage of recounting" (227).

The dominance of visual media in Holocaust discourses and the move towards video-testimony in the 1980s have transformed the memory of the Holocaust and fate of DPs to a hyper-imaged event in global history. Oral history and audio testimony are deemed important in mediating the Holocaust. Nevertheless, video testimony and the added voice-overs to silent newsreel footage proved to be the most accessible format, pushing audio testimonies to the margin.[6] The recent republication of interviews with displaced persons that Boder conducted in 1946 represents an unusual, but nevertheless all the more striking case study in the age of digital archives in the public domain. Here the commentary track for the Holocaust and its visual imagination is not left to professional newsreel announcers, but to the voices of the survivors. *Die Toten habe ich nicht befragt* is a fascinating case in oral history because it offers a venue into the earliest recorded memories of the Holocaust and challenges us to approach a complex digital oral history archive by relying on traditional print media. The transcriptions and the resurfacing of the audio interviews in the digital archive also illustrate how film, despite its *longue durée*, has been an inadequate, or at least problematic, mediator of the Holocaust.

Again, what is gained and what is lost in the current first German edition of Boder's interview project? The selection of texts is very limited: the collection of eight interviews in the first German edition is hardly a representative cross-section of Boder's work. Most of the 130 interviews were conducted in Paris, and the city functioned as a hub for Boder's manifold visits to other shelters on sixteen different interview sites in four countries including France, Switzerland, Italy, and Germany.[7] Five of the eight interviews published in *Die Toten habe ich*

---

[6] Gigliotti asks a crucial question regarding the function and value of audio testimony by comparing it to video testimony: "Is it [video testimony] a response to the failure of previous narrative practice to enter the epicentre of suffering declared unreadable by historians and survivors?" (204-18).

[7] The selection of eight interviewees, however, is hardly representative if compared to the entire project in terms of age, political and religious backgrounds, or the geographic location in which the interview took place. However, it offers a glimpse at the breadth of the topics. Boder was particularly interested in the Jewish suffering under the Nazi regime, and six interviews are conducted with Jewish DPs. In addition, the book features a transcription of interviews with a

nicht befragt were conducted in Germany. The fact that the transcriptions are now available for the first time not in translation but in the original language provides an opportunity to get a better understanding of the suffering of DPs and their struggles under extreme conditions of concentration camps.

Linguistic authenticity forms a basis for a literary experiment. The interviews in *I Did Not Interview the Dead* were conducted in German, Yiddish, and Russian. As an international migrant, Boder was fluent in these languages as well as in Latvian, Lithuanian, Polish, French, and Spanish, and was therefore able to conduct all of the interviews in the corresponding language albeit with idiosyncratic aberrations due to Boder's stay in the United States after his emigration via Mexico. In a 1948 radio interview called "Your Right to Say It," Boder explained that he had actually lived among and with the displaced persons in the summer of 1946: "I listened to the rank and file of martyrs who have seen men and women marched into gas chambers, children burned in open fire pits, and youths killed at electrified fences in desperate bids for freedom" (qtd. in Rosen 138). Boder's multilingual background and the technological means that he brought to the DP shelters allowed him to record interviews with survivors in their own languages. Scholars such as James E. Young have argued that by turning to English as the preferred language of testimony the stories offer survivors a productive sense of neutrality (160). Boder, however, recognized that by allowing interviewees to use their own language they could tap deeper into the socio-cultural dimensions of their autobiographical experience.[8]

Boder listened not only to the DPs, he also listened to the recordings. The different cover designs for his book publications pay tribute to this circumstance. The original cover shows a phantom-like figure behind barbed wire with empty, dark hollow eyes. The right hand clutches desperately at a wire fence. The faceless figure is accentuated with stark green contours harking back to the Munich Secession and Brücke artists who often captured the sense of desolation and isolation of German urban dwellers after World War I. By the late 1940s, barbed wire had become a well-known symbol for concentration camps and had achieved iconographic status in Holocaust representations. The new cover of the German edition, however, features a full-body photograph of Boder in his role as an interviewer and recorder of testimonies. Our attention is drawn to the very media device that made the transcriptions and the sense of immediacy possible: a then state-of-the-art wire recorder.

Ukrainian Mennonite and a woman from Estonia. Their accounts broaden the perspective on the DPs and the Holocaust by including voices that describe *en détail* the suffering under the socio-political conditions of the Soviet terror regime in which the German invasion functioned as a chance of escape. The latter two interviews shift the perspective of victimhood from the Nazi terror regime to suffering under Soviet oppression.

[8] A similar function can be ascribed to the act of singing. Boder asked several interviewers to remember and perform songs that reflected their experience in the camps.

Fig. 1: David Boder, *I Did Not Interview the Dead*. First Edition (1949).

Fig. 2: David Boder, *Die Toten habe ich nicht befragt*. First German Edition (2011).

At first glance, the device is reminiscent of a reel-to-reel magnetic tape recorder. On closer inspection, however, it becomes clear that the reels consist of wire spools. The large recording device had several functions, the first of which is technological innovation: sound and film records that form the basis of our global knowledge of the Holocaust and the fate of DPs. A second function is media transmission. The image on the cover of *Die Toten habe ich nicht befragt* reminds us that Boder used technology to help him disseminate the stories via print media, and the recordings offered the basis for transcribing the stories from the audio recordings. In this process of remediating, the stories are made accessible for the then most effective media distribution channel: book publication.

A third advantage of using the recording device is the attraction of the technology itself. In the past (and today, as well) the wire recorder functioned as an effective tool of advertisement for Boder's interview project. He used the recording device to gain attention by showcasing the power of his technological apparatus. For the people who had been in camps for years, the device had a magical quality, and in order to persuade them to meet with him and tell him their stories, Boder staged little demonstrations in which he recorded and then played back the material to great effect: "I would meet a colony of DPs in a particular shelter house for lunch or dinner. After the meal I would ask them to sing and, with their knowledge, I recorded the songs. When I played these back, the wonder of hearing their own voices recorded was boundless. Then I would explain my project and ask for volunteers" (Boder, *Dead* xii). Boder knew that the media device functioned as an attraction that he could channel into active participation for his interview project. The "wonder of hearing their own voices" must have been more than a technical wonder;[9] it also elevated those who had been pushed into the realm of death and forgetfulness. Their stories are now remembered, archived, and disseminated via modern mass media. Boder's decision to use songs as the medium to gain attention and interest reveals his keen understanding regarding the power of mediated emotions, stories, rituals, and traditions.

A fourth function is technology as opposite. The presence of the cumbersome recording device had a particular impact on the interview situation, which sometimes took place in very small, makeshift rooms. The wire spool recorder operates as a third interview partner who silently records the data for the future. The rotating wire spools surely created a particular tension in the interview situation since the process of recording gave particular weight to the very moment of speaking about one's life experience. Some interviewees took the opportunity to officially thank Boder at the end of the conversation for his efforts, thereby acknowledging the historical weight of the recording process. For example, Jürgen Gastfreund explained:

> Ja, vor allen Dingen danke ich Ihnen dafür, dass Sie mir Gelegenheit gegeben haben, hier noch einmal über diese ganzen Erlebnisse aus dem Lager zu sprechen und damit die Leute, damit man ihnen man mal ein Bild geben kann, von dem was wirklich geschehen ist, und das, was ich gesagt hab, sind nur einzelne Fälle und es ist nicht übertrieben, das kann ich mit gutem Gewissen sagen. Im Gegenteil man kann es nicht so schildern, wie es wirklich gewesen ist.
>
> I wish to thank you first of all for giving me the opportunity to talk about my experiences in the camp so that people can get a picture of that which has really happened. What I have told you are only isolated incidents, and I can tell it with a clean conscience that nothing is exaggerated. On the contrary one cannot describe these things the way it really happened. (*Die Toten* 87-88)[10]

Here, Gastfreund is talking as much to Boder as to the recording device.

Recording and transcribing dialogical situations is a fifth function of the device, as the literal transcriptions retain information on the conductor of the interviews. Thus, the recordings provide us with more than details about the situation of the concentration camps. Boder's questions, his repeated insistence on certain patterns of information, his interruptions, pauses, comments, and general conduct also shed revealing light on the interviewer. In some cases he even provides information on American culture and professional opportunities for those willing to emigrate. Thus, Boder's presence is also recorded. This kind of additional information about the interviewer is often lost or considered unwelcome in contemporary video interviews. By recording both the interviewer and the interviewee, the

---

[9] Rosen uses this media effect as a part of the title for his comprehensive account on Boder's life and work.

[10] This and the following translations are based on the translation of the transcripts in the digital archive of *Voices of the Holocaust*.

medium enables us to characterize and critically engage with Boder's project, his approach, and the function of media in understanding trauma.

Sixth: recording and transcribing emotions. Boder's transcriptions provided information on the emotional state of the specific interview situation and the conduct of the interview. He sometimes interrupts the flow of conversation to make sure that he (as well as the listener/reader) understands the report. In other instances Boder describes the way in which the information is presented. His interview with Anna Kovitzka is a good example: at some point while delivering her report, she is crying incontrollably ("Sie weint krampfhaft") and is in such an agitated state that the recording is difficult to understand (33). Boder therefore makes assumptions about the contents:

> Hier beginnt sie heftig zu schluchzen, und der gesamte Satz ist zusammenhanglos. Die letzten Worte klingen wie, "ich sah ihn überall unter den Leuten."
>
> Here she begins to sob violently, and the whole sentence sounds incoherent. The last few words seem to sound like: "I saw him everywhere among people." (35)

In other instances, Boder calls attention to the tone and melody of the voice, be it full of surprise, with a slight hint of radiance, or with laughter or joy in her voice: "hier imitiert Anna einen Tonfall extremer Überraschtheit" ('and here she imitates a voice of extreme surprise'; 37), "dies mit einem verhaltenen Strahlen in ihrer Stimme" ('this with some hiden light in her voice'; 37), "Anna setzt fort mit einem Lachen in ihrer Stimme" ('Anna continues with laughter in her voice'; 41), "Mit Freude in ihrer Stimme" ('with joy in her voice'; 42). Boder's almost obsessive concern to transcribe as literally as possible leads to a sometimes awkward reading experience: the narrative is full of fissures and break-ups which, as Frank Kelleter recently observed, prevents the interviews from aestheticizing the events.

A seventh function is that of footnotes. Boder uses footnotes to explain words that might be unfamiliar to the reader or are part of another language (such as the English word 'shops' used in an interview conducted in Yiddish). The editors also preserved Boder's use of italics to indicate emotions and linguistic emphasis in the textual translation of the oral account: "Wir wuschen uns! *Mit Seife*, warmem Wasser, einem sauberen Handtuch, *reine* Unterwäsche. Ach!" ('We washed ourselves! *With soap*, warm water, a clean towel, *pure* underwear. Oh!'; 43). In order to translate the peculiar ways of narration into writing, Boder takes advantage of blank space on the page to provide a sense of the aural experience. When Anna Kovitzka tells her stories via direct speech re-enacting dialogue situations—for example, an interrogation between a Gestapo officer in the presence of a Polish policeman and Kovitzka's husband—Boder disentangles the report by adding line breaks and quotation marks to provide a sense of drama (33).[11]

How can we take into account the temporal distance of more than half a century in order to properly approach and understand the testimonies of Holocaust survivors? What is the impact of these testimonies on our understanding of trauma and belonging? On the one hand the testimonies function as memory aids. The

---

[11] Greenspan (see *On Listening*) ranks among those scholars who have paid particular attention to the function and changes of the Holocaust and oral history.

archival media need to be distinguished from traditional broadcast media such as film and television, which more often than not require a passive reception mode. In an "ecology of associated hypomnesic milieus," a term I borrow from Bernard Stiegler (64), we encounter living conditions of digital citizens who engage in a network of communication based on a procedural logic of sending and receiving of information. Here the digital archive of Boder's interview project has a lot to offer. The embedding of memories—such as those of Holocaust survivors—within technological systems, and organizing memories according to systemic logics such as age, gender, country of origin, and alphabetical lists of names and places represent new digital mnemotechniques that hold the promise to remediate memory, give way to (self-)expression, and offer ways of (self-)exteriorization.

On a less positive note, the exteriorization of memory can also result in a loss of memory. With the introduction of personal digital assistants such as smart phones with their access to global knowledge on web-based encyclopedia, GPS controlled digital maps, and concise personal data on social networks, we have undergone a shift from practicing mnemotechniques to becoming mere exteriorized media ourselves and to a mnemotechnology that even collects and structures our memories for us (e. g., Facebook's Timeline diary). In such an industrial model of memory, we run the risk of anamnesis. Today the Holocaust is remembered mainly via visual sources. The "psychological methods and corresponding tools," which Boder deemed crucial to complement the filmmaker's desires to document, proved less decisive in the memorialization of the Holocaust than expected.

In our digital age, how can we approach, use, and make sense of hundreds of hours of audio files with often difficult-to-understand recording quality? The discrepancy between transmitting, transcription, and translation of interviews encoded in the history of *Die Toten habe ich nicht befragt* redirects our attention to some of the earliest recordings of Holocaust survivors. It asks us to rediscover the effects of trauma and displacement on complex layers of acoustic narration. To do so, we need to rely on non-visual information to decode the information provided. The multilingual recordings tell of the European dimension of the Holocaust, adding a new element to the nexus of testimony and media representation. By putting the acoustic recording device at the center of Holocaust testimonies, we need both digital literacy and intercultural competence to understand human memory and the impact of catastrophic events.[12] Therefore, Boder's interview project emerges as an inter-media project.

The two recent publications in the medium of print, *Die Toten habe ich nicht befragt* and *The Wonder of Their Voices*, provide a gateway to engage with Boder's trajectory, his cultural background, and the particular conditions under which he conducted the interviews. The print medium enables both scholars and the in-

---

[12] Boder introduced far-reaching theoretical concepts in his trail-blazing article "The Impact of Catastrophe," in which he combines an analysis of content with the function of trauma based on audio recordings of displaced persons immediately after the liberation of the Nazi concentration camps in 1946 and survivors of the Kansas flood in 1951. His comparative approach to patterns of traumatization in man-made catastrophes in a hostile environment and nature-made catastrophes in a friendly and intact environment can provide a new basis to rethinking models of Holocaust testimony.

terested public to approach the comprehensive digital archive with specific questions and background information. In the digital realm, the user is now in a better position to contextualize and analyze Boder's media project, to make informed selections based on parameters defined by the interview (selections offered by filter parameters based on date, location, or language) or the interviewee (with selections offered regarding name, age, birthplace, nationality, religion, gender, marital status, camps and ghettos of internment, location at the time of Nazi occupation, and location at the time of liberation). This triangular approach holds the promise to uncover an intermediary reservoir of early voices of the Holocaust. The editors—Julia Faisst, Alan Rosen, and Werner Sollors—deserve the highest praise for creating new research opportunities and for making accessible these remarkably rich multilingual sources.

Works Cited

Alexander, Jeffrey C. *Trauma: A Social Theory*. Cambridge: Polity, 2012. Print.

Assmann, Aleida. *Erinnerungsräume: Formen und Wandlungen des kulturellen Gedächtnisses*. München: Beck, 1999. Print.

Assmann, Jan. *Das kulturelle Gedächtnis: Schrift, Erinnerung und politische Identität in frühen Hochkulturen*. 5th ed. München: Beck, 2005. Print.

Bathrick, David, ed. *Visualizing the Holocaust: Documents, Aesthetics, Memory*. Rochester, NY: Camden, 2012. Print.

Boder, David P. *Die Toten habe ich nicht befragt*. Ed. Julia Faisst, Alan Rosen, and Werner Sollors. Heidelberg: Winter, 2011. Print.

---. *I Did Not Interview the Dead*. Urbana: U of Illinois P, 1949. Print.

---. "The Impact of Catastrophe: I. Assessment and Evaluation." *The Journal of Psychology: Interdisciplinary and Applied*. 38.1 (1954): 3-50. Print.

---. "Traumatic Inventory of the Assessment and Evaluation of Interviews with Displaced Persons." *Topical Autobiographies of Displaced People Recorded Verbatim in Displaced Person Camps, with a Psychological and Anthropological Analysis*. Vol. 16. Chicago, 1950-57. 3141-59. Self-published. 16 vols.

Bolter, Jay David, and Richard Grusin. "Remediation." *Configurations* 4.3 (1996): 311-58. Print.

Ebbrecht, Tobias. *Geschichtsbilder im medialen Gedächtnis: Filmische Narrationen des Holocaust*. Bielefeld: Transcript, 2011. Print.

Frank, Anne. *Anne Frank: The Diary of a Young Girl*. New York: Pocket, 1958. Print.

Gigliotti, Simone. "Technology, Trauma and Representation: Holocaust Testimony and Videotape." *Temporalities, Autobiography and Everyday Life*. Ed. Jan Campel and Janet Harbord. Manchester: Manchester UP, 2002. 204-18. Print.

Greenspan, Henry. "'An Immediate and Violent Impulse': Holocaust Survivor Testimony in the First Years after Liberation" *Remembering the Future: The Holocaust in an Age of Genocide*. Ed. John K. Roth and Elizabeth Maxwell. London: Palgrave, 2000. 108-16. Print.

---. *On Listening to Holocaust Survivors: Recounting and Life History.* Westport, CT: Praeger, 1998. Print.

Kaplan, E. A. *Trauma Culture: The Politics of Terror and Loss in Media and Literature.* New Brunswick, N.J: Rutgers UP, 2005. Print.

Kelleter, Frank. "David P. Boder: Die Toten habe ich nicht befragt Als Begriffe für das Grauen noch fehlten." *Frankfurter Allgemeine Zeitung.* 30 Nov. 2011. Web. 25 August 2012.

Kushner, Tony. "Holocaust Testimony, Ethics, and the Problem of Representation." *Poetics Today* 27 (2006): 276-78. Print.

Mitchell, W. J. T., and Mark B. N. Hansen. *Critical Terms for Media Studies.* Chicago, IL: U of Chicago P, 2010. Print.

Rosen, Alan. *The Wonder of their Voices: The 1946 Holocaust Interviews of David Boder.* Oxford: Oxford UP, 2010. Print.

Semprún, Jorge. *Literature or Life.* New York: Viking, 1997. Print.

Stiegler, Bernard. "Memory." *Critical Terms for Media Studies.* Ed. W. J. T. Mitchell and Mark B. N. Hansen. Chicago, IL: U of Chicago P, 2010. 64-87. Print.

Voices of the Holocaust. Paul V. Galvin Library, Illinois Institute of Technology, 2009. Web. 17 Oct. 2013.

Wieviorka, Annette. *The Era of the Witness.* Ithaca, NY: Cornell UP, 2006. Print.

Young, James E. *Writing and Rewriting the Holocaust: Narrative and the Consequences of Interpretation.* Bloomington: Indiana UP, 1988. Print.

Zelizer, Barbie. *Visual Culture and the Holocaust.* New Brunswick, NJ: Rutgers UP, 2001. Print.

Reviews

CHARLOTTE A. LERG, *Die Amerikanische Revolution* (Tübingen: Francke, 2010), 128 pp.

CHARLOTTE A. LERG, *Amerika als Argument: Die deutsche Amerika-Forschung im Vormärz und ihre politische Deutung in der Revolution von 1848/49* (Bielefeld: transcript, 2011), 391 pp.

Probably no event in American history has had as long-lasting and wide-ranging consequences for European and indeed world history as the American Revolution. By founding a large territorial state upon the sovereignty of the people and creating a democratic system of government based upon the consent of the governed and responsible to the will of the people, the American Revolution "proved that the liberal ideas of the Enlightenment might be put into practice," as Robert A. Palmer put it in his comparative study of the Atlantic Revolutions in the late eighteenth century.[1] The American Revolution thus posed a direct challenge to Europe's feudal order, to unaccountable absolutist government, to inherited rights and privileges, and to entrenched social hierarchies. It not only inspired liberal reformers and revolutionaries seeking political participation in Europe in the late eighteenth and the nineteenth centuries, it would also serve as an example to colonial liberation movements seeking independence and self-government in Latin America in the early nineteenth century as well as in Africa and Asia in the twentieth century.[2] Charlotte A. Lerg's aim to provide German readers with a readable introductory survey of the events of the American Revolution in *Die amerikanische Revolution* is therefore highly legitimate and—since the last concise overview of the American Revolution in German dates back to the 1980s—also timely and indeed warranted.[3] After all, not all interested general readers and B. A. students in Germany—which the UTB Profile series, as part of which Lerg's volume was published, targets—speak English proficiently enough to be able to use one of the many excellent overviews that are available in English.[4]

Lerg provides a knowledgeable and eloquent recount of all the major events surrounding the American Revolution. In the first two chapters, Lerg describes the events leading to the Declaration of Independence, before she summarizes the major battles of the War of Independence. The Constitution is the subject of the fourth chapter. Finally, she thoughtfully discusses the situation and role of blacks, women, and Indians in the American Revolution. Numerous illustrations and an appendix with concise biographies of important American and British actors in the American Revolution complete the account. In sum, Lerg produced an easy-to-access and reliable introduction to important events of the Revolution. There is only very little inaccurate information. For example, Lerg writes

---

[1] Robert A. Palmer, *The Age of Democratic Revolution: A Political History of Europe and America, 1760 - 1800*, Vol. 1 (Princeton: Princeton UP, 1959/1964): 239-40. 2 vols.

[2] See David Armitage, *The Declaration of Independence: A Global History* (Cambridge: Harvard UP, 2007).

[3] See Horst Dippel, *Die Amerikanische Revolution, 1763-1787* (Frankfurt/M.: Suhrkamp, 1985). See also, Hans-Christoph Schröder, *Die Amerikanische Revolution: Eine Einführung* (München: Beck, 1982). German translations of major documents of the American Revolution can be found in Angela Adams and Willi Paul Adams, eds., *Die Amerikanische Revolution und die Verfassung, 1754-1791* (München: DTV, 1987). Hermann Wellenreuther's excellent study on the American Revolution is probably too sophisticated and detailed to arouse the laymen's interest. *Von Chaos und Krieg zu Ordnung und Frieden. Der Amerikanischen Revolution erster Teil, 1775-1783* (Münster: LIT, 2006).

[4] Gordon S. Wood, *The American Revolution: A History* (New York: Modern Library, 2002). Robert Middlekauff, *The Glorious Cause: The American Revolution, 1763-1789*, rev. and expanded ed. (New York: Oxford UP, 2005). Francis D. Cogliano, *Revolutionary America, 1763-1815: A Political History*, 2nd ed. (New York: Routledge, 2009). Robert J. Allison, *The American Revolution: A Concise History* (New York: Oxford UP, 2011).

that the Seven Years' War began already in 1754 (cf. 12; 102). While the first hostilities of the so-called French and Indian War in North America indeed occurred that year, the Seven Years' War only began officially in 1756.

Yet the strength of the book—the chronological description of all the important legislative acts, declarations, battles, and treaties—also deprives it of some of its potential, since it is a very traditional 'history of events.' It seems that Lerg all too closely followed Jefferson's prediction about how the American Revolution would fare in historical scholarship: "On the subject of the history of the American Revolution, you ask who shall write it? Who can write it? And who will ever be able to write it? Nobody; except merely its external facts," he told John Adams in 1815.[5] In the rather short introduction Lerg identifies some of the crucial questions historians have asked in regard to the revolution: Were political ideas or economic interests dominant? What was the ideological foundation of the Patriots' rebellion against the mother country? Who was the driving force behind the revolution? Was it a 'gentlemen's revolution' by the social elite or a revolution from below? How far-reaching were the social and cultural changes that the American Revolution triggered? Did the American Revolution transform a feudal society into a democratic-egalitarian one within a few decades, or had American society already been liberal in the colonial period such that the Revolution only made 'official' what had de facto already been there before? After mentioning some of these hotly contested issues in the introduction, Lerg, however, does not address them in the main part of the book, nor does she synthesize the scholarship on them. Granted, while an introduction to the American Revolution cannot delve deeply into scholarly debates, one could nevertheless have raised awareness that questions about underlying causes and effects or about structure and agency have given rise to extensive debate to date.

One could also have marked out the problems historians of the American Revolution face when deciding at which point to begin and to end their narratives. Lerg, for example, simply claims that the Boston Tea Party in 1773 marked the beginning of the American Revolution (cf. 9). How so? Most scholars start their narratives of the American Revolution in 1763, when the end of the Seven Years' War removed the French enemy, relieving colonists of the need for British protection, and when King George's Proclamation of 1763 forbade the colonists to settle on the land west of the Appalachians.[6] One could also consider the resistance to the Stamp Act in 1765, which set in motion the dynamic culminating in the Declaration of Independence, or the meeting of the First Continental Congress and the commencement of hostilities at Lexington and Concord in 1774 as the beginning of the Revolution.[7] When did the American Revolution end? With the attainment of independence in 1783? With the ratification of the Constitution in 1787/88? After the Constitution had been put to practice in the 1790s?[8] The fact that the periodization of the American Revolution is not scrutinized is related to the absence of a discussion of the term and concept of revolution. What was the American Revolution after all? Is it synonymous with the War of Independence? Was it the creation of the United States? Was it the democratization of British North America?[9] How does the American Revolution relate to

---

[5] "Thomas Jefferson to John Adams, August 10, 1815," Paul Leicester Ford, ed., *The Works of Thomas Jefferson*, Vol. 11 (New York: Putnam, 1904-05): 485. 12 vols.

[6] Cf. Dippel, *Die Amerikanische Revolution, 1763-1787*. Middlekauff, *The Glorious Cause*. Cogliano, *Revolutionary America, 1763-1815*.

[7] Cf. Pauline Maier, *From Resistance to Revolution: Colonial Radicals and the Development of American Opposition to Britain, 1765-1776* (New York: Knopf, 1972). Douglas Bradburn, *The Citizenship Revolution: Politics and the Creation of the American Union, 1774-1804* (Charlottesville: U of Virginia P, 2009).

[8] Scholars increasingly emphasize the need to overcome the rigid separation of the American Revolution from the Early Republic. Cf. Gordon S. Wood, "The Significance of the Early Republic," *Journal of the Early Republic* 8.1 (1988): 1-20. Bradburn, *The Citizenship Revolution*.

[9] To Gordon S. Wood, for example, the American Revolution was the rapid and profound democratization of American society in *The Radicalism of the American Revolution*.

the French Revolution? Was the American Revolution a revolution at all?[10]

Finally, while the repercussions of the American Revolution are not the topic of the book, it would have been interesting for German readers to learn about what effects the American Revolution had on political developments in Germany.[11] In a conclusion, which the book is lacking, Lerg could have sketched the implications and consequences of the American Revolution for European and world history in a few broad strokes. This omission is rather surprising since Lerg herself wrote her dissertation on the role that the example of America's political and social system emerging from the American Revolution played in the German Revolutions of 1848 and 1849.

In her dissertation, published as the book *Amerika als Argument*, Lerg analyzes how 'America' was used as an argument in the National Assembly in Frankfurt in 1848/49, which was elected to create a modern constitution as the foundation for a unified Germany. During this assembly, various members referred to the American political system in order to legitimize their political positions (cf. 12-13). Invoking the American example was an obvious rhetorical strategy, since the political concepts discussed in the National Assembly had been put into practice across the Atlantic. By pointing to certain aspects of the American system, members of the Assembly sought to legitimize their political positions or discredit those of their opponents. Lerg focuses on representatives who had received an academic education, who had dealt with America's system of government before the Revolutions of 1848/49, and who made up a sizable part of the so-called 'Professorenparlament' ('professors' parliament'). Her in-depth analysis not only encompasses the debates in the National Assembly but also investigates numerous documents produced by scholars of political science, law, and history on the United States between 1750 and 1850 (cf. 14).

The first part of the book features a comprehensive and knowledgeable discussion of the preconditions and antecedents of the discussion about America in the National Assembly. It sums up the academic literature on the German emigration to the United States; travel literature and guidebooks on America; the importation, translation, and edition of American sources; the first German magazines focusing on America; and the emerging research on America at German universities. Lerg demonstrates that the pursuit of American studies has always had a political dimension, since—to liberal intellectuals—the American republic proved that civic participation and a change of government was possible without the excesses of the French Revolution (cf. 70).[12] At the same time, she makes clear that the academic discourse was not necessarily dominated by enthusiasm for America, as many scholars found numerous aspects of American society deplorable. She also shows that making a positive reference to American conditions was not tantamount to demanding their transfer to Europe (cf. 87-91).

In the second part, Lerg analyzes how the American paradigm was invoked in the debates of the National Assembly in 1848 and 1849. After a short introduction to the quasi-diplomatic relations between the National Assembly and the American government,[13] she examines how its members used America as

---

[10] Cf. Georg P. Meyer, "Revolutionstheorien heute: Ein kritischer Überblick in historischer Absicht," *200 Jahre amerikanische Revolution und moderne Revolutionsforschung*, ed. Hans-Ulrich Wehler (Göttingen: Vandenhoeck, 1976): 122-176. Dick Howard, *Die Grundlegung der amerikanischen Demokratie* (Frankfurt/M.: Suhrkamp, 2001).

[11] For the influence of the American Revolution in Germany, see: Horst Dippel, "Die Wirkung der amerikanischen Revolution auf Deutschland und Frankreich," *200 Jahre amerikanische Revolution und moderne Revolutionsforschung*, ed. Hans-Ulrich Wehler (Göttingen: Vandenhoeck, 1976): 101-21. Horst Dippel, *Germany and the American Revolution, 1770-1800: A Sociohistorical Investigation of Late 18th Century Political Thinking* (Chapel Hill: U of North Carolina P, 1977): especially 329-32.

[12] For this point see also: Elisha Douglass, "Sturm und Drang: German Intellectuals and the American Revolution," *Liberté, Egalité, Fraternité: The American Revolution & the European Response*, ed. Charles W. Toth (Troy: Whitston, 1989): 48-63.

[13] This topic is investigated in detail in: Günter Moltmann, *Atlantische Blockpolitik im 19. Jahrhundert: Die Vereinigten Staaten und der deutsche Liberalismus während der Revolution von 1848/49* (Düsseldorf: Droste, 1973).

an argument when arguing over the constitution. In the first empirical chapter called "Defensive Revolution," Lerg explores the debates over the characteristics and the legitimacy of revolutions. Liberals mostly considered the American Revolution legitimate, since it had been moderate and 'defensive': it upheld traditions, while promoting necessary reforms (cf. 193). The American Revolution was thus regarded as standing in stark contrast to the French Revolution, which was understood as an attack on traditions and laws and which— to conservatives—served as proof that a revolution seeking to abolish monarchy in Europe would fail. For this reason, it was important for liberals to have the example of the American Revolution at hand, since it represented a moderate alternative to the French Revolution (cf. 177). In fact, liberals frequently denied the revolutionary character of the American Revolution and portrayed it as the outcome of a natural process: a young but mature nation cutting the chord to the mother country and becoming independent (cf. 180-81).

In the second empirical chapter entitled "Republikanische Monarchie," Lerg investigates the debates over the meaning of the ambivalent concept of the Republic. Conservatives and liberals rejected the French egalitarian and democratic model of republicanism but applauded the elitist model of republicanism which the Constitution of the United States institutionalized in America (cf. 196-98). The American presidential system had such particular appeal as it could potentially be adapted to create a republican monarchy in Germany (cf. 205; 217; 234), especially when considering the sweeping powers of the American President and his depiction as a quasi-monarch (cf. 234). Liberals and conservatives, however, noted the increasing democratization of American society in the nineteenth century with consternation (cf. 212; 216-17; 243), a development which only the democrats welcomed (cf. 217).

The third empirical chapter called "Föderativer Einheitsstaat" examines how the model of American federalism was invoked during the discussions over the divisions of power between the central government and the state governments. The American example was instructive, since Americans had debated the nature of their union—federal state versus federation of states—ever since the founding of the United States. Aside from the Constitution of the United States, the *Federalist Papers* were an important source for these discussions, although they had not yet been translated into German but had to be read in the English original or in French (cf. 248). Even though the example of an American federal union found more supporters than the French centralized state, most representatives emphasized that it was not possible to copy the American model directly, since the historical and cultural conditions in Germany were just too different.

The last chapter entitled "Geordnete Freiheit" traces the debates over the concept of liberty. The American example again played an important role in the discussions when it was argued that Americans had put the idea of a social contract into practice upon the founding of the United States, evidenced by the American states having adopted catalogs of civil rights in their constitutions and a Bill of Rights having been amended to the Constitution of the United States. On one point, however, the members seemed to agree: they all condemned America's system of institutionalized slavery.

With *Amerika als Argument*, Lerg has produced a study investigating the manner in which America was invoked as an example in the discussions of the National Assembly in 1848/49, which is based on a large amount of primary sources and which is broadly contextualized with the help of a wide array of secondary literature. Her sources include not only the protocols of the debates in the National Assembly but also political, legal, and historical treatises, pamphlets, and the transatlantic correspondences of the representatives. Lerg has consulted both German and American archives. Her study shows a vast variety of the different ways in which the American example was used in the political discussions in 1848 and 1849. She avoids mono-causal explanations and makes clear that referring to America could serve various intentions. Conservatives pointed to more negative aspects of American society than liberals but also used the United States as a positive foil against which to condemn the radicalism of the French Revolution. Liberals had the most positive attitude towards America but were cautious to recommend a direct replication of the American model in Germany. Democrats were more critical of the American system, which they considered too elitist, but welcomed the progressive democratization of American society in the nineteenth century. Lerg convincingly demonstrates that the discursive formations overlapped and that it depended on the situational context how, by whom, and to what effect America was used as an argument.

The influence the American model had on what representatives conceived as desirable or possible in Germany—by contrast—is not the topic of her book, as she herself makes clear (cf. 23). It thus remains unclear what significance the American example really had. When reading the book, one gets the impression that making references to America fulfilled exclusively functional purposes. Lerg analyzes how political positions, which had formed before, were afterwards legitimized by making partisan use of the American example. We therefore do not learn how the study of America on the part of the 'political professors' shaped their political positions and how the debates over America defined their political differences. How were political concepts revaluated and developed after those pursuing American studies had analyzed their practical application in the United States?[14] Scrutinizing the political system of the United States helped the emerging political camps of democrats, liberals, and conservatives develop a political agenda and build up political identities in the first place, as Volker Depkat demonstrated for the period between 1789 and 1830.[15] Showing the interplay of how political ideologies shaped the perception of America and how the American example in turn influenced the political orientations of the 'political professors' would have provided a more comprehensive picture of the role the American example played in the Revolutions of 1848 and 1849.

In conclusion, Lerg has supplied a readable, comprehensive, and multifaceted analysis of how and to what purposes America and its political system were invoked by members of the National Assembly, which met in Frankfurt in 1848 and 1849. It becomes abundantly clear that 'America' was put to various uses and that America's political system was frequently referred to in the debates over a constitution for a unified Germany. The significance the American Revolution had on Germany's political development in the mid-nineteenth century could, however, have been demonstrated more clearly.

Berlin   Jasper M. Trautsch

---

[14] For this question see for example Horst Dippel, *Die amerikanische Verfassung in Deutschland im 19. Jahrhundert: Das Dilemma von Politik und Staatsrecht* (Goldbach: Keip, 1994). Jürgen Heideking, "Das 'Modell Amerika' in der deutschen Verfassungsgeschichte vom Vormärz bis zur Weimarer Republik," *Amerikanische Einflüsse auf Verfassungsdenken und Verfassungspraxis in Deutschland*, eds. Werner Kremp and Gerd Mielke (Kaiserslautern: Atlantische Akademie Rheinland-Pfalz, 1997): 7-34. Herbert Reiter, "Amerikabilder der Revolution von 1848/49," *Mundus Novus, Amerika oder die Entdeckung des Bekannten: Das Bild der neuen Welt im Spiegel der Druckmedien vom 16. bis zum frühen 20. Jahrhundert*, ed. Peter Mesenhöller (Essen: Klartext, 1992), 76-91. Anton Scholl, *Einfluß der nordamerikanischen Unionsverfassung auf die Verfassung des Deutschen Reiches vom 28. März 1849*, Diss. Eberhard Karls Universität Tübingen, 1912. Thomas E. Ellwein, *Der Einfluß des nordamerikanischen Bundesverfassungsrechts auf die Verhandlungen der Frankfurter Nationalversammlung im Jahre 1848/49*, Diss. Friedrich-Alexander-Universität Erlangen, 1950. Eckhart G. Franz, *Das Amerikabild der deutschen Revolution von 1848/49: Zum Problem der Übertragung gewachsener Verfassungssysteme* (Heidelberg: Winter, 1958).

[15] Volker Depkat, *Amerikabilder in politischen Diskursen: Deutsche Zeitschriften von 1789 bis 1830* (Stuttgart: Klett-Cotta, 1998): 14-15.

UDO SCHEMMEL, *Laien in lutherischen Kirchenordnungen: Die unterschiedliche Entwicklung ihres Beeinflussungspotentials auf Gemeindebelange im 18. Jahrhundert in Pennsylvania im Vergleich zu Kirchenordnungen des Landesherrlichen Kirchenregiments—dargestellt an der Genese der Kirchenordnung der St.-Michaelis-Gemeinde in Philadelphia, Pennsylvania* (Würzburg: Ergon, 2012), 272 pp.

Das Buch widmet sich einem Thema mit einigem Potenzial für komparativ-interdisziplinäre Studien in Geschichte und Sozialwissenschaften. Der Ansatz, die Kirchenordnung der lutherischen St.-Michaelis-Gemeinde in Philadelphia von 1762 aus der Tradition des landesherrlichen Kirchenregiments zu deuten, um dann das wegweisend Neue dieses Statuts herauszuarbeiten, ist geeignet, die Forschung zum deutschen Luthertum in Nordamerika stärker auf das reformatorische Erbe hin zu orientieren. Allerdings unterliegt der Autor zwei Fehlannahmen, die seinen Erkenntnisgewinn unnötig begrenzen. So erklärt er die Franckeschen Stiftungen in Halle zu einer "Mutterkirche" (vgl. 152–53, 164, 203) der deutschen Lutheraner in Pennsylvania und den Leiter dieses karitativen, pädagogischen, missionarischen und kommerziellen Konzerns sowie den eng mit ihm kooperierenden lutherischen Hofprediger in London zu "Kirchenführern" (165). Anders als Schweden, Niederländer und Engländer, die ihre Kirchen im Zuge ihrer Landnahme Amerikas etabliert hatten, waren die deutschen Lutheraner nämlich allein auf sich gestellt und nach ihrer Auswanderung keiner Obrigkeit in der Heimat mehr untertan. Deshalb zielt Schemmels Argumentation mit deutschem Kirchenrecht ins Leere.

Wenn der Autor resümiert, "[d]ie Kirche wurde zu einer Sache der freiwilligen Selbstverpflichtung ihrer Mitglieder" (202), dann übersieht er, dass sich das Freiwilligkeitskirchentum nicht entwickelte, sondern ein eherner Grundsatz religiösen Lebens in Pennsylvania war. Auch ist ihm offenbar der Unterschied zwischen 'Gemeindeglied' und "Gemeindemitglied" (vgl. 186, 188, 190, 194–98) nicht bewusst. Daher fällt ihm nicht auf, dass das Statut der St.-Michaelis-Kirche von 1762 durchgängig von "Gemein-Gliedern" oder "Gliedern der Gemeinde" (vgl. Kirchenordnung, I [Präambel], § 9; II [Präambel], §§ 3 (1), 5; III, §§ 1–2) spricht und damit am Kirchenverständnis vom Hineingeborenwerden des Gläubigen in eine mystische Verbindung mit Jesus Christus festhält (1 Kor 12, 12–31), was dem voluntaristischen Prinzip bloßer Mitgliedschaft—also der Gruppenzugehörigkeit mit Kündigungsvorbehalt—zuwiderläuft. In einer Gemeinde jedoch, in der "einer des andern Glied" ist, "viele ein Leib in Christus" sind, "aber nicht alle Glieder einerlei Geschäft haben," (Röm 12, 4–5) kommt der Austritt einer Amputation gleich, die den ganzen Körper schwächt, weil sie ihm die Gottesgaben ebenjenes Gliedes entzieht. Es war diese paulinische Körpersymbolik, die beim Abfassen des Ausschlußverfahrens in den Kirchenordnungen hallescher Pastoren Pate stand.

Wo zudem Röm 12, 3 gebietet, dass "niemand höher von sich halte, als sich's gebührt zu halten," steht jeder Versuch, die Tektonik innerkirchlicher Herrschaft zu ändern, im Verdacht von "Umsturz und Verwirrung."[1] Indem pennsylvanisches Recht dem Pfarramt seinen Schutz versagte und jedermann gestattete, Taufe und Abendmahl als Dienstleistungen feilzubieten, trieb es die Profanierung dieser Sakramente und damit die Demystifikation der Kirche voran. Weil Schemmel diese soteriologische Dimension des Ringens um das Kirchenstatut von 1762 nicht sieht, verharrt er in der bekannten Diskussion oligarchischer Tendenzen, erstarkenden Selbstbewusstseins der Laien und schwindender Autorität der Pfarrer. Dabei wäre es aufschlussreich gewesen, die Ordnung von St. Michaelis mit deutschen Regelwerken, zum Beispiel mit dem vom Autor erwähnten Leisniger Statut, zu kontrastieren, um ihren kirchengeschichtlichen Stellenwert genauer auszuloten.

Leider weist die vorliegende Studie erhebliche formale wie inhaltliche Mängel auf. Bereits die barocke Epik des sperrigen Untertitels lässt eine umständliche Gliederung der Studie ahnen, die sich im Inhaltsverzeichnis vollauf bestätigt: Rigoros werden knapp 190 Textseiten inklusive 1.100 Anmerkungen in 74 Kapitel, Unterkapitel und Zusammenfassungen zerstückelt. Mag eine solche Kleinteiligkeit einer Dissertation angemessen sein, so hätte dieses Dickicht spätestens für die Druckfassung radikal zurückgestutzt werden müssen. Die hohe Fußnotendichte in der ersten Hälfte des Bandes legt den Schluss nahe, dass in diesem Teil ein Kompilat aus Sekundärliteratur unter weitgehendem Verzicht auf originär eigene Gedanken referiert wird. Dieser Abhandlung ein Literaturverzeichnis von 43 Seiten mit 730 Titeln beizugeben lässt jede vernünftige Proportion vermissen. Dagegen wäre ein Personen- und Sachregister aller Mühen wert gewesen.

Dringend hätte es auch einer redaktionellen wie inhaltlichen Überarbeitung bedurft. Zwei bis drei Fehler in Syntax, Orthografie oder Grammatik pro Seite verdrießen selbst den geduldigsten Leser. Noch ärgerlicher ist die Fülle grober Schnitzer, die Schemmel unterlaufen. Gleich in der Einleitung taucht

---

[1] Vgl.: Johann Friedrich Handschuh an Heinrich Melchior Mühlenberg, Philadelphia, 3.6.1761, *Die Korrespondenz Heinrich Melchior Mühlenbergs*, Kurt Aland and Hermann Wellenreuther, eds., Vol. 2 (Berlin / New York: de Gruyter, 1986–2002): 462.

Gotthilf August Francke als Heinrich August Francke auf (vgl. 18). Später verwechselt ihn der Autor dann zweimal mit dessen Vater August Hermann (vgl. 128; 202). Aus dem Londoner Hofprediger Anton Wilhelm Böhme macht er einen Anton Jacob Böhme (vgl. 122). Die in Ostpreußen angesiedelten Salzburger Emigranten verpflanzt er ins polnisch-katholische Litauen, ohne darauf hinzuweisen, dass er hier natürlich das überwiegend evangelische 'Preußisch-Litauen' im damaligen Königreich Preußen, der späteren preußischen Provinz Ostpreußen, meint (vgl. 89). Pennsylvanias Provincial Council tauft er in Provincial County um (vgl. 183; 191). Auf Oktober statt August 1748 datiert er die Gründung eines "Deutschen lutherischen Ministeriums von Pennsylvanien und angrenzender Staaten" (155; 162; 168; 184; 202), die unter diesem fiktiven Namen allein schon deshalb nicht hat erfolgen können, weil 'Staaten' in Nordamerika zu jener Zeit bekanntlich noch gar nicht existierten.

Dass Schemmel die Inkorporation der St.-Michaelis-Kirche in Philadelphia 1765 unzutreffend auf alle "Vereinigten Gemeinden" (149-50) bezieht, nährt weitere Zweifel an seiner Sachkenntnis. Anders als er hervorhebt, verfügten Pfarrer in Pennsylvania, wie etwa Mühlenberg, durchaus über Grundbesitz (vgl. 153). Auch hatte der jüngere Francke mitnichten Pastor Weygand entsandt (vgl. 153-54). Vielmehr warnte er frühzeitig vor ihm, weil Weygand "eine ordentliche vocation ausgeschlagen" und "den Antrag solcher Leute, die selbst keinen Beruf haben, derselben vorgezogen" habe.[2] Während es in Kapitel neun zutreffend heißt, der erste vom Ministerium ordinierte Kandidat sei "allein ihm gegenüber verantwortlich" (169) gewesen, behauptet das "Fazit" in Kapitel elf irrtümlich, er sei "allein Mühlenberg gegenüber verantwortlich" (202) gewesen. Untragbar werden solche Patzer dort, wo sie Aussagen Dritter entstellen. So liest Schemmel in Franckes Antwort auf eine Bitte aus Amerika um einen Pastor die Bedingung einer "Ordination der Pfarrer in Halle" (132) hinein. Dabei hatte Francke lediglich verlangt, dass Prediger für den Dienst dort "in hiesigem Lande vorhero ordiniret werden,"[3] besaßen doch weder die Stiftungen noch sonstige Institutionen in Halle das Ordinationsrecht. An anderer Stelle schreibt Schemmel beim Paraphrasieren eines Fremdzitats dem Sendschreiben Mühlenbergs von 1741 theologische Positionen zu, die jener Autor aber gerade nicht ihm, sondern einem orthodoxlutherischen Gegner attestierte (102n58).[4] Im Vergleich dazu erscheint die munter wechselnde Schreibweise von Ortsnamen wie New Hanover oder Providence nurmehr als störende Lässlichkeit (127-63). Zu begrüßen ist Schemmels Versuch, den Inhalt seiner Studie grafisch zu verdeutlichen. Leider enttäuscht Abbildung 1 zu Kirchenaustritten in Deutschland sogleich mit einem weiteren Lapsus, fehlt doch der Hinweis, dass alle Mitgliederzahlen mit dem Faktor 1.000 zu multiplizieren sind (vgl. 213). Die nächste Nachlässigkeit folgt in Abbildung 2 zur Mitgliedschaft in US-Kirchen (vgl. ebd.). Hier muss der zu ergänzende Faktor stillschweigend gar auf 1.000.000 quadriert werden, um die korrekten Jahresdaten zu erhalten.

Insgesamt muss man bedauern, dass Schemmel nicht mehr aus seinem Thema gemacht und nicht sorgfältiger gearbeitet hat. Während die Unachtsamkeiten in Orthografie und Grammatik von Flüchtigkeit bei der Manuskripterstellung zeugen, führen die vielen Sachfehler zu handfesten Falschinformationen. Dass diese meist nur kundigen Lesern auffallen werden, kann nicht trösten, zumal die Zahl der in Deutschland angefertigten Studien zum deutschen kirchlichen Protestantismus in Nordamerika vor 1800 ohnehin schon recht gering ist.

Halle   Wolfgang Splitter

---

[2] Vgl.: Gotthilf August Francke an Peter Brunnholz und Heinrich Melchior Mühlenberg, Halle, 23.7.1748, *Die Korrespondenz Heinrich Melchior Mühlenbergs*, Vol. 1, 311.

[3] Vgl.: William J. Mann et al., eds., *Nachrichten von den vereinigten Deutschen Evangelisch-Lutherischen Gemeinen in Nord-America, absonderlich in Pen[n]sylvanien*, Vol. 1 (Allentown, PA: 1886): 54.

[4] Vgl.: Thomas J. Müller, *Kirche zwischen zwei Welten*, Transatlantische Historische Studien 2 (Stuttgart: Franz Steiner, 1994): 87–88. Vgl. bes. 87 Mitte.

AXEL JANSEN, *Alexander Dallas Bache: Building the American Nation through Science and Education in the Nineteenth Century* (Frankfurt/M./New York: Campus, 2011), 353 pp.

Alexander Dallas Bache (1806-1867) war eine Schlüsselfigur in der amerikanischen Wissenschaftsorganisation und -politik im zweiten Drittel des neunzehnten Jahrhunderts: Er wurde 1843 zum 'Superintendent' des US Coast Survey ernannt und stand damit der damals größten "science-related federal institution" vor (197). Bache war zudem von großem Einfluss auf die American Association for the Advancement of Science (AAAS) und er gehörte schließlich zu den Gründern der National Academy of Sciences, deren erster Präsident er 1863 wurde. Axel Jansen unternimmt im vorliegenden Buch, das auf seine Frankfurter Habilitationsschrift zurückgeht, den Versuch, Bache als genuinen Repräsentanten einer Wissenschaft zu sehen, die nur universal gedacht werden konnte und sich zugleich "intrinsic to national development" verhielt (105). Den Impuls zur Verbindung von Wissenschaft und 'nation building' deutet Jansen aus der familiären Konstellation heraus: Bache war ein Urenkel von Benjamin Franklin und die Familie der Mutter gehörte über Generationen hinweg zur politischen Elite Pennsylvanias. Das zentrale Problem, vor das sich Bache gestellt sah und das Jansen ins Zentrum seines Arguments stellt, war die Fragilität der 'American nationhood.' Jansen, der bereits in seinem ersten Buch am Beispiel des Einsatzes von Amerikanern auf dem europäischen Kriegsschauplatz und in der französischen Armee in den Jahren von 1914 bis 1917 nach der Bindungskraft der amerikanischen Nation gefragt hat,[1] sieht einen engen Zusammenhang zwischen dem "lack of a consolidated national perspective" (19) vor dem Bürgerkrieg und einer unzureichenden nationalen politischen Vergemeinschaftung. Die Ungleichzeitigkeit von Wissenschaftsentwicklung und 'nation building' wurde zur großen Herausforderung: "To Bache, the problem was not how to implement the profession in the nation, but how to implement a nation that could provide the institutional framework for the profession" (238). Bache fürchtete, dass das Desinteresse des Staates an der Wissenschaft die amerikanische Profession auf lange Zeit in Abhängigkeit von europäischen Kollegen und Institutionen halten werde. Die Gründung der National Academy 1863—auch als Bekenntnis der Wissenschaft zur Union— war ein persönlicher Erfolg und doch auch nur eine weitere Bekräftigung des 'Vorsprungs' den die Profession vor dem 'nation building' hatte: "the Academy stood for the profession's support of the American nation state rather than for the nation's support of science as a profession" (310).

Jansens Ausleuchtung der Person Bache und die Technik des close reading (in der Anwendung sequenzanalytischer Verfahren der von Ulrich Oevermann entwickelten objektiven Hermeneutik) sorgen für ein ungemein präzises, nuanciertes und auch empathisches Porträt von Bache. Freilich bleibt in Jansens Analyse bisweilen zu wenig Raum für jene, die mit und neben Bache für ähnliche Ziele eintraten: Sie bleiben nicht unerwähnt, bilden aber fast nur Kulisse und Stichwortgeber für Bache, der in Jansens Buch immer zentral und führend ist. Die Frage nach Baches Bedeutung für die amerikanische Wissenschaft kann aber nicht ausschließlich mit der Darstellung seiner eigenen intellektuellen Entwicklung und seiner organisatorischen Arbeit beantwortet werden—mitunter müssen Akteurskonstellationen und politische Zusammenhänge, wie zum Beispiel Whiggism, Henry Clays 'American System' und machtpolitische Schwächen des Bürgertums in der demokratisierten Gesellschaft in Rechnung gestellt werden, die gegebenenfalls auch eine Relativierung seiner Bedeutung zulassen können. Bache wirkt in Jansens Buch sehr 'perfekt' und immer passgenau für das Analysefeld aus 'nation building' und Wissenschaftsorganisation. Dass sich Bache und die gleichgesinnten Wissenschaftler Joseph Henry, Benjamin Peirce und Louis Agassiz in den 1850er Jahren selbst als Gruppe verstanden und sich ironisch 'Lazzaroni' nannten—nach dem Begriff für jene Unterschicht Neapels, die in den Jahren der Französischen Revolution auf Seiten der Monarchie bzw. der Bourbonen standen— erwähnt Jansen und deutet es als "romantic reference to a band of outsiders" (250). Außen vor bleibt aber, wer in diesem Zusammenhang die 'insider' sind. Meist erweckt Jansen den Eindruck, als ob Bache und seine Mitstreiter gegen Gleichgültigkeit, Selbstgenügsamkeit und einen an Intervention und Wissenschaftspolitik uninteressierten Staat anzukämpfen

---

[1] Vgl. Axel Jansen, *Individuelle Bewährung im Krieg: Amerikaner in Europa 1914-1917* (Frankfurt/M.: Campus, 2003).

hatten. Das ist sicher nicht falsch, aber die Postulierung eines am europäischen Beispiel orientierten engen, gewissermaßen notwendigen Zusammenhangs aus 'nation building' und Wissenschaft lässt von vornherein eine Alternative zur nationalen Organisation und zum staatlichen Horizont der Wissenschaft nicht zu. Jansen kann am Beispiel Baches und seiner Mitstreiter denkbar klar analysieren, warum ein Teil der amerikanischen Wissenschaft exakt jenen Nexus aus Nation, Staat und Wissenschaft zum wechselseitigen Vorteil betrieb. Die Ursachen für das Desinteresse eines anderen Teils der amerikanischen Wissenschaft am Staat wird dadurch freilich nicht erklärt. Waren jene Wissenschaftler, die unter dem Ausbleiben einer National Academy offensichtlich nicht gelitten haben, nur Repräsentanten einer unfertigen Nation? Lässt sich von einer in den Interessenslagen der Wissenschaft (und vieler privater Institutionen) begründeten Verspätung der nationalen Wissenschaftspolitik reden? Oder boten die USA ein Beispiel für eine Wissenschaftsorganisation, die sich im Unterschied zu den traditionellen europäischen Nationalstaaten nicht nur durch Fragmentierung, sondern dadurch auch durch eine stärkere Pluralisierung auszeichnete — mit Folgen für die Qualität der Wissenschaft? Wie viel Staat und Nation braucht die Wissenschaft im neunzehnten Jahrhundert wirklich? Jansens Buch liefert ein wichtiges Stück der Wissenschafts(organisations)geschichte der USA und verhilft zu neuen Fragen — in beidem liegt kein geringes Verdienst seiner Studie.

Linz   Marcus Gräser

ANDREA MEHRLÄNDER, *The Germans of Charleston, Richmond and New Orleans during the Civil War Period, 1850 – 1870: A Study and Research Compendium* (Berlin/New York: de Gruyter, 2011), 442 pp.

If there is one thing that is wrong with this book, it is most likely the fact that it was originally published as a dissertation. If this is the form in which it was submitted, it should have been on the habilitation level. In terms of thoroughness, diligence, depth of research and insight, and usefulness, there are very few like it that I am aware of.

Having started to love the South through watching *Gone with the Wind* at age ten is not the usual point of origin for an academic career. In this case, however, Andrea Mehrländer did not stop with a romantic infatuation (though she still likes *Gone with the Wind*), but travelled through the South, did extensive research in archives and museums, coaxed dozens of German-stock families to share their private documents, letters, diaries, memoirs, and photographs related to the Civil War period, and worked this into a path-breaking book. In his foreword, Robert N. Rosen, President of the Fort Sumter / Fort Moultrie Historical Trust, also calls it "the most authoritative study, indeed the definite work" (v) on the Germans in the Confederacy. This is probably true, even though Mehrländer's is also the first book on the Confederate Germans anyway.

The eight major (Roman numeral) chapters are devoted to German antebellum immigration, the urban South as a settlement ground, Nativism in Richmond and New Orleans, and the comparable lack thereof in Charleston, Antebellum militia organisations in all three cities (somewhat incongruously New Orleans gets a whole chapter by itself this time), a long chapter on the participation of the Germans from these three cities in the Civil War, Southern urban Germans under siege conditions, and the first phase of reconstruction. Bibliography and sources take up some forty pages, another forty go to material such as company rosters, with twenty more being devoted to comparative population statistics — great and ample material not just for historians but also for sociologists and for urban and migration studies in general.

Andrea Mehrländer, currently managing director of the Berlin-based Checkpoint Charlie Foundation, has delved into every detail of her subject. She knows exactly how many of the high-profile German Forty-Eighter refugees settled in the Southern States — there were eight (cf. 24) — and of them, most went to Texas or stayed in urban New Orleans. It is highly interesting to see how the Germans, most of whom were either adverse to slavery or at least not disposed favourably to it, negotiated urban spaces in the South. There is a lot of background information on the cities themselves, the general situation of their inhabitants, the number of volunteer fire companies in Charleston — there were twenty (cf. 33), including a German one (cf. 41) — and their quality (they were more like sports clubs), as well as the number of German churches in New Orleans, of which there were twenty-nine (cf. 69).

The parts that come close to Clifford Geertz' 'thick description' are of course the personal life-stories, which are based on a variety of sources and in their vast majority presented here for the first time. It is amazing how deep Mehrländer has delved into the family histories of many people, and quite surprising that much of this material was available at all—the Civil War itself left much less archival material in the South than what was amassed, catalogued, and bound together with the eponymous 'red tape' in the Union states. The 'German scare' of 1917 also contributed to the obliteration of a lot of material pertaining to and signalling German ancestry. Stories like the one of seafaring Captain Heinrich Wieting, who personally accounted for three out of four of Charleston's Germans (cf. 37-38), of Christian Roselius from Bremen, who was a foreigner and a Know-Nothing representative, slaveholder and Unionist (cf. 70-72), and the Melchers and Wageners of Charleston are not just well-researched and presented as scholarly material, they also make 'rattling good history' as the late Shelby Foote would have said.

The massive focus on the military (cf. 77-212) is owed to the topic and its temporal range on the one hand, and the availability of records on the other. In this field, differences are also most easily visible: while Germans formed a score of regiments within weeks of the outbreak of hostilities in Missouri, Pennsylvania, Ohio, and New York, Louis Hellwig complained bitterly about the hesitancy of Germans in New Orleans to form as much as a battalion (cf. 130). Only the third attempt, under the auspices of the Prussian consul Augustus Reichard, proved successful: the German companies became part of the twentieth Louisiana (cf. 141). To arrive at tenable numbers for the German participation in the Confederate war effort is difficult for a variety of reasons. However, Mehrländer's research produces a number of highly interesting insights that range far beyond previous scholarship to include not just the highly visible observers and participants like Scheibert, von Borcke, or Buchel (cf. 147). She goes into personal detail and not only provides a first insight into a unit like Captain Bachmann's 'German Volunteers' from Charleston but also unearthed what is likely the only diary extant from this unit (cf. 161-62). These stories are set off again against detailed charts and lists giving information on age, occupation, number of slaves owned, and the like. Analogous chapters and figures are available for the 'Virginia' and the 'Marion Rifles' as Co. K of the First and Fifteenth Regiments of the Virginia Volunteer Infantry.

The conclusion that the hitherto maintained insignificance of the German ethnic communities in the South has been revised by this book is entirely justifiable. The pro-slavery and pro-Southern attitude of Germans settling in the three cities (other than e.g. in Texas) can be assumed for the simple reason that they might have settled elsewhere and knew what they were doing. However, to speak of 'the' Germans means to neglect the differences between the life and the experiences of native Germans in these three cities.

By comparison, there are few if any grievances. Chapter 6.1 mentions among the anti-German sentiments in the South reactions to Sherman's March, which, having taken place late in 1864, would hardly have registered (cf. 149), while missing out on the German reputation as 'nigger-lovers.' In chapter 8 on the early reconstruction period, the chapter is limited to 1865-70, but the first subchapter deals with New Orleans 1862-65. There are some formally maudlin points ('ibid.' refers to place, not person, and an occasional relative clause beginning with 'who' preceded by a comma, as in German) but nothing serious or detracting.

Of course, the thoroughness of this thesis-turned-book is somewhat aided by the fact that there were, according to census data, only 71,962 native-born Germans in the eleven States that seceded in 1860-61. Anything planned on a similar scale for the Germans in—and for—the Union would have to be gigantic in scale: where there were twelve ethnic German Confederate companies (cf. 9) that form the core of Mehrländer's research (cf. 143-212), there were thirty-five regiments for the Union, and about 200,000 German-born men who fought to suppress the rebellion. However, whoever might attempt a similar study for individual cities, or states, will have to look to Andrea Mehrländer's book as the measuring rod. In any case, this will be a tough act to follow.

Freiburg i. Br.   Wolfgang Hochbruck

EVE TAVOR BANNET, *Transatlantic Stories and the History of Reading, 1720–1810: Migrant Fictions* (New York: Oxford UP, 2011), 295 pp.

Eve Tavor Bannet's book *Transatlantic Stories and the History of Reading* is a survey of the political and social implications of eighteenth century narratives that have been reprinted, adapted, or edited on both sides of the Atlantic. Bannet divides these narratives into three thematic clusters on the Atlantic trade, different types of servitude, and sentimentalism to show how each variation and generic change of a story offers a different point of view on them. By employing a discursive-analytical approach, Bannet probes the possible functions that each narrative may fulfill in conversations about war, liberty, and captivity and regards them as expressions of a "transatlantic subaltern subculture" (4) uniting the poor and enslaved from both sides of the Atlantic. Bannet constructs these narratives as socially engaged literature that is concerned with the roles of men and women, transculturation, and the possibility of a transatlantic union of the poor, enslaved, and suppressed. Next to discussing their content and the historical context, Bannet often refers to paratextual elements to indicate changes of print-format and genre. Epitomes, versions, and reprints in collections present only a few of the strategies for reframing and adapting stories for the print markets in Britain and North America. Bannet calls these "native fabrications," (3) a claim to literary independence, and explores the various ways in which texts became transatlantic, either by topic, author, or by the fact that they were appropriated or adapted by printers on the other side of the Atlantic. At the same time, each re-use and adaptation of a story represents a materialized reading. These readings are, according to Bannet, highly indebted to their respective context and often address issues or views not entailed in the original text, confounding the modern notion of original and copy.

The book is divided into three sections, each beginning with a short introduction that breaks down the chapter's theme into specific issues and types of prints that are explored in the subsequent chapters. The first part maps the Atlantic as a space for sea voyages, adventure, and captivity and revolves around narratives of traders, Barbary captivity, piracy, and island retreat. Comparing a number of epitomes and versions of Defoe's *The Life and Strange Surprising Adventures of Robinson Crusoe*, Bannet finds that they seek to rectify the absence of issues such as piracy, slavery, transculturation, or the roles of men and women in captivity by adding a larger Atlantic panorama to Crusoe's travels. Making their protagonists at turns slaves, slave holders, traders, pirates, or hermits, the narratives under survey modify these roles as fortune and power relations shift and even weak positions allow for new forms of agency. For example, Penelope Aubin's *Noble Slaves* shows how female captives could protect their honor and even escape to Britain whereas William Chetwood's Captain Boyle acts as a merchant and pirate while trading in smuggled goods with various colonies. In the second part, Bannet examines different kinds of servitude, exploring the lives of indentured servants, convicts, free blacks, and women. Because the distinction between servants and slaves was not reflected in their living and working conditions but merely employed by the slave owners for ideological reasons, Bannet assembles a number of texts that unite these groups and also includes the relationship between Christianized Natives and European missionaries as in the autobiography of Samson Occom and *The Female American*. According to Bannett, these transatlantic narratives show the plight of the poor and those without a voice as they struggle for recognition and freedom in America and Britain alike. America more often than not emerges as a replication of social and legal conditions of England where real liberty can only be reached outside its borders. By contrast, the America portrayed in *Elizabeth Canning* and *Mr. Anderson* offers a bond between the poor and subservient but also the possibility of raising their masters' respective moral awareness.

The last section shows how Robert Bell's compilation *Miscellanies for Sentimentalists* criticizes and comments on the Revolutionary War through a number of works influenced by sentimental discourse. His collection at once disparages the immoral pursuit of pleasure by British polite society while it uses its very codes of honor and gentility to instill bravery and discipline into the American army. Hence, while *The Pupil of Pleasure* and *The Man of the World* apply Chesterton's principles of politeness to the ruin of a family, a number of English military handbooks should teach American officers the rules of warfare as well as gallant behavior in the face of danger. *Emma Corbett*, by contrast, attacks this shared "soldierly ideal" (216) by showing the repercussions on individual members of a family spanning Britain and America and fighting on both sides.

Transatlantic Stories makes an important argument for the inclusion of the various forms and adaptations of an eighteenth-century story into literary scholarship by capturing the different viewpoints and generic qualities that emerge from the then far greater influence of printers and editors. Bannet maintains that, "[o]ur post-romantic emphasis on originality has fostered denigration and exclusion from 'literature proper' of works resulting from practices of imitation [...] which were fundamental to all forms of eighteenth-century writing, as well as the [...] book trade" (10). Taken together, her analyses show how much each actualization of a story is engrained in the context of its time and place of publication. Introducing techniques of versioning and epitomizing as some of the ways in which stories were changed and reprinted over time, Bannet generally deduces genre distinctions from titles and other paratexts and—though the term is not defined in more detail or related to larger generic developments—implicitly defines 'stories' as individually published prose narratives. Concentrating on Anglo-American prints, *Transatlantic Stories* does not include transatlantic narratives or translations from other European sources as well as those adapted for publication in literary magazines. Yet for those interested in the history and publications of the eighteenth century as well as in opportunities for further study, Bannet's ample and detailed account paints a rich picture of the historical background of printing as well as individual narratives, relating them to Federalist politics, to smuggling, the English penal code, or Barbary captivity.

In her introduction, Bannet argues that rather than for formal or aesthetic reasons, these narratives were marginalized because they "tell us something about experiences [...] that we do not normally read and teach" (3) and "people who experienced and portrayed empire from below" (4). To rectify this point, Bannet uncovers and aptly selects an interesting blend of primary sources along with an impressive amount of documentary evidence and secondary sources. This very strength makes Bannet's account at times rather descriptive, and the diversity of issues and methodology create an impression of heterogeneity that makes it difficult to establish a "master-narrative," (18) as Bannet admits in her introduction. While Bannet's approach to create a history of reading by analyzing versions and reproductions of a story is worthwhile, given the lack of other data, her assumptions of how a given text resonates with a particular audience—however convincing—are difficult to verify. Generally, Bannet matches political and social issues with the natural concerns of specific readerships without paying much attention to the texts' entertainment value, the study of reading habits, or reader comments and marginalia in the copies. While she stresses the importance of not reading these texts according to modern notions of literature, Bannet uses concepts like abolitionism and feminism to evaluate the likes of *Mr. Anderson* and Pratt's *Emma Corbett*, long before these movements came into being. To be fair, Bannet understands her book as a starting point for exploring the variety of intentions, values, and market conditions involved in reprinting and editing eighteenth century narratives. Especially its breadth of material and topical issues make it valuable to scholars of eighteenth-century English and American literature, history, and print culture.

All in all, *Transatlantic Stories* brings together a host of primary and secondary sources to show how marginalized narratives and print products offer alternative experiences and evaluations of political and social issues of the day. As a study of eighteenth-century transatlantic print culture, Bannet's book sheds new light on the various genres, market conditions, and historical contexts involved in the adaptation of existing narratives in England and America. It not only raises the issue of how much we overlook by concentrating on a canon based on originality but also of how to describe and analyze the various print genres of the eighteenth century without applying modern notions of art and literature on them.

Mainz   Martin Seidl

NICOLE WALLER, *American Encounters with Islam in the Atlantic World* (Heidelberg: Winter, 2011), 257 pp.

As is so often the case in times of national crisis, the events of 9/11 and the following years have caused the United States to look back on historical episodes of conflict with Islam. Such analyses commonly focus on violent episodes that reveal a clear discrepancy between U.S. culture and that of its enemy. In contrast, this study of captivity narratives ranging from the seventeenth to the twenty-first century—written by Nicole Waller, Professor of American Cultural Studies at the University of Potsdam—suggests that "American nationhood was not only created, tested, and contrasted against Islam, it was also examined, critiqued, and even undermined" (3). As a classic genre of cultural encounter (the most famous of which certainly being that of Mrs. Rowlandson), the captivity narrative's typical plot narrates the attack, captivity, physical and spiritual trials, and eventual release, rescue, or escape of an innocent individual at the hands of the savage. In Waller's reading, these narratives, and the entailing identity crises of Americans following captivity by Muslims, might be seen as constitutive for the American consciousness as a whole, and thereby "establish Islam as one of the driving forces in American history and culture" (8). Waller hopes to establish a counterpoint to isolationist interpretations of American history and to maintain a perspective on American encounters with Islam that might open up intercultural discourses with what is still most often presented as the savage yet exotic 'other.' As her terminology reveals, the author draws upon the historical and theoretical works of Ammiel Alcalay, Paul Baepler, Thomas R. Kidd, Timothy Marr, Walter D. Mignolo, and Edward Said in her analysis of these captivity narratives. Following a two-fold approach, Waller first argues that such narratives were employed to negotiate varying elements of Americanness against a purposefully constructed 'other,' i.e. "situating Islam as geographically elsewhere and envisioning the American nation's relationship to this elsewhere," a "global matrix" (26) there for the United States to fill as needed. Simultaneously, she attempts to read "maps as narratives and texts as mental maps" (38). This approach allows her to portray the (mind-) mapping and worldviews of the individual authors, describing the continuous shift from a Mediterranean towards an Atlantic center of the world, and the subsequent geographical adjustment of the borders of civilization to the U.S. nation situating its alternating spheres of influence within a global world. The constant repositioning of boundaries and the displacement of home, nation, and sacred spaces onto the foreign maps in captivity narratives are read as crises of security, religion, and identity. In Waller's methodological description, "this means a move from the levels of both identity politics and national historiography to the level of epistemology and cosmology in our analysis of intercultural encounters" (38-39).

Following this theoretical introduction, Waller begins with a concise discussion of John Smith's *True Travels* (1630), which tells of his enslavement by Muslim corsairs. In Waller's reading, Smith's descriptions of the Barbary States and their slave trade reveals an overlap in his mental map of the Medieval conflict of faith between Muslims and Christians, fought out around the Mediterranean, and the Early Modern shift following the Reformation and Western Christian schism, as well as the 'discovery' of the American continent and the subsequent shift towards an Atlantic world. This tension within the narrative hints at the future struggles of American authors to locate Islam at the physical, cultural, and religious edge of their world map despite constant cultural interaction.

In the following chapter, Waller discusses late seventeenth century captivity narratives in relation to Cotton Mather's millennialism. Drawing on recent scholarship on the typology of New England Puritanism, Waller demonstrates how Mather employed the fate of Puritans enslaved in North Africa as a theological tool to map out a 'sacred geography' in which Muslims had their own particular part as instruments of God's providence. As Waller correctly argues, North America itself held no particular importance in Mather's millennialism. Rather, the global community of visible saints, which included the elect anywhere in the world, was the foundation for his mind-map. Mather's faith therefore allowed him to move beyond Smith's depictions of Christianity versus the heathenish 'other,' including Islam as part of an uniformly sinful world, rather than excluding and relocating it to the fringes of civilization. In Mather's analogy, the Barbary States serve as a manifest location of spiritual tribulation, in which enslaved Puritans nonetheless remained connected to the global community through spiritual ties not severed by distance and dislocation. In this manner, Waller describes Mather's theologically inspired mental map, which incorporated Muslims and Islam into God's providence, as an unidirectional mode of cultural contact in a global world of potential faithful.

While depictions of the social and religious structures of the Islamic states generally served as projections of cultural and political anxiety during the negotiation of American nationhood in the young Republic, Waller's example, James Leander Cathcart's narrative *The Captives*, allows a more complex perspective. In her reading, Cathcart undermines the construction of cultural binaries, as he not only sees his own identity altered by his contact with Islam when it slips into his language and affects his opinions of non-American 'Western' nations, but he also subverts religious and national identity building as a whole. This is made especially clear when Waller offers a later geographical journal, in which Cathcart describes his travels through the newly acquired Louisiana territory, while creating a discursive closeness between the wilderness and slavery system of the area and that of the Barbary Coast. Here, the seemingly clear-cut distinction between American national identity and Christian morality located on the one side of the Atlantic, and the 'tyranny' of North African slave states and the Muslims' barbarism on the other, is thrown into disarray. Finally, Waller juxtaposes Cathcart's writings with the slave narrative of Omar ibn Said, a North African Muslim enslaved and brought to the United States, whose own identity was marked by violent yet ultimately integrated experiences of cultural border-crossing. Both authors situate religion between these cultural spheres by reducing each to central religious beliefs compatible with both faiths. In conjunction, both captivity narratives demonstrate how models of cultural cohabitation and identification were created despite ideological attempts of cultural and religious segregation in the formation of U.S. nationhood. In fact, these narratives of intercultural dialogue by Cathcart and ibn Said would have been well worth more discussion.

Waller's final chapter, chronologically set almost two centuries later, is an analysis of two narratives concerned with the captivity of Jessica Lynch in the second Iraq War that continue the logic of cultural isolationism, and one novel which attempts to overcome such limitations. The omniscient narrator of *I Am a Soldier Too: The Jessica Lynch Story*, written by Rick Bragg and authorized by Lynch, offers a seemingly truthful description of this capture, depicting Iraq as a wasteland frontier where even the sand and soil themselves are at war with the soldiers, and 'the others' capture helpless women in service. Contrasting Iraq with the 'true America' of West Virginia, Lynch's home state, the narrative follows the well-established geographical separation of American and enemy territory. In this account, Lynch is pulled from her Christian home and family, and brought into the war zone through a geographical mistake rather than as part of an invasive force. While Bragg's narrator is at times at odds with Lynch's actual memory, the general narrative of the American soldiers liberating both Lynch and Iraq is corroborated by Mohammed al-Rehaief, whose own narrative *Because Every Life Is Precious* highlights his part in Lynch's rescue. Rather than complicating the clear separation between American and Iraqi citizens or Christians and Muslims, Waller reads his narrative as neatly fitting into the overall narrative of America's war against Islamist terror. Waller here contrasts such clear distinctions of religion and culture with the novel *Crescent* by Diana Abu-Jaber, which continues the tradition of ibn Said and Cathcart. Her characters, developed in two strands of narratives, reveal 'true' Arab-American hybrid identities, including a typical trickster figure who frustrates all attempts at cultural homogeneity and in turn evokes troubling images of such transatlantic topics as the American slave trade and imperialism. While the narrative of Jessica Lynch depicts the Atlantic as both a natural and a cultural boundary, Abu-Jaber's protagonists hint at a more complex perspective on the Atlantic Ocean as a space of fluid identities. In a nutshell, Waller contrasts depictions of cultural division and of Islam as the projection space for American authors with discourses of genuine cultural crossings. Her attempt to construct a counterpoint to ideologies of culture wars here merges with her hope for future research that might bridge the gap between Western and Islamic readings of such cultural contacts from a different perspective and offer new historical material between the beginning of the nineteenth and the close of the twentieth century.

Tübingen   Michael Dopffel

BRADLEY A. JOHNSON, *The Characteristic Theology of Herman Melville: Aesthetics, Politics, and Duplicity* (Eugene, OR: Pickwick, 2012). iii + 168 pp.

Bradley A. Johnson investigates Herman Melville's characteristic (a term Johnson keeps intentionally ambiguous) theology by examining the ways in which Melville's novels "model the aesthetic-theological dimensions of subjectivity and in the process 'characterize' [...] theology as a revolutionary Subject" (8). Both Melville the author and the characters in his fiction emerge as subjects only when they invent, relate, and narrate themselves and, through this creative activity, become theological. Johnson balances a plethora of philosophical and narratological discourses in his study. However, readers expecting yet another chronological investigation of the sediment of Melville's religious views in his fiction will search in vain here. About halfway through the book, Johnson notes that while his "inquiry is thoroughly theological in its scope, it is assuredly not so in its genre" (77). Rather, he characterizes his project as an attempt to refute the tendency within Melville studies to connote discussions of faith in Melville's fiction with the frustrating realization of "one's epistemic inability to see beyond the mask of phenomenal limitation" (8). In contrast, Johnson proposes that the Melvillean subject productively arises from "the unthinkable [...] possibility of freedom that unavoidably emerges from the material, creative processes at work in self-characterization" (8). Johnson's programmatic aim is "to revaluate the immanent, self-creative potential of the masquerade as a whole" (150) by suggesting that the subject 'per excellence' can only ever be the subject playing a character, for only in aesthetic creation and performance can the subject be itself and for another, i.e. occupy "the twin matrices of subjective agency and its power of objectification" (8).

Chapter one, entitled "Melville and the Problem of Self-Representation," suggests that while drafting his south-sea adventurer protagonist in his first novel, *Typee* (1846), Melville simultaneously drafts himself as adventure novelist. Tommo, the protagonist, was loosely based on Melville's own experiences as a sailor in the Marquesan isles. This blending of character and author caused controversy upon the novel's publication. Johnson compellingly combines the issue of subject formation with well-researched expository notes on Melville's writing career to illustrate how the authenticity of Melville's account becomes a hotly contested issue in the critical reception of *Typee*. From these early endeavors, Melville learns that he can be "never entirely himself" as an author (29). For Johnson, this realization sets in motion a perpetual process of self-construction. Compared to the others, this chapter is lightly theorized, due to its focus on *Typee*'s textual history.

Chapter two, named "Melville and German Romanticism," argues somewhat obliquely that *Mardi* (1849) and Melville's review essay "Hawthorne and His Mosses" share "with German Romanticism a conceptualization of the self and the Absolute," while his materialism ultimately sets Melville apart from such idealism (46). Johnson utilizes Fichte and Kant's ideas about subject formation, as well as Schlegel's system of aesthetics to describe how Melville's earlier realization about the self-alienation of authorship produces subjective and creative excess in his fiction. *Mardi*, contrary to *Typee* an expressly fictitious account, ultimately proves too small a vessel for Melville's continuous intellectual unfolding within himself. Johnson maintains that, to cope with this excess, Melville begins emphasizing "irony, duplicity, and disguise" (75) in his plots and artistic process and develops a programmatic ambiguity that sets up the subject positions of both author and audience. Accordingly, we "can engage a text by Melville only insofar as we are uncertain where or how to begin it" (76) and how to situate ourselves in it.

Chapter three, "Melville and Dialectical Materialism," contemplates the inevitability of masquerade as a strategy for aesthetic and subjective expression in light of Schelling's philosophy, which casts even God as the function of a consciousness expressing itself (cf. 87). At intervals, Johnson's philosophic excursions lead him off the beaten path of Melville's midway novels, *Moby-Dick* and *Pierre* (1852), into investigations of beginnings and ontological origins, which are not identical for Johnson. The "unthinkable absolute singularity that beckons us to begin" and repress all other beginnings constitutes for Johnson the "primordial intensity of an active [...] condition for the creative possibility of beginning at all" (79). *Moby-Dick* and *Pierre* are still integrated here, even if their discussion is comparatively global: To illustrate how Melville carries out his authorial struggle in his fiction, we are briefly reminded not to dismiss Ishmael's "reflective complexity," through which "Ishmael-as-character retroactively [. . .] informs his own characterization by Ishmael-as-narrator" (80). However, this chapter takes unconventional and sometimes surprising detours. For instance, Johnson employs the 2005 Bush Inaugural Address to illustrate the self-perpetuating logic of "The Call," which apparently fuels conservative administrations, Captain Ahab, and creative subjects alike. With the help of Plato and Žižek—again quite independently of Melville's texts—Johnson concludes that the authorial and creative subject only becomes itself by being for another. In this paradox Johnson finds Melville's final embrace of the "affirmative potential of a self-becoming that is also a self-creation" (111).

Chapter Four, "Melville's Aesthetic Theology," explores the masquerade in *The Confidence-Man* as the actualization of this proposed paradoxical, dualistic, and creative subject. With the aid of Derrida's concept of the secret, Johnson postulates the intersubjective "giving and taking of truth and of lie" (114) as Melville's assumed default social condition in his fiction. In *The Confidence-Man*, Melville becomes interested in the "social bonds that govern this virtual economy of secrets" (114), rather than in the imbalance of power and knowledge that secrecy creates. The limited access of characters to each other, which results from this economy, ultimately indicates the limited access of the subject to itself: "the Subject is its own stranger" (125). Johnson goes on to show that the subject's "essence is not concealed by the mask but *is itself* [emphasis in original] precisely as it is masked" (126). This "theatrical role-play" reveals "a certain aesthetic theological intensity immanent in life itself" (126). Melville constructs an alternative to Judeo-Christian desire-based ontology, which has its subjects perceive reality as a veil to be pierced. In *The Confidence-Man* "malleability and potential" (135) are therefore given materialistic gravity and thus get "privileged over essence" (135). This reshuffling of epistemological hierarchies sets up "subjectivity qua characterization" (135).

The stratagem of reading Melville's fiction retroactively through the lens of masquerade and ambiguity crafted in *The Confidence-Man* (1857) is intriguing insofar as it departs from canonical readings of Melville's work through the lens of *Moby-Dick* (1851).[1] However, Johnson's characterization of Melville's work as a system that linearly approaches a sophisticated, philosophical end often ignores the multifarious cultural and personal influences to which Melville finds himself subjected. Occasionally, Johnson seems less interested in the impact of German Romanticism on Melville's fiction than in examining Romanticist subject formation in terms of Lacanian 'jouissance.' (Johnson cautiously distances himself from the term, arguably in order to preclude the implied sense of confinement for artistic production). Nevertheless, Johnson later declares that his project consists of the "casting of theology as a Subject through the frame of Herman Melville" (146). Despite this issue of emphasis, Johnson's readings of Melville's early and last novels are convincingly researched and argued, and operate under the compelling premise that Melville "was astutely attuned to the dialectical dynamics at work in the process of self-creation" (7). Johnson's conclusion that Melville ultimately abandons the Calvinist search for universal Truth in favor of a complex notion of empowerment derived from the manipulation of surfaces might seemingly fall into the trap of mistaking German Romantic idealism for Melville's own. While it is accurate to say that Melville never fully abandoned his metaphysical project, assigning a final comfortableness, even with the creative praxis of ambiguity, seems uncharacteristic for this author.

Literary critics, such as Nathalia Wright, Lawrance Thompson, T. Walter Herbert,[2]

---

[1] See Lawrance Thompson, *Melville's Quarrel with God* (Princeton: Princeton UP, 1952), in which Thompson shows how Melville uses the figure of the Confidence-Man—the swindler representing God because he too operates by methods of misrecognition and ambiguity—to cope with the increasingly "misanthropic notion that the world was put together wrong, and that God was to blame" (425).

[2] See Wright's *Melville's Use of the Bible* (Durham, NC: Duke UP, 1949), Thompson's *Melville's Quarrel with God* (1953), and Herbert's *Moby-Dick and Calvinism* (New Brunswick, NJ: Rutgers UP, 1977) respectively. While sharing Johnson's notion of Melville's theology as preoccupied with performance, Thompson considers in greater detail Melville's awareness of his reading public and social conventions, as well as his concurrent

and recently theologians, such as Ilana Pardes and Robert Alter,[3] have investigated how institutionalized faith, economic constrictions, and autodidactic philosophic studies impact Melville's fiction. Johnson importantly contributes to this project by connecting subject philosophy in Melville's fiction to German Romantic idealism. Theorizing these connections is the greatest accomplishment of Johnson's book, even when we consider its occasional detachment of philosophic observation from literary analysis. And while he predicts his work will be grouped with other postmodernist studies on Melville, postmodernist tools merely underscore the book's real strong suit: the sketching of the complex interlocking subject philosophies of Kant, Fichte, Schlegel, Schelling, and Melville. Beyond a plot-level understanding of Melville's major works to fill in the blanks in Johnson's—sometimes global—readings, readers should approach *The Characteristic Theology* with a solid grasp of Hegelian Phenomenology, (Post-)Structuralism—specifically the issue of the subject in language philosophy of Jacques Derrida, Jacques Lacan, and Slavoj Žižek.

Despite its relative brevity, the book forges several useful theoretical tools that I would have enjoyed seeing Johnson apply to some of Melville's shorter fiction and poetry. Particularly, a reading of *Clarel* (1876) under the auspices of Johnson's character theology might have shed light on whether Melville, having turned to poetry, further modifies his technique of subjectivity through artistic production. Despite its genre-centered focus, Johnson's is an original, theory-driven approach that often successfully transcends the standard biographical readings one has come to expect from studies dealing with Melville's novels. At its best, *The Characteristic Theology of Herman Melville* is as much a riveting investigation of the philosophic history of subject formation as it is a study arising necessarily from the subject philosophy inherent in Melville's novels.

Atlanta   Damien Schlarb

GÜNTHER LEYPOLDT, BERND ENGLER, eds., *American Cultural Icons: The Production of Representative Lives*, ZAA Monograph Series 11 (Würzburg: Königshausen, 2010), 501 pp.

From its founding at the dawn of the nineteenth century, the pinnacle of nationalism and the nation state, the United States was faced with the task of finding its own, independent iconography. The new nation required a recognizable national character, a cultural memory and archive to set itself apart from its ancestor England and from the continental fashion hub of France. In the absence of a longstanding poetic tradition, the quest for a genuinely 'American' cultural tradition was omnipresent, founding myths were fabricated and promulgated swiftly, and the concept of an 'American character' became inscribed in the nation's most exemplary citizens and their "representative lives" (5).

The volume *American Cultural Icons*, edited by Günther Leypoldt and Bernd Engler, takes a closer look at these representative lives from the viewpoint of iconicity studies. It discusses the contestation and consecration of historical figures as American 'live icons', and, by extension, as embodiments of American cultural identity. The volume thereby presents a fresh approach to the study of icons and the much traveled path of the pictorial turn: it focuses on individuals and biographies that were made larger than life. The contributions from established scholars and young researchers cover American history from the Colonial period to the present day. They examine icons from pop culture as well as the literary and political realms (ranging from Pocahontas to Madonna, from Abraham Lincoln to James Dean). The essays are grouped in two parts, respectively based on their subjects' provenance from cultural production ("Literary and Cultural Icons") and their investment in social action ("Political Icons and Founding Figures").

Günther Leypoldt's introduction frames the volume by successfully mapping the difficult territory of theoretical inquiry and by contextualizing live cultural icons. Leypoldt productively locates the concept of "represen-

---

conception of his audience as goatish (receptive of subversive and blasphemous ideas) and sheepish (theological literalist) readers. Cf. Thompson, 164 ff.

[3] See Pardes for Melville's use of exegetical tropes of Jonah and Job in *Melville's Bibles* (Berkley, CA: U of California P, 2009) and Alter on *Moby-Dick*'s exegetical polyphony in *Pen of Iron* (Princeton, NJ: Princeton UP, 2010).

tative lives" at the intersection of the pictorial turn, authenticity, and iconic charisma. The latter, identified by Leypoldt as the non-quantifiable currency of icons, gains crucial meaning for the study of live icons:

> the charisma of cultural icons depends on how they refer to imaginary spaces outside quotidian economies—as when gentleman presidents begin to embody civil religious ideals (Washington, Jefferson), professional politicians an 'American Camelot' (JFK); or commercially successful entertainers 'black resilience' (Josephine Baker) or 'existentialist non-conformism' (James Dean). (13)

Beyond these examples of charismatic personae, readers might wonder how icons refer to other discursive frameworks and what triggers this referral. It seems that the people-as-icons approach hinges on the relationship between the icon as image and the life story as narrative. How do life stories become charismatic? How do they 'script' icons? How are group-specific interests narrated into pre-existing biographical stories? The mechanics of this sense-making through storytelling are at the core of some contributions in the volume, for example the essays on Squanto by Ralph Bauer and on Pocahontas by Jan Stievermann.

The interesting point about icons is that they carry an aggrandizing, exaggerated content as well as a reference to their culture of origin: they speak both to trends and fashions at a historical cultural moment and to the nation's desire of seeing itself. In this context, one might ask what is special about American cultural icons? Leypoldt observes that after 1800 the notion of "great men" (6) has been linked to national specifics but does not discuss this any further (cf. 7). Given the historical and cultural void described above, it seems that the nascent American cultural industry was specifically prone to produce and disseminate icons, a legacy that appears to persist well into twenty-first-century popular culture: from the obsession with Michelle Obama's fashion to reality TV shows like the 'Real Housewives' series, Americans seem deeply invested in life stories and a multilayered notion of charisma. *American Cultural Icons* offers an intriguing pioneering effort in this direction that invites more detailed explorations of the cultural specifics of American icons.

One of the volume's strong points is the controversial reflection on 'greatness' expressed in the contributions. They represent valuable case studies of the palimpsestic nature of icons. Among their many intriguing insights, the essays foreground the interaction between individual agency and inscription by others, such as Gerd Hurm's analysis of James Dean and the notion of authenticity pinned onto his persona. Nadja Gernalzick's article about Madonna is noteworthy because it argues that the artist's iconization is staged in the context of aesthetic performance art, which in turn induces a process of postmodernist meta-iconization. That different historical and national moments garner diverse rhetorics of iconization is illustrated by Bernd Engler, who discusses how William Shakespeare was de-nationalized in the United States and then inscribed into nineteenth-century American culture. The essays also illuminate the relation between the United States and other cultures, such as in the contributions on the reception of James Fenimore Cooper, Napoleon of France or Oliver Cromwell.

Readers from an extended field of literary and cultural studies will find *American Cultural Icons* inspiring both for its fresh treatment of iconicity, its reimagining of the dated yet resilient concept of 'great men,' and for the many personas chosen for analysis in the contributions. Encountering these American cultural icons from a viewpoint of iconicity and charisma opens up a new field of inquiry about who is iconized and how, and, last but not least, about an American culture that continues to try to picture itself in a mirror of myriad faces and life stories.

Jena   Stefanie Schäfer

ULRICH ESCHBORN, *Stories of Survival: John Edgar Wideman's Representations of History*, Mosaic: Studien und Texte zur amerikanischen Kultur und Geschichte 42 (Trier: WVT, 2011), ix + 198 pp.

At the beginning of the 1990s, a dissertation investigating the writings of John Edgar Wideman was considered pioneering work.[1] Ironi-

---

[1] See Klaus [H.] Schmidt, *"The Outsider's Vision": Die Marginalitätsthematik in ausgewählten Prosatexten der afro-amerikanischen Erzähltradition: Richard Wrights* Native Son, *Toni Morrisons* Sula *und John Edgar Widemans* Reuben (Frankfurt/M.: Lang, 1994). For my discovery of Wideman's oeuvre in the

cally, this is still true two decades later because the body of Wideman criticism has grown more slowly than expected. If one excludes edited collections and studies dealing with several authors, Eschborn's *Stories of Survival* turns out to be the fifth of only six monographs published on Wideman since the latter entered the literary scene forty-six years ago.[2]

The fact that Wideman's contributions to (African) American literature are so strikingly underrepresented in Americanist scholarship may be due to the unusual complexity and experimental nature of this important writer's art and epistemology.[3] The exceptional level of competence that the author's demanding oeuvre requires of prospective critics makes publishing on Wideman a risky business. A case in point is Doreatha Drummond Mbalia's *John Edgar Wideman: Reclaiming the African Personality* (1995), a booklet I had the dubious pleasure of reviewing in 1998. In this deplorable study, Mbalia, unable to grasp the author's thinking and philosophy or understand the inner logic of his style and narrative technique, reduces Wideman to his personal biography and alleged obligations as a spokesman for the black community.[4]

Relying on prodigious research, extended conversations with the author[5], and a deep exploration of John Edgar Wideman's far-reach-

---

1980s, I am indebted to the late Michel Fabre (1933-2007; Université de la Sorbonne Nouvelle [Paris III]), who was gracious enough to give me a decisive hint while chatting over a coffee at the 1988 James Baldwin Conference in Heidelberg.

[2] In addition to Schmidt (1994) and Eschborn (2011), there are twelve books (or book-length assessments) fully or partly devoted to Wideman's work: Coleman (1989); Mbalia (1995); Byerman (1998); TuSmith (1998); Rowell (1999); Bidinger (2006); TuSmith and Byerman (2006); Okonkwo (2008); Russell (2009); Coleman (2010); Guzzio (2011); and D'Amore (2012). The scandalous neglect of Wideman's writings becomes even more evident if one compares the volume of secondary sources that relevant databases contain for major African American authors. Under the heading "Primary Subject Author," the *MLA International Bibliography*, for instance, offers 2,084 entries for 'Morrison, Toni,' 641 entries for 'Walker, Alice,' and a mere 164 entries for 'Wideman, John Edgar' (search date: March 12, 2013).

[3] For Wideman's unique position as literary craftsman and intellectual, see my article "Reading Black Postmodernism: John Edgar Wideman's *Reuben*," *Flip Sides: New Critical Essays on American Literature*, ed. Klaus H. Schmidt (Frankfurt/M.: Lang, 1995), 81-102. As to the categorization of Wideman's oeuvre in terms of either modernism or postmodernism, Ulrich Eschborn offers a fresh and more precise view: "I argue that, even though Wideman's work is embedded in a broader American trend towards an increased interest in historical reflection, his literature does not belong to a certain literary school or style such as the black arts movement, the realist strand in African-American literature or postmodernism but retains a modernist core while also incorporating certain postmodern elements" (6).

[4] See Klaus H. Schmidt, Review of *John Edgar Wideman: Reclaiming the African Personality*, by Doreatha Drummond Mbalia (Selinsgrove: Susquehanna UP; Associated UP, 1995), and *Langston Hughes and the Chicago Defender: Essays on Race, Politics, and Culture*, edited by Christopher C. De Santis (Urbana: U of Illinois P, 1995), *Amerikastudien / American Studies* 43 (1998): 538-42. My negative assessment of Mbalia's simplistic approach was later confirmed by Susan M. Pearsall: "Mbalia's *John Edgar Wideman* is of limited use for literary scholars due to its questionable scholarly apparatus and overt attempt to reclaim Wideman for political purposes" (44; qtd. in Eschborn 11); see Pearsall, "'Narratives of Self' and the Abdication of Authority in Wideman's *Philadelphia Fire*," *MELUS* 26.2 (2001): 15-46. Ulrich Eschborn arrives at a similar conclusion (cf. *Stories of Survival* 11). That the writer himself rejects any attempts at instrumentalizing his art is demonstrated by Wideman's response to a question by Charles Rowell: "I don't respond well to anybody who tells me what to do [...] certainly not in something as personal and intimate as literature" (Wideman, "An Interview with John Edgar Wideman" 93; qtd. in Eschborn 4); see TuSmith, *Conversations with John Edgar Wideman*, 86-104.

[5] From these conversations also resulted a published interview. See John Edgar Wideman, "'To Democratize the Elements of the Historical Record': An Interview with John Edgar Wideman about History in His Work," Interview with Ulrich Eschborn, *Callaloo* 33.4 (2010): 982-98.

ing literary universe, Eschborn aptly avoids such fallacies.[6]

Stories of Survival[7] is divided into seven parts: In his "Introduction," Eschborn manages to combine a concise presentation of his subject matter and methodology with a balanced report on the current state of research. "Wideman's Literary Concept of History" (I), which marks the beginning of the study's main part, provides the reader with an excellent introduction both to historiography as a topical site of theoretical contestation and to history as a central theme in the author's work. Of particular importance for Eschborn's analysis is a) Wideman's view of history as a "collective enterprise of mind" (Wideman, *Fatheralong*[8] 102; qtd. in Eschborn 27) and a "record of survival" (Wideman, "Frame and Dialect"[9] 34; qtd. in Eschborn 32), b) the Igbo proverb "all stories are true" (Wideman, *Fatheralong* 62; cf. Eschborn 158-59) that underlies the writer's attempt at decentralizing historical "truth" by using multiple perspectives, and c) his concept of "Great Time" (*Fatheralong* 102; qtd. in Eschborn 27), which helps to explain the simultaneity of different temporal levels that has puzzled so many readers of Wideman's fiction:

> Great Time is the ancestral time. It's nonlinear. It is, if anything, like a river, like the sea [...]. It is the medium which holds everything and always has. So there is no beginning, no end. You are just as likely to bump into someone from fifty years ago as to bump into someone you saw the day before. Not only the living, but the dead—everything that has ever happened—is floating around in this medium of time. (Wideman, "Storytelling and Democracy [Interview]"[10] 267; qtd. in Eschborn 35)

In the following parts (II-V), Eschborn examines representations of history in *The Lynchers* (1973), the 'Homewood Trilogy'[11] (1981-83), *Philadelphia Fire* (1990), and *The Cattle Killing*[12] (1996). While *The Lynchers* (II) is read as a metahistorical novel that, due to the increasing role of the black vernacular, "must be regarded as a transitional work leading to a new phase in Wideman's writing" (68), the 'Homewood Trilogy' (III), "characterized by its focus on poor, marginalized characters in a local setting" (71), emerges as a celebration of family, community, and oral history by which the artist-intellectual "reconnects to his African-American cultural roots" (118). *Philadelphia Fire* (IV), a "contemporary novel with historical elements" (123), and *The Cattle Killing* (V), "a historical novel" (123), are seen as interconnected "meditations on [...] catastrophe, loss, and survival" (121). In both of these novels—masterpieces abounding in self-reflexivity, metafictionality, and intertextuality which have rightly been classified as belonging to Wideman's most demanding works—, catastrophic events function as "historical metaphors of black-white relations [...] throughout American history" (121).[13]

---

[6] The only aspect of the book that occasionally detracts from the pleasure of reading Eschborn's lucid analysis derives from the relatively high number of stylistic and content-related redundancies.

[7] *Stories of Survival* originated as a dissertation supervised by Oliver Scheiding, himself a leading expert on representations of history in American culture. See Oliver Scheiding, *Geschichte und Fiktion: Zum Funktionswandel des frühen amerikanischen Romans* (Paderborn: Schöningh, 2003) and *Reel Histories: US History in Film, Zeitschrift für Anglistik und Amerikanistik* [Special Issue, edited by Oliver Scheiding] 53.3 (2005). For the significance of the former in Early American Studies, see my review in *Literaturwissenschaftliches Jahrbuch* 45 (2004): 374-84.

[8] See John Edgar Wideman, *Fatheralong: A Meditation on Fathers and Sons, Race and Society* (New York: Vintage, 1995).

[9] See John Edgar Wideman, "Frame and Dialect: The Evolution of the Black Voice in American Literature," *American Poetry Review* 5.5 (1976): 34-37.

[10] See John Edgar Wideman, "Storytelling and Democracy (in the Radical Sense): A Conversation with John Edgar Wideman," Interview with Lisa Baker, *African American Review* 34.2 (2000): 263-72.

[11] *Damballah* (1981, short story cycle), *Hiding Place* (1981, novel), and *Sent for You Yesterday* (1983, novel).

[12] Eschborn's examination of the historical novel *The Cattle Killing* (1996) also includes a discussion of the short story "Fever" (1989), which is seen as the nucleus from which this novel grew.

[13] What Eschborn, referring to *The Cattle Killing*, calls the novel's "global setting" (176) could have been linked to approaches in 'Atlantic studies,' particularly to concepts such as the 'black Atlantic' and 'circum-Atlantic

Eschborn's "Conclusion" contains a useful summary of the various ways in which history and historiography are inscribed in the texture of the author's literary cosmos:

> Wideman's literary concept of history forms a unique combination of various elements: the concept of Great Time, the saying "all stories are true," storytelling, individual, family, and community, the double perspective of the artist-intellectual, the emphasis on local settings, [...] the focus on the view of poorer African Americans, intertextuality, and African-American culture as a means of the preservation of the ethnic group. (186)

Wideman's overall objective in entering the conversation about the implications of history for the makeup and further development of Western culture is interpreted as a contribution to what has been called 'history from below.' By writing his family and community back "into history" (184), Wideman subverts "the kind of historiography which has excluded African-American voices" (186).

The true measure of Eschborn's achievement is the author he has chosen to tackle. Wideman's literary work rests on an intricate combination of several complex components: the experimental use of time inspired by African cosmology; the innovative play with blurred boundaries between fact and fiction, including metafictional games, the self-ironic staging of an elusive "Wideman persona" (6), and the narrativization of historical events by way of "literary historiography" (6) and "historical metaphor" (19); the double vision and self-reflexivity of Widemans's hybrid narrators; the radical foregrounding of the African American vernacular and the multiperspectivity inherent in oral storytelling; the extensive employment of intertextual allusions and intratextual references; as well as the ambivalent blending of African, African-American,

___

memory'; cf. Paul Gilroy, *The Black Atlantic: Modernity and Double Consciousness* (Cambridge: Harvard UP, 1993), and Joseph R. Roach, *Cities of the Dead: Circum-Atlantic Performance* (New York: Columbia UP, 1996). For the beginnings of this ever-expanding field of study, see Klaus H. Schmidt, Review of *The Creation of the British Atlantic World*, edited by Elizabeth Mancke and Carole Shammas (Baltimore: Johns Hopkins UP, 2005), *Amerikastudien / American Studies* 51 (2006): 621-26.

European-American, and European cultural traditions.

Eschborn's ability to master all these challenging components and incorporate them into a convincing study of a key theme in Wideman's oeuvre has resulted in the first book that covers virtually every facet of Wideman's narrative technique and epistemological agenda. As a volume that also deals with much broader issues, Eschborn's *Stories of Survival* deserves to be read not only by Africanists but by anybody interested in configurations of history in contemporary culture. For specialists on Wideman, this monograph is nothing less than a must-read, a text to be consulted and quoted for decades to come.

Germersheim   Klaus H. Schmidt

JARED GARDNER, *Projections: Comics and the History of Twenty-First-Century Storytelling* (Stanford: Stanford UP, 2012), 240 pp.

Laments about the dearth of substantial scholarship and the lack of perceptive publications on comics are about as common as knee-jerk accounts of the medium's triumphant transformation from trashy children's entertainment to serious graphic literature. In fact, the bulk of research that has come to represent the growing field of comics studies has labored rather hard to recover from what is often described as the scholarly neglect and critical disdain with which the medium has grappled throughout most of the twentieth century.[1] It seems, however, that such assumptions no longer hold true (if they ever have) and that the field of comics studies is currently being mined and cultivated by so many scholars across national contexts and academic disciplines that a review such as this one can cut right to the chase, offering its conclusion at the outset: Jared Gardner's *Projections: Comics and the History of Twenty-First-Century Storytelling* contains some of the most fascinating and theoretically advanced writing about comics to date, and it marks a watershed moment not only in comics studies but also in

___

[1] See also: Daniel Stein, Christina Meyer, and Micha Edlich, Guest Editors, *American Comic Books and Graphic Novels*, special issue of *Amerikastudien / American Studies* 56.4 (2011): 501–29.

postclassical narratology, American Studies, and related areas of research.

Gardner, an Professor of English and Film at The Ohio State University, makes two crucial claims: First, American comics have already worked out, and found solutions for, many of the narrative conundrums we encounter in the digital age and thus offer "a treasure chest of experience, cautionary tales, and possibilities for engaging with new narrative media" (xiii). Second, American comics are an inherently participatory narrative form shaped by the manifold interactions among authors and readers, producers and consumers. In order to substantiate these claims, Gardner digs deep into the history of American comics from the late nineteenth century onwards, tracing their aesthetic and narrative evolution throughout the twentieth century. The preface acknowledges that the aim of the book is not "to provide a comprehensive history of the various forms and mediums in which comics have operated" (x), but rather to tell "the tale of how comics creators have engaged with their readers, how readers have responded to the demand that they project themselves actively into comics, and how this history helps us imagine the future of storytelling" (xiii). *Projections* tells this tale masterfully, and it is most compelling whenever it leaves the worn-out paths of conventional comics history and weaves its own, original way through the maze of materials that constitute the ephemeral archive of the medium.

The first chapter, "Fragments of Modernity, 1889-1920," views the American comic strip as "the first and arguably most important of the new vernacular modernisms" (7). The weekly and daily comics of the urban mass tabloid newspapers, Gardner suggests, were "dedicated to diagramming the serial complexities of modern life and fixing the fragments of modernity on the page" (7). They accomplished this through their particular storytelling apparatus: narrative progression through sequential panels that required readers to project their own meanings into the spaces between panels, the so-called gutters, as well as into the necessarily unfinished—that is, cartoonish—visual-verbal content of these panels. Moreover, comic strips offered an antidote to the ravages of modern life by visualizing the recurring resilient body of hapless characters (think of Frederick Burr Opper's *Happy Hooligan*) as pleasurable figures of identification. Gardner maintains that early comic strips from Winsor McCay's *Little Nemo in Slumberland* to George Herriman's *Krazy Kat* established new types of serial storytelling, such as "recursive seriality" (21) and "discontinuous seriality" (24), where the story always ends in more or less the same way, and the "open-ended serial narrative" (47), which came to dominate comics by the 1920s and 1930s in strips such as Frank King's *Gasoline Alley* and Milton Caniff's *Terry and the Pirates*. The turn towards open-ended storytelling marks the parting of ways between comic strip and film, the latter eventually moving away from the narrative structures of the early popular film serial and toward the self-contained feature film, only returning to the possibilities of open-ended storytelling through Hollywood's recent obsession with the "new serial cinema," often of the superhero genre (183).[2]

The convergences and interdependencies of the early film serials and comic strips lie at the center of Gardner's second chapter, "Serial Pleasures, 1907-1938." The film serials of the 1910s and later decades were part of a larger media ecology that included the newspaper, where editorial columns, news features, and contests among readers compensated for the lack of film's participatory potential. As such, these serials shared many of the comic strip's most interactive features, for instance, the overlap between comics' content in Bud Fisher's *Mutt and Jeff* and the sports pages, as well as the national news covered elsewhere in the paper. Here, the principle of open-ended serial narrative found its full realization, with strips like Sidney Smith's *The Gumps* establishing most of the interactive parameters of today's serial entertainment: letters to the editor, the explicit encouragement of reader feedback within the strips themselves, fantasies of shared author- and ownership of characters and series on the part of vast audiences, to name a few. Most rewarding in this chapter is Gardner's awareness that these kinds of readerly engagement are not only central to

---

[2] Gardner's focus on film comes with a slight disadvantage: It disregards the connections among comics, modernist literature, and modernist art. See also: Daniel Stein, "The Comic Modernism of George Herriman," Jake Jakaitis and James F. Wurtz, eds., *Crossing Boundaries in Graphic Narrative: Essays on Forms, Series and Genres* (Jefferson: McFarland, 2012): 40-70.

the history of American comics, and in many ways prefigure the digital culture of our contemporary world, but that they also produce self-conscious readers who perform their role as active (co-)producers of popular culture knowingly and purposely, rather than being mere dupes of the culture industry.

The third chapter, "Fan Addicts and the Comic Book, 1938–1955," provides a counter-narrative to the conventional origin story of the comic book. According to Gardner, the comic book of the late 1930s and 1940s emerged from attempts to reign in the overly active readers of science-fiction magazines and comic strips by producing monthly installments of superhero exploits that initially possessed little continuity beyond the individual story. Yet as serial entertainment, these comic books ultimately afforded authors, editors, and readers their very own interactive culture, complete with specific loci of engagement, such as letter columns, editorials, and fanzines, as well as authorial performances from creator biographies to the editorials of Marvel Comics' Stan Lee, covered in the following chapter. Ironically, we learn that it was not only the fans of these comics who acted upon the medium's propensity to heighten readerly projections into the storyworld, but some of the staunchest critics of comics, such as the German-born Fredric Wertham. Readers whose academic background is American Studies will find Gardner's close readings of Wertham's *Seduction of the Innocent* (1954) and its relation to the work of the New Critics worth their while; for students of comics, the careful treatment of Wertham's theory of comics reception will surely be a revelation.

Chapter four, "First-Person Graphic, 1959–2010," begins with an assessment of Marvel's self-doubting superheroes of the 1960s, Spider-Man in particular. Gardner's observations about the serial universe created by the Marvel authors and the ways in which these comics mobilized their youthful readers are highly insightful, but they do not always stray far enough from established comic book history. To boot, at least this reader would have liked to know how the story of the superhero genre generated new modes of creator-reader interaction beyond the 1960s.[3] But, as Gardner states in his preface, any book that deals with the 'longue durée' of American comics is bound to produce a narrative "marked by gaps and omissions" (x). We are compensated for these gaps and omissions by case studies of central figures from the underground 'comix movement' and its antecedents, such as Robert Crumb, Justin Green, Aline Kominsky, Harvey Pekar, Art Spiegelman, and Alison Bechdel. Gardner's knowledge of autobiography theory and its nuanced application to his material will prove extremely useful for critics working on comics autobiographies: "The compressed, mediated, and iconic nature of the testimony (both text and image) in comics denies any collapse between autobiography and autobiographical subject," Gardner suggests, and he concludes that the split between autobiographer and subject "is not a casualty or regrettable *cost* of the autobiographer's chosen form, but is instead precisely what motivates the drive to tell the self in comics form" (131).

The fifth chapter, "Archives and Collectors, 1990–2010," turns to the "structural affinities" between comics and the Internet as a digital archive of popular culture ephemera (149). The analyses focus on creators such as Ben Katchor, Kim Deitch, and Chris Ware, who are positioned simultaneously as collectors of comics and other items from the popular culture archive and as creators of their own comics archives. As in all previous chapters, Gardner's insistence on, and explication of, the specific ways in which comics mediate new modes of storytelling leads to profound conclusions: "The comics form is forever troubled by that which cannot be reconciled, synthesized, unified, contained within the frame," he writes toward the end of the chapter; "but it is in being so troubled that the form defines itself" (177) and speaks to many of our contemporary concerns vis-à-vis the digitization of history in the Internet age.

Projections ends with a final chapter, "Coda: Comics, Film, and the Future of Twenty-First-Century Storytelling," which is both retro- and prospective in that it ponders a crucial paradox: While comics have

---

[3] For an approach that reads the arrival of the Marvel heroes and the new author and reader roles that emerged out of the authorization conflicts these narratives generated, see Frank Kelleter and Daniel Stein, "Autorisierungspraktiken Seriellen Erzählens: Zur Gattungsentwicklung von Superheldencomics," Frank Kelleter, ed., *Populäre Serialität: Narration—Evolution—Distinktion: Zum Seriellen Erzählen seit dem 19. Jahrhundert*, (Bielefeld: transcript, 2012): 259–90.

anticipated many narrative developments of the digital age, from the loop aesthetic to practices of remixing, they have also proven staunchly resistant to digital conversion, with webcomics not having garnered much popular appeal. But instead of lamenting the fact that the future of print comics looks dire and that webcomics may never catch on, Gardner ends on a positive note: "The future of storytelling in the twenty-first century lies in the history of comics and its audiences. It is in everyone's interest that we nurture this unique narrative medium—and attend to its history—as it helps us imagine what comes next" (193). I can only add that what comes next may increasingly depend on the ability to move from the predominantly American perspective that shapes Gardner's fascinating account to a transnational vantage point from which we can trace the history and envision the future of comics.[4]

Berlin   Daniel Stein

---

[4] See also: Shane Denson, Christina Meyer, and Daniel Stein, eds., *Transnational Perspectives on Graphic Narratives: Comics at the Crossroads* (London: Bloomsbury, 2013).

Contributors

DOPFFEL, Michael; American Studies Program, English Department, Eberhard Karls Universität Tübingen; Wilhelmstraße 50, 72074 Tübingen (michael.dopffel@uni-tuebingen.de)

GRÄSER, Univ.-Prof. Dr. Marcus; Institutsvorstand, Institut für Neuere Geschichte und Zeitgeschichte, Johannes Kepler Universität Linz; Altenberger Straße 69, 4040 Linz, Austria (Marcus.Graeser@jku.at)

HEINZ, Jun.-Prof. Dr. Sarah; Anglistische Literatur- und Kulturwissenschaft, Universität Mannheim; Schloss EW 268, 68131 Mannheim (sarah.heinz@uni-mannheim.de)

HOCHBRUCK, Prof. Dr. Wolfgang; Department of English, Albert Ludwigs University Freiburg; Rempart Straße 15, 79098 Freiburg i. Br. (wolfgang.hochbruck@anglistik.uni-freiburg.de)

LATSIS, Dimitrios; Department of Cinema and Comparative Literature, University of Iowa; Iowa City, IA 52242-1498, USA (dimitrios-latsis@uiowa.edu)

MEHRING, Prof. Dr. Frank; North American Studies, English Department, Radboud University; PO Box 9103, 6500 HD Nijmegen, Netherlands (f.mehring@let.ru.nl)

MILLER, DR. Andrew; Department of English, Germanic and Romance Studies; University of Copenhagen; Njalsgade 128, 24.2, 2300 København S, Denmark (amiller@hum.ku.dk)

NAGL, Dr. Dominik; Neuere und Neueste Geschichte, Historisches Institut, Universität Mannheim; 68131 Mannheim (nagl2001@yahoo.de)

POLLEY, Jason S. Polley; Associate Professor, Department of English Language and Literature, Hong Kong Baptist University; Kowloon Tong, Hong Kong (jspolley@hkbu.edu.hk)

PUXAN-OLIVA, Dr. Marta; Postdoctoral Marie Curie Research Fellow, Department of Comparative Literature, Harvard University / Department of Filologia Romànica, Universitat de Barcelona; Dana Palmer House, 16 Quincy Street, Cambridge, MA 02138, USA (puxanoliva@fas.harvard.edu)

SCHÄFER, Dr. Stefanie; Assistant Professor of American Studies / Wissenschaftliche Assistentin; Institut für Anglistik und Amerikanistik, Friedrich-Schiller-Universität Jena; Ernst Abbe Platz 8, 07743 Jena (schaefer.stefanie@uni-jena.de)

SCHLARB, Damien B; PhD candidate Georgia State University Atlanta; American Studies, Department of English and Linguistics, Johannes Gutenberg-Universität Mainz; Jakob Welder-Weg 18, 55128 Mainz (schlarbd@uni-mainz.de)

SCHMIDT, Dr. Klaus H.; Abteilung für Anglistik, Amerikanistik und Anglophonie, Johannes Gutenberg-Universität Mainz, Fachbereich Translations-, Sprach- und Kulturwissenschaft; An der Hochschule 2, 76711 Germersheim (schmikla@uni-mainz.de)

SEIDL, Martin; American Studies, Department of English and Linguistics, Johannes Gutenberg-Universität Mainz; Jakob Welder-Weg 18, 55128 Mainz (Martin.Seidl@uni-mainz.de)

SPLITTER, Dr. Wolfgang; Franckesche Stiftungen zu Halle; Franckeplatz 1, Haus 37, 06110 Halle (Saale) (wsplitt1@jhu.edu)

STEIN, Dr. Daniel; John-F.-Kennedy-Institut für Nordamerikastudien, Abteilung Kultur, Freie Universität Berlin; Lansstraße 7-9, Raum 323, 14195 Berlin (Daniel.Stein@fu-berlin.de)

TRAUTSCH, Dr. Jasper M.; Deutsches Historisches Institut in Rom; Via Aurelia Antica 391, 00165 Roma, Italy (trautsch@zedat.fu-berlin.de)

Anglistik/Amerikanistik

Universitätsverlag
WINTER
Heidelberg

GERNALZICK, NADJA
PISARZ-RAMÍREZ, GABRIELE
(Eds.)

Transmediality and Transculturality

2013. XXIX, 444 Seiten, 57 farbige, 8 s/w Abbildungen. (American Studies – A Monograph Series, Volume 233)
Geb. € 52,–
ISBN 978-3-8253-6108-2

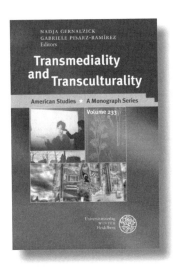

The terms transmediality and transculturality by the ambiguity of the prefix denote transcendence as well as procedurality and provisionality. Since the mid-20th century, transmediality and transculturality have been launched into debates about cultural and medial sectionalisms when competing terms such as inter- or multiculturality and inter- or multimediality entrenched virulent distinctions for the organization of privilege and hierarchy. The volume comprises essays by scholars from American Studies, Inter-American Studies, Media Studies, and Comparative Literature and Culture which explore transmediality and transculturality from different perspectives and in various cultural contexts and languages, covering a timespan that reaches from the Renaissance to the 21st century and a provenance of works from Europe, the Caribbean, and the United States.

Anglistik

Universitätsverlag
WINTER
Heidelberg

FREITAG, KORNELIA
REED, BRIAN (Eds.)

Modern American Poetry

Points of Access

2013. 212 Seiten, 5 Abbildungen. (anglistik & englischunterricht, Volume 79)
Kart. € 22,–
ISBN 978-3-8253-6169-3

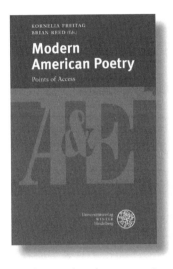

How to read – and how to teach poetry? The present volume on 'Modern American Poetry' assembles ten essays that distill and share tips, facts, arguments, interpretations, and techniques that a number of German and American scholars believe to be helpful when reading and teaching American poetry. The essays introduce topics such as the poetry of war and postmodern poetic experimentation, dwell on teaching Emily Dickinson, Gertrude Stein, and Frank O'Hara, and relate the experiences of translating texts by the African American poet June Jordan in the classroom. Imagism and confessionalism are re-negotiated while more recent developments, such as slam poetics and South Asian diasporic verse are introduced. All essays share a single goal: to provide 'Points of Access' for interested readers and especially instructors to transform an exciting, chaotic, contested field of study into lessons that are enlightening and, ideally, enjoyable.

D-69051 Heidelberg · Postfach 10 61 40 · Tel. (49) 62 21/77 02 60 · Fax (49) 62 21/77 02 69
Internet http://www.winter-verlag.de · E-mail: info@winter-verlag.de

Visibility beyond the Visible

The Poetic Discourse of American Transcendentalism

Albena Bakratcheva

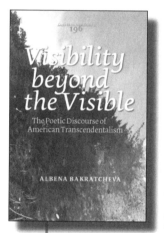

Visibility beyond the Visible. The Poetic Discourse of American Transcendentalism is the first study to entirely deal with the poetics of American Transcendentalism. The author takes it for granted that the major New England transcendentalists were writers of utmost literary significance and so focuses thoroughly on their extremely rich and many-sided poetic discourse. The book's inevitable European perspective only enhances its preoccupation with the Americanness of the New England Transcendentalists, thus making it emphasize, in all the aspects of its concern, the uniqueness of the interrelation between place-sense and artistry which the transcendentalists' writings offer. Because most of these writings hold iconic stature as American masterpieces, both scholars and lay readers will welcome *Visibility beyond the Visible. The Poetic Discourse of American Transcendentalism* as opening novel horizons for greater insights, deeper understandings, and further exploration of the poetic complexities of Emerson's, Thoreau's, M. Fuller's, and their co-thinkers' work.

Albena Bakratcheva is Professor of American Literature at New Bulgarian University, Sofia, Bulgaria. She is member of The Thoreau Society U.S.A. and Executive Council member of the International American Studies Association (IASA). Her work includes: *Similarities in Divergences* (1995), *Potentialities of Discourse* (1997), *Visibility Beyond the Visible* (Bulg., 2007), *The Call of the Green* (2009).

Amsterdam/New York, NY
2013. XII, 268 pp.
(Costerus 196)
Paper €59,-/US$80,-
E-Book €53,-/US$72,-
ISBN: 978-90-420-3556-0
ISBN: 978-94-012-0831-4

USA/Canada:
248 East 44th Street, 2nd floor,
New York, NY 10017, USA.
Call Toll-free (US only): T: 1-800-225-3998
F: 1-800-853-3881

All other countries:
Tijnmuiden 7, 1046 AK Amsterdam, The Netherlands
Tel. +31-20-611 48 21 Fax +31-20-447 29 79
Please note that the exchange rate is subject to fluctuations